Dr Peter Savage trained as an architect and town planner and is a graduate of the Universities of Liverpool and Edinburgh. He worked in architects' offices in England and Scotland, and taught in two colleges of art and the Universities of Edinburgh and New Mexico, as well as the Technical College of Nova Scotia.

A general interest in conservation and in garden design led him to Robert Lorimer's work in 1968, and he contributed articles on this subject to a number of journals including *Country Life*. This study began with Lorimer's drawings and papers and widened to his buildings, gardens and furniture and, finally, to his writings, which reveal so much of the inner feelings of this richly diverse designer.

Married with six children, for the last thirty-five years Dr Savage has divided his time between Edinburgh and South East France.

Frontispiece: *Robert Lorimer aged twelve painted by his brother John.*

R.C.A.M.

PETER SAVAGE

LORIMER

AND THE EDINBURGH CRAFT DESIGNERS

Steve Savage
LONDON AND EDINBURGH

Steve Savage Publishers Ltd
The Old Truman Brewery
91 Brick Lane
LONDON
E1 6QL

www.savagepublishers.com

Paperback edition published in Great Britain by Steve Savage Publishers Ltd 2005

First published by Paul Harris Publishing 1980
Copyright © Peter D Savage 1980

Photographs © Peter D. Savage and Patricia Macdonald
unless otherwise credited

ISBN-13: 978-1-904246-14-5
ISBN-10: 1-904246-14-1

Design by Patricia Macdonald
Cover and prelims design by Stephen Strong

British Library Cataloguing in Publication Data
A catalogue entry for this book is available from the British Library

Printed and bound by The Cromwell Press Ltd

PUBLISHER'S NOTE
The first edition of this book contained a series of plates on glossy art paper as well as a separately numbered series of figures alongside the text. The plates in this edition are printed on the same paper as the text, and there are two series of numbering running in parallel. The two may be distinguished because the figure numbers are enclosed in square brackets.

Preface to the First Edition

The fiftieth anniversary of the death of Robert Lorimer fell on 13 September, 1979, so it is appropriate that a fresh appreciation of his architectural work should be published and it is extremely fortunate that an Edinburgh architectural historian has been able to undertake this formidable task. In 1931 Country Life *published an excellent book by Christopher Hussey, but now Peter Savage has been able to look back over the years, and draw upon the many letters which Robert Lorimer wrote to his architect friend R. S. Dods in Australia. These letters were never seen by Hussey, and there has been time also for detailed examination of the drawings of the office which number many thousands.*

For making this book possible readers are indebted to the Moray Fund of the University of Edinburgh and the Carnegie Trust for the Universities of Scotland, the Scottish Arts Council, the Hope Scott Trust, the British Academy and the Jocelyn and Katharine Morton Charitable Trust, who have given generous financial assistance towards a book worthy of the subject.

Christopher Lorimer
Gibliston, Fife, January, 1979

To Catriona

Contents

List of Plates

ABBREVIATIONS used for sources of illustrations:

A.R.	Architectural Review.
A.N.	Architects' News.
B.C.	Glasgow Museums: The Burrell Collection.
C.L.	Country Life, Magazine and books.
C.W.G.C.	Commonwealth War Graves Commission.
E.F.	Elizabeth Farfan.
L.S.	Lindsey Stewart.
N.L.S.	National Library of Scotland (from *The Builder*).
N.T.S.	National Trust for Scotland.
O.D.	Drawing from Office of Sir Robert Lorimer.
P.M.	Patricia Macdonald.
P.S.	Peter Savage.
R.C.A.M.	Crown copyright: Royal Commission on the Ancient and Historical Monuments of Scotland.
R.S.L.	Office records of Sir Robert Lorimer.
S.C.L.	Scottish Colorfoto Laboratories, Alexandra.
S.R.M.	Stuart Matthew.

List of Figures

Introduction

The single book to have been written previously on the work of Sir Robert Lorimer appeared in 1931 and was written by Christopher Hussey. He wrote vividly but in haste, and with a concentration on Lorimer's restoration work, but he did visit Scotland to talk to the colleagues and friends who had known Lorimer for a long time, so that his book, despite its gaps, has served to preserve their memories of Lorimer. The need remained, however, to review the full breadth of this important Scottish architect's work and to make use of other sources not so far used. They include the recollections of a number of people who worked for or with him, the surviving drawings of the office (rumoured to total about thirty thousand and now deposited by Stuart Matthew as a memorial to the office in the Royal Commission on Ancient Monuments, Scotland), and the surviving office letters numbering several thousand (which have been given by him to the library of the University of Edinburgh, where they form part of the Edinburgh Collection). On Lorimer's personal matters I have relied mainly on his correspondence with R. S. Dods, which was lent to me by Elizabeth Farfan now removed to Brisbane. The letters will not be available publicly during the lifetime of his family, but will become so when they pass to the Edinburgh Collection to which they have been left.

The family history in Chapter One is based on the family papers of Christopher Lorimer of Gibliston (including a volume of obituary cuttings and letters of condolence which have been put on microfilm by the Edinburgh Collection with his permission); of Hew Lorimer, R.S.A., curator of Kellie Castle in Fife for the National Trust for Scotland, who provided the text of his father's lecture on William Morris and who allowed the 'Red Book', a family history, to be put on microfilm by the University of Edinburgh Library. Details of Lorimer's and his brother John's careers at the University of Edinburgh were provided by its former keeper of manuscripts, Charles Finlayson. The late Morton Cowie recounted Lorimer's reminiscences of waiting to enter Bodley's office. The account of Lorimer's stay in Maclaren's office was put together with the help of Anne Riches of the Historic Buildings Branch of the Scottish Development Department. The late John Begg gave details of life in London with Lorimer and Dods in an interview with the Glasgow *Sunday Post* in September, 1929, as J. Wilson has given details of Sir G. W. Browne in the obituary in the Journal of the R.I.B.A. (17 July, 1939), and Sir John Stirling Maxwell's *Shrines and Homes of Scotland* ((1937) provides short biographical sketches of both Sir Robert Rowand Anderson and Sir Robert Lorimer. David Walker of the Historic Buildings Branch of the Scottish Development Department informed me of Lorimer's part at Tilliefour, and the lead to

Lorimer's first house design was provided by Sir John Summerson, Curator of the Soane's Museum, who had visited it after the war. Some drawings of it were traced by the planning department of the London Borough of Merton and photographed for me. Christopher Lorimer has made available the sketch books of his father which are now in his possession.

Lorimer's connections with the Edinburgh Architectural Association in his first years in practice are traced in Chapter Two from the published transactions of the Association, copies of which are held by its library. Lorimer's work at Earlshall was written up by Lawrence Weaver for *Country Life* in 1905, and further details are given by Inigo Trigg's book *Formal Gardens* (1901). Dr Ronald Cant, formerly Reader in Scottish History and Archivist of the University of St Andrews, provided details of Earlshall's owner R. W. Mackenzie. Professor Gordon Donaldson and John Simpson of the Department of Scottish History in the University of Edinburgh provided further details of Clousta Hotel, Shetland. Stuart Matthew has made available the notes on the office written by his father J. F. Matthew in his last years.

The development of Lorimer's Colinton manner in Chapter Three has been traced by myself before, but more briefly, in an article in the *Scottish Georgian Society's Bulletin*, Vol. 3 1974–5. Miss Catherine Cruft, Curator, the Royal Commission on Ancient Monuments, Scotland, which holds the Lorimer office drawings, and Richard Emerson formerly of the Commission helped in innumerable ways to cope with this unwieldy mass of paper. Rowand Anderson's many houses in Colinton appear on the valuation rolls at Register House, Edinburgh, but with addresses too cryptic for all of them to be identified. J. J. Stevenson's *House Architecture* of 1888 has been referred to for the architectural fashions in materials of the time. Many of the Colinton cottages appeared in the *Builder* in the eighteen nineties with the briefest of comments by its editor H. H. Statham. A slightly wider discussion of their period and some comment on them is provided by the books edited by Shaw Sparrow: *The British Home of Today* (1904) and *The Modern Home* (1906). *Our Homes* (1909) has a few illustrations of them, and *Hints on Home Furnishing* (1909) a few pieces of Lorimer's furniture. *Modern Cottage Architecture* by Maurice Adams (2nd ed. 1912) includes two lodges by Lorimer, as does Weaver's *Country Life Book of Cottages* (1913).

The development of Lorimer's Baronial manner in design is traced in Chapter four from his correspondence, Weaver's articles in *Country Life* (Lympne, 12 November, 1910; The Architectural Supplement on the work of Sir Robert Lorimer 27 September, 1913). *The House and Its Equipment* by Weaver (*c.* 1912) includes interior work by Lorimer at Lympne, Laverockdale and Ardkinglas. *Small Country Houses*, also by him, includes Briglands, Pittencrieff House and Barton Hartshorn. *Domestic Architecture in Scotland*, edited by James Nicoll (1908) includes Ardkinglas, Wemyss Hall and Pitkerro. Most of these buildings were also illustrated by the *Architectural Review*. The text on Rowallan closely follows that of two articles by myself in *Country Life* (21 and 28 December, 1978). Details of the family are drawn from conversations with the late Lord Rowallan and from his autobiography (1976).

The part of craftsmanship in Lorimer's design in Chapter Five had been written from a wide series of interviews with people associated directly with Lorimer in his last years in practice, and those connected indirectly through other people, many of them drawn to my attention by the late Sir Robert Matthew. They include George Hay, formerly of Scott Morton and later in Lorimer's office; Elspeth Hardie, née Scott Morton, who provided details of that firm (showing that despite Lorimer's special attachment for the Clow brothers, Scott Morton undertook far more work for him than Hussey suggests); William Laing, of Nathaniel Grieve and formerly director of the rival firm; Campbell and David Reid of Whytock and Reid, as well as John Todd, formerly a carver in their firm. Lorimer's association with William Burrell is treated at greater length by myself in two articles in *Country Life* (27 January and 3 February, 1977) which included material supplied by Magnus Magnusson and William Wells, formerly Keeper of the Burrell Collection. Many of Lorimer's churches appeared in the *Architectural Review*, starting with the Church of the Good Shepherd (1901) which was included also with St Peter's Morningside in *Recent Ecclesiastic Architecture* by Nicholson and Spooner (*c.* 1911). Lorimer gave his own views on stained glass in an article he wrote in 1915 for *Country Life*.

Both secondary sources and primary sources have been used in Chapter Six to write up Lorimer in mid-career. The dates of all the buildings will not be finalised until all the office's papers have been found. So far the dates in Lorimer's letters and account books suggest that Hussey's dates are for the final certificate for payment which, in some cases, was delayed long after the building was completed. Interviews with the late John Noble and Mr McVicar, mason, who worked on its construction, are part of the material from which Ardkinglas was written up. The layout of the gardens and the grounds of those houses was researched by myself and written up in a report presented for the Thomas Ross award of the Royal Incorporation of Architects in Scotland in 1975 and is held in its library. Eve Haig of the National Library of Scotland has helped guide me through the necessary search of the early Ordnance Survey maps, and Eileen Finlayson who works on the *Dictionary of the|Older Scottish Tongue*, has searched the office letters in the Edinburgh Collection for references. The conclusions of this study have been published by the *Journal of the Garden History Society* (Vol. 5, No. 2, 1977) and a further article will be found in the *Journal of the Royal Horticultural Society* (Summer 1979).

The war years in Chapter Seven are described from the Design and Industries Association's papers in the library of the R.I.B.A., located with the help of Sir Nikolaus Pevsner, his own paper on the D.I.A.'s proceedings and discussions with Jocelyn Morton, as well as his book *Three Generations in a Family Textile Firm* (1971). A more detailed study of Lorimer's role as a Principal Architect for the Imperial War Graves Commission forms part two of my Ph.D. Thesis (in the Library of the University of Edinburgh). It is based on letters and office correspondence, as well as much material provided by the Commonwealth War Graves Commission through Nancy Bowden. Articles on later country houses which appeared in *Country Life* on 3 September, 1921 on Dunrobin and on 28 February and 7 March, 1925 on Marchmont, have been used.

Lorimer's last decade in practice was overshadowed by the National Memorial which is discussed in Chapter Eight. The controversy upon it was discussed at length in part three of my thesis and was based on the office scrap book of press cuttings, notes and memoranda lent to me by the late Margaret Swan, née Brown, and the picture of the office is given as she saw it. Command 279 of 1919 gives the details of Lorimer's first scheme. A photograph of the second scheme is shown by Hussey, and the third and final scheme is described by the numerous illustrated guides which were published. I have used those of Sir Lawrence Weaver (1927), Major Beith (Ian Hay's *Their Name Liveth*, 1931), Sir Ian Hamilton (1932) and Frank Deas (1930, 2nd ed.). I was also guided by the late James Richardson who only wanted, he said, 'to show me both sides of the picture'. The late Phyllis Bone, Pilkington Jackson, and Miles Johnson discussed their experiences working on the National Memorial, and James Clark of working with Lorimer on memorials, as did the late Alfred Lochead, Morton Cowie and Leslie Graham MacDougall of working in his office in the early twenties. Alan Reiach and George Lyall, Lorimer's last two pupils, and the late Margaret Swan have commented to me on how much conditions have changed in offices since those spartan days, and yet she told me such was Sir Robert's leadership that 'We were all wrapped up in the work'.

Finally, in addition to all those people who have contributed information, mention must be made of my publishers for their support since the first proposals, Pat Macdonald for her design and for coping so well with the large and heterogeneous collection of photographs old and new which were available, the photographic department (E. U. Library) for its work in rephotographing old prints, and Margaret Geddes for typing the manuscript with its many many alterations. It has been read by quite a number of people and particular thanks are due to Christopher Lorimer for his suggestions on family affairs, George Hay and David Walker and Richard Emmerson on architectural matters, and Catherine Cruft on anything from illustrations to punctuation. As time began to run out David Walker, Maurice Lindsay and John Gerrard (Director and Assistant Director of the Scottish Civic Trust) all demanded more notation, and David Walker, the external examiner for my thesis on Lorimer, allowed Richard Emmerson (now on his staff at the Historic Buildings Branch of the Scottish Development Department) to provide some of them from his copious notes on all Scottish architects while adding innumerable other details from his prodigious memory. Lastly my wife Catriona, who is a historian herself, read the manuscript and rightly insisted that certain things had to be rewritten. To all these people my thanks.

Peter Savage
Edinburgh, 1979

I

Robert Lorimer's Formative Years

Robert Lorimer was born in Scotland, where he lived and worked for most of his life. At his death he had become the country's foremost architect. The age of the Enlightenment, the flowering of Scottish culture which had begun in the late eighteenth century was over, and the eclecticism of the Victorian age was ebbing. Scotland, from the example of Sir Walter Scott and others, was a little less affected by it than England but, as Lorimer trained, attention was being directed again to the heritage of the buildings and gardens of the past. He loved the genius of the country and he came to believe that each building should grow naturally from its surroundings by making use of the materials of its locality, fashioned by its craftsmen to the forms traditional to it. As he found his inspiration in the people, the land of Scotland provided sites amid mountains for hill-top houses gazing on magnificent views across gardens striding the slopes in terraced banks; for mansions beside sea lochs like fiords and windswept moorlands and gardens in the far from flat lowlands like private arcadias sheltered behind high walls, as well as for long low unobtrusive cottages planted thick with rhododendrons and roses, the many dormers pushing against deep set sheltering roofs.

The palette Lorimer used, though limited mainly to stone and wood, employed every subtle nuance of regional style. There was grey Craigleith stone of Edinburgh, the cold sparkle of Aberdeenshire granite, the golden stone of Argyllshire, and everywhere, from Dumfriesshire in the south to the far north, other buildings harled (roughcast) against the weather on exposed sites, their walls whitewashed and gleaming in the distant spaces of the landscape, capped by roofs of ragged light-dappling grey slates from Ballachulish or Stobo, and also by the smoother warm coloured Easdale slates, as well as by great calm Caithness slabs in the north east.

Robert – or Robin as he was known as a boy – Lorimer was born in Edinburgh on 13 September, 1864, and was brought up with his five brothers and sisters in a pleasant but undistinguished Georgian house in Hill Street, which is one of the narrowest streets of the New Town. When he was nine the family moved to a larger house designed by David McGibbon who later produced the definitive book on the *Castellated Architecture of Scotland* with Thomas Ross.[1] The house at the end of Bruntsfield Crescent, as might be expected, is a scholarly exercise in the revival Baronial style, with a larger garden and the benefit of an open outlook to the north over Bruntsfield Links which provide a pleasant walk to the University.

His parents liked to get out of Edinburgh for the long holiday in the summer and rented country houses (Cockenzie House and Whinney Hall). In 1877 they bought about forty

Antique tile

1 OPPOSITE *Kellie Castle, Fife* c. *1885.* R.C.A.M.

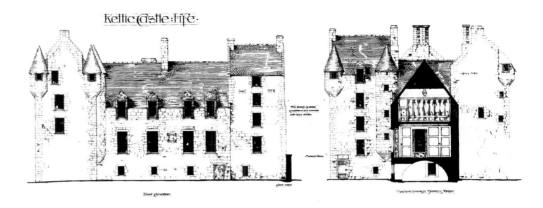

[1] *Kellie Castle, measured and drawn by Lorimer as an apprentice.* R.C.A.M.

Kellie Castle Fife

[2] *Professor James Lorimer by William Hole.* Quasi Cursores, Edinburgh 1883.

acres of land at Auchentrail near Upper Largo in Fife after they had rented a house called the Priory in Pittenweem for the summer. Although Auchentrail occupied their thoughts, according to his sister Louise, they were all immediately taken with Kellie[2], *Pl. 1*, a disused castle near Pittenween, when they happened to come across it on a walk. Professor Lorimer, a distinguished lawyer, suffered from asthma and as the climate of Fife had been recommended for its cure he decided to take a long thirty-eight-year lease of the castle to use as a summer holiday home.

If neither the Hill Street nor the Bruntsfield Crescent houses could have been described as cramped, Kellie offered a quite different experience. The vaulted undercrofts (at the ground floor level), the turnpike (spiral) stone stairs leading to a vaulted hall above, and tiny lookout rooms set within the huge thickness of the walls, the bedrooms with seventeenth century enriched plaster ceilings and the wide outlook from the bartisans (corner pepper-pot turrets) at the roof – all these features combined to give fresh insights into Scottish architectural history, and the influence of Kellie was to be profound on all the family.

Scottish professors in those days gave the introductory course of lectures in their subjects, no light load, but Professor Lorimer thereafter spent late spring and summer at Kellie, resolutely refusing to return to Edinburgh before November to start his lectures on Public Law. The task of running this rambling and beautiful, but in most ways inconvenient, establishment fell on his wife. It was a formidable task. The Victorian zeal for improving old buildings out of all recognition by virtually rebuilding them was passing out of fashion, and was not possible or financially feasible at Kellie, yet the swing back to merely repairing old derelict buildings and enjoying them for what they were, and accepting many of their limitations, was only beginning. Louise wrote in the family history that the condition in which they found this ancient building was such that neighbours like Sir Robert Anstruther, who had long regarded Kellie as a ruin, 'thought us daft'. All the windows were broken, the roof leaked like a sieve, and the fireplaces were stacked with fallen nests of decades of jackdaws and rooks. The Earl of Mar agreed, however, to have it made weather fast for them and on 'The glorious first of September in 1878' the family took

KELLIE CASTLE · FIFE
THE VIEW FROM THE GARDEN

R S Lorimer Delt

[3] LEFT *Realistic draughtsmanship by Lorimer; Kellie Castle.*   R.C.A.M.
[4] ABOVE *Factual draughtsmanship by Scott Morton; Edzell Castle.*   E.A.A., S. Bk *1875–1876.*
[5] BELOW *Lyrical draughtsmanship by W. Leiper; Allardyce Castle.*   E.A.A., S. Bk *1875–1876.*

possession and, after a candle lit supper, retired to bed tired but happy. Living conditions were to be spartan and basic. An earth closet in the garden for the men, no baths with running water or electric light, just candles and paraffin lamps.

Robin's oldest brother James had already followed his father into the law and was working in Leith. John, the next eldest, who was making his way as a painter, had entered the University of Edinburgh at fifteen, but also attended classes at the School of Design and later, in 1874, the life class at the Royal Scottish Academy. He did well enough in his studies at University despite a weakness in maths but, as his interests in art took over more of his time, he did not graduate but turned to painting full time. He was soon elected a member of the Royal Water Colour Society and in 1882 became an associate member of the R.S.A.[3] He also became very knowledgeable about antiques and helped find suitable pieces for Kellie.

John, Robin and Louise, who all shared an inclination to the arts, were all to spend much time on Kellie, and Robin began by plotting the garden and drawing out its plan. As a lad of thirteen, *frontispiece*, he had been too young to do more than observe the work of repair and restoration of Kellie, but the contrast between their Baronial town house and this genuine piece of Baronial history seems to have given him an insight which was to be the foundation of his success as an architect from which he went right to the top of his profession.

It is believed that his parents had known the architect William Burn, who had played such

[6] ABOVE *Design for a bedspread for Kellie Castle by Lorimer.*   R.C.A.M.

[7] BELOW *Plasterwork details of Kellie Castle drawn by Lorimer.*   R.C.A.M.

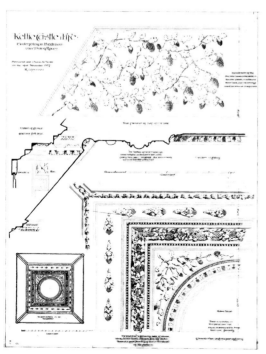

an important a part in the Baronial revival, and had pondered whether young Robin might be apprenticed to him, or to his nephew and successor MacVicar Anderson (Burn himself died at the age of eighty in 1870 when Robin was only six), but eventually he was entered at the University of Edinburgh, where his progress followed a similar pattern to John's. He took courses in the Humanities and Greek, passing all his courses but always low in marks, until having taken Fine Art as well in his third year, he persuaded his father to let him leave in 1884 without graduating and to take articles with the architect Hew Wardrop. Professor Lorimer knew the Professor of Fine Art, there being only forty professors in all at that time (who were known as the forty thieves), and as Professor Baldwin Brown would have met Wardrop and his partner Rowand Anderson through their work on the new medical school in Teviot Row, it is likely that he helped Professor Lorimer to his decision. Indeed, Brown's interest in architecture was such that he was to become President of the Edinburgh Architectural Association in 1890.

Maitland Wardrop, Hew's father, was among the foremost exponents of the Baronial revival in the middle of the nineteenth century, and if this revival had been strengthened by the writings and example of Sir Walter Scott,[4] it was also part of a general European swing towards nationalism and the use of national forms of expression. Hew Wardrop had not long taken over his father's practice when young Robin joined him as apprentice in 1884. There is no doubt that they got on well together. Wardrop's central belief that the roots of design lie in proportion was one which Lorimer came to share, and Tilliefour in Aberdeenshire, *Pl. 3*, one of the very few designs credited to Wardrop, was given a long, low white harled extension of many gables (to a small existing tower house), a theme which appears in Lorimer's early design for the Grange, North Berwick, *Fig. 20*. Years later Lorimer was to name his second son Hew after him.

The office was a good one for a young man beginning his career since the two junior partners were also exceedingly able men who were rising fast in the profession. Rowand Anderson was an older architect who had emerged from a specialised practice in episcopal churches (and he gave Lorimer his thorough grounding in the Gothic style) to become Edinburgh's leading architect on winning the 1874 competition for a new Medical School. George Washington Browne who was third partner, was also a firm man but one with a courtly manner and great personal dignity. He, like Anderson had begun to play a leading part in the affairs of the Edinburgh Architectural Association,[5] and went on to become the first architect to become President of the Royal Scottish Academy, both institutions with which Lorimer was to have close associations. If Browne as third partner seems to have had less to do with Lorimer, the young apprentice had an affectionate respect for him and his ability as a designer, because he believed that Browne could 'do the whole thing'. Browne had worked for J. J. Stevenson and W. Eden Nesfield in London before becoming Anderson's chief draughtsman on the Medical School; he became his partner in 1881 before they both joined Hew Wardrop as partners in 1884. If Browne could produce excellent Scots houses like Johnsburn at Balerno plainly relying on form and proportion, his own tastes ran to the richer modelling of the François Premier Architecture of France, which he used extensively for banks as well as for the Central Library in Edinburgh. J. Wilson who had worked for him has recalled how Browne felt that architecture was not something to be talked about but rather that 'the work was itself a message and an inspiration to all of us', and his belief in history was such that he was critical of 'the originality which has no origin'. Design had to evolve rather than revolve, a belief which he and Anderson instilled in Lorimer.

After Wardrop's early death Lorimer came mainly under Anderson's influence since Browne left the partnership not long afterwards. The carcase of the Medical School was finished by the time Lorimer joined the office, so the six months he spent on it were no doubt devoted to its fitments. The style of the building is fifteenth century Italian, which was but one of the many styles in which Anderson worked. His churches were in Gothic of various periods, his schools G. G. Scott midpointed, and his houses anything from the Butterfield Gothic to Jacobean Baronial. His country house work included Mount Stewart for the Marquis of Bute and as in any substantial Scots practice of that time, a number of baronial mansions being refurbished and extended, of which Tilliefour, which he had inherited from Wardrop, was one, and Lorimer had worked on this building in the office before being sent up to act as site agent during the construction, giving him a foretaste both of the problems of building on remote sites and of informal design, by which separate blocks were loosely grouped together to suggest a building which had been added to several times over the years. The new lodge, which was added, was half-timbered.

If Browne was a superb draughtsman, Anderson, too, drew competently and meticulously, as shown by his drawings for his book of *Municipal Architecture in France and Italy*. Lorimer learned rapidly from their example measuring buildings in Edinburgh and Fife, including his parents' home Kellie, all of which he drew out meticulously. His drawings, like Anderson's, are good archaeological records in which little or no effort was expended on artistic effects, and the style of drawing of Lorimer's office later owes much to his apprenticeship.

Plumbing and other technical subjects were taught at the Heriot Watt Institute in Edinburgh to which Lorimer repaired for classes first thing in the morning or in the evenings. He learned all about traditional construction in the office, Anderson being about the first Victorian architect in Scotland who tried in his restorations to leave the building as close to its original design as possible. Anderson had also built the Burgh Hall of Pollockshaws, which is transitional Baronial with features modelled on those of the old Glasgow College which had been pulled down to make way for a railway yard. Yet he remained a typical Victorian architect whose buildings are substantial and carefully modelled, and when asked on one occasion by Stirling Maxwell what he might have done had he had more money for a building he replied, with a shake of his head and a cheerful sigh, that he thought he 'should make the walls thicker'. Yet despite the care with which he planned his buildings, he failed sometimes, as with the McEwan Hall for the University of

[8] *Robin reading to 'the Prof' drawn by his brother John.*   R.C.A.M.

Edinburgh, to provide the lighting necessary to bring out the spatial effects, but his high respect for the best in traditional form was also something which his young apprentice respected.

There is a story that Lorimer did not get on well with Anderson, who had a firmness in manner verging on vehemence. Anderson, like Lorimer, came from a legal family, and he had completed his law articles before turning to architecture, after which he rose steadily in his adopted profession, though not without some upsets. He was elected an associate of the Royal Scottish Academy in 1876 but resigned seven years later when he considered that he had been passed over for full membership. Then as he rose rapidly to become the doyen of the profession in Scotland the Academy reinstated him as an honorary member. His partnership with the two Bryces lasted but months in 1870, with Browne about four years, and with Simon and Crawford his partnership was ended in between two and three years by a lawsuit of 1901. He was called in to make alterations at Balmoral and was invited to enter a limited competition for laying out the Mall from Buckingham Palace to Admiralty Arch (which he did not win). He set up a dynastic office, and near the end of his life, after taking the leading role in setting up the Royal Incorporation of Architects in Scotland in 1916, he then gave the Incorporation the building it occupies in Rutland Square next door to his own office, of which William Laing remembers that it 'had a dignity of its own, a sort of class distinction, where I was made to feel what I was, a small boy. Sir Robert Lorimer's office was much freer in atmosphere'.

Anderson, who was the very opposite of Browne in temperament, was nevertheless very interested in the training of his young apprentices; within a year or two of Lorimer leaving his office, he succeeded in 1892 in setting up a school of applied art[6] at the Royal Scottish Academy where he assisted with the teaching for a while. He felt that too great an importance could not be put on history, which was taught in all schools of design of the day as though it were the only springboard of invention. If Robert Lorimer subsequently has not earned the reputation for being easy of temperament, he managed not only to complete his articles with Anderson after Wardrop's death, but then even to stay on for a further year as improver (an improver was one who worked up and improved the rough sketches passed to him by his principal).

History in those days was not only the central force in building design. It governed the choice of much of the contents also, and Anderson and Lorimer shared a keen interest in antique furniture, Anderson leaving some of his choicest pieces to Holyrood House.[7] Towards the end of Lorimer's stay with him an event occurred which gave the final direction to Lorimer's career when among other things he turned to furniture design: The National Congress for the Improvement of Art was held in Edinburgh and to it came all the leading figures of the Arts and Crafts movement. As his brother John was secretary to the painters' section, he was in a position to introduce his young brother to many visiting dignitaries. Anderson gave an optimistic and confident talk on the state of British architecture and predicted a great future for it. George Frederic Bodley, a leading Arts and

Crafts architect from London, attended the conference and it was to his office that Lorimer moved a year later. He had to wait for the opening, but filled his spare time with a study of Bodley's work so thorough that he used to boast that when he got there he found that he knew more about the past work of the office than the staff who were already there.

Bodley saw every building as an artwork fashioned democratically by a band of craftsmen of whom the architect was but one. His Arts and Crafts approach in design was the reason for Lorimer being in London, but Bodley did not offer much by way of instruction (according to one of his notable pupils) he gave them instead the run of his house with its exquisite fabrics and furnishings which was an education in itself. Christopher Hussey has stressed Bodley's influence on Lorimer's woodwork details but all that is common to their work is the Gothic play of craftsmanship.

Walter Tapper, from Bodley's office, remained Lorimer's close friend for life but there is an indication of some resentment when Lorimer chose to move, in rather less than a year, to another office which not only practised Arts and Crafts methods but which also had strong Scots connections. He had spent much of his spare time in London with his fellow expatriates among whom Norman Shaw was most notable, and he had been recommended for associateship with the R.I.B.A. by J. J. Stevenson, who declared he had known him a year by 1890. By 1891 he had moved to the office of the late James Maclaren which had been taken over by Bob Watson and William Dunn, who both became firm friends. If there is some affinity with their work it derives from their backgrounds which shared so much in common. Other architects from Scotland with whom he mixed were John Begg, who had trained with Hippolyte Blanc, Robin Dods, *Pl. 275*, an Australian who had trained with Hay and Henderson, and Roger Kitsell, who had been at university with him, and was also apprenticed to Rowand Anderson.

This set of London friends was hardworking yet found time for much else besides. They scoured the antique shops and Begg has told how Lorimer and Dods stopped 'to gaze into the window of an antique shop in the King's Road. Suddenly their eyes lighted at the same time on a Chippendale tray, and both made a dive to get in. They got jammed in the doorway and they struggled for a moment, but Dods was the smaller and thinner, and he got in first and snatched the tray.' Lorimer and 'his wee boxes' had become a standing joke with them but their deep interest in the antique took them frequently to the Victoria and Albert Museum to measure and sketch.

Lorimer found the time, as well, to design a house for an uncle who was a doctor in Wimbledon, *Fig. 9*. This first design in Arthur Road is set like so many of his later buildings on the brow of a hill, although uncharacteristically for him, it is built of brick and in the revival Queen Anne style, which had been characteristic of Bodley's domestic practice since the 1860s. The only drawings extant are those submitted for bye-law permission which then called only for details of the drainage, so that the front elevation was included to show the stand pipes. The draughtsmanship is rough and shows many changes to windows, and the elevation does not entirely correspond with the plan, all of which suggests that Lorimer

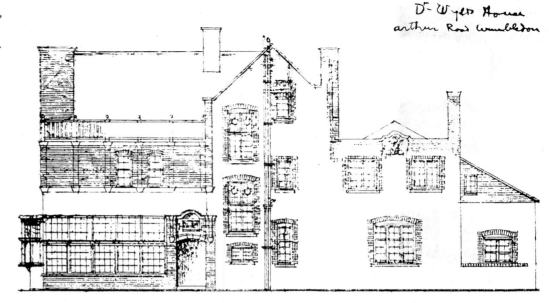

[9] *Fieldhead, Lorimer's first exercise in Queen Anne, a house for an uncle in Arthur Road, Wimbledon.*

O.D.

Antique tile.

rushed this scheme out quickly amid all the other things he was doing in London. The composition does not recall any other particular building, but there are features, like the wood balustrade around the flat roof in the corner of the L-shaped block, which are similar to those used by Norman Shaw. The overall massing, however, is more casual and less well ordered than any of Shaw's houses of similar scale (at Bedford Park), with a freedom of grouping which may owe something to Maclaren, but might equally well derive from the Baronial.

Everywhere Lorimer and his friends went, they carried sketchbooks, incessantly measuring and jotting down details. The Edinburgh Architectural Association and the London Architectural Association sketchbooks include many examples of their industry. In later years the first thing Lorimer would tell a new apprentice entering his office was to have a pocket for a footrule made in his trousers. Lorimer had his down the seam of his right leg below the side pocket. A 'poacher's pocket' was also required to be made inside the jacket to take a 'bushey' notebook with a fabric loop to prevent the sheets becoming creased.

Whether Lorimer intended to pass more than an interlude with Bodley to gain experience in Arts and Crafts methods is unlikely in view of his deep love of Scotland and its own architecture, and his stay in Maclaren's office ended after he was asked by R. W. Mackenzie (a friend of his parents) if he would undertake the restoration of a sixteenth century tower house in Fife. The house, Earlshall,[8] was only eleven miles from Kellie, and had a considerable enclosure surrounded by a high stone wall in which a garden was to be laid out. He began the designs in London and had made a preliminary scheme by the time he left in 1892 on his return north to set up office on his own account in Edinburgh, which he did at 49 Queen Street in May 1893.

2 *Lorimer while an apprentice painted by his brother John.* C.L.

3 *Tilliefour, Aberdeenshire, for which Lorimer was site agent.* P.S.

2

Practice in the Nineties

Professor Lorimer had died in 1890 but the family's winter house was still in Bruntsfield Crescent and there Lorimer stayed on his return from London. Although his sister Louise spent much of her time there, since his father's death his mother lived most of the time at Kellie, which Robin himself began to frequent at the week-ends. He would take the train to the nearest point on the main line north, and after retrieving his bicycle from the guard's van, would pedal the rest of the journey. At Kellie he would think nothing of cycling the eleven miles across to Earlshall to take more dimensions before returning to Kellie to work out further details.

Lorimer became involved with the educational affairs of the Edinburgh Architectural Association soon after his return when he agreed to conduct a competition for a Presbyterian Church. In 1892 Rowand Anderson became Vice-President and Lorimer one of the six members of council and they both served on the sketchbook committee. Earlshall, *Pl. 4*, had attracted attention even in dereliction. The members had sketched it and proposals to remodel it entirely fortunately came to nought, *Fig. 10*. In the late spring of 1893 he conducted a visit by members of the Association around Earlshall, at which time he gave a paper describing its history since it was built in 1497. The actual work of restoration appears to have been discussed as they walked around the building and only in one comment in his paper did his own attitude to restoration emerge as he told how Earlshall, like Kellie, had been empty for more than seventy years before its restoration was begun, and as the roof had become dilapidated parts of a unique black and white distemper pattern on the wooden plank ceiling of the second floor gallery had been effaced, *Pl. 17*. He described how only the work which remained 'clearly legible' was re-touched and that no attempt was made to fill in those parts which had disappeared, since, in his view, such recreation often destroys the character of the old work. The remark shows a young architect alert to the dangers of restoration, yet today no obvious gaps remain which were not filled in. This delicate work was entrusted to Mr Nixon of Moxon and Carfrae, who had also a measured drawing of the ceiling to guide him drawn out some years earlier by Thomas Bonnar, *Fig. 13*, possibly the architect of that name but, more probably, the earlier principal of the firm of decorative designers.

Earlshall is arranged in an L-shaped block with the longer wing housing the main apartments facing south across the former barmican (a walled enclosure forming an entrance court), *Pl. 6*, which was enclosed by walls east and west and by a range of out-buildings to the south, and which allowed the main door to be put at ground level

4 OPPOSITE *Earlshall of yesteryear, engraved by Joseph Swan.* P.S.

9

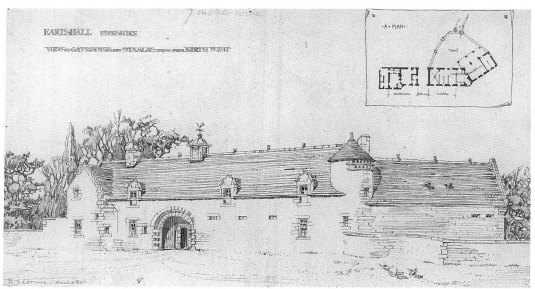

[10] LEFT *Earlshall, Fife, a late Victorian scheme in the 'Old Balmorality'.* R.C.A.M.

[11] RIGHT *Earlshall, the first unrealised scheme for the Lodge.* R.C.A.M.

conveniently close to the wellhead. The west wall of the barmican which had been replaced already by a lower stone wall was again replaced, this time by an open stone balustrade affording views of the garden beyond it, whereas the house itself, apart from routine repairs to such things as woodwork, required nothing of importance to be added except an openwork screen across one end of the hall, *Pl. 19*. He took as his model a screen in Falkland Palace[1], the only addition being some carving including an inscription upon the transome to give its date.

Earlshall, Lorimer's first restoration, thus shows him working with so light a touch that the only obvious sign of his involvement internally is the stained glass with its arts and crafts manner which was put in the peep holes on the turnpike stairs. The antique furniture and tapestries, of which Mackenzie was so keen a collector, may be seen in all the early photographs of the interior taken after the restoration. The cottages on the south side of the barmican were slightly remodelled and given quite plain dormer heads which also carry the date of their execution, and the kitchen inside shows one of Lorimer's first essays in furniture design, *Pl. 20*. The table and benches are probably to his design, the bink (long bench) and shelves carrying pottery produced at Wemyss[2] are certainly his because all his earliest pieces are scaled for cottages or farm houses.

The garden enclosure, which was then under grass, left Lorimer free to suggest what he wanted for it. Interest in the little of Scotland's ancient walled gardens which the zeal of the picturesque improvers had not swept away was strong in the nineties. The Baronial revivalists had usually followed the eighteenth century practice of detaching the house amid open landscaping, looking for all as if, Lorimer said, the house were set upon a Sunday airing. He much preferred the snugness of a walled garden which opened from the foot of a turnpike (or spiral) stair as it did at Edzell Castle[3] which he admired so much. It represented

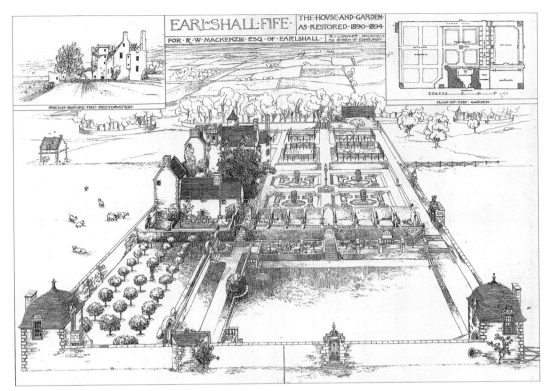

an earlier form of Scottish garden better adapted to the windy climate of the east coast of Scotland, and which provided an outdoor room within the shelter and security of its walls, or an enclosed paradise in which to stroll to watch the changes of the seasons. The enclosed area at Edzell was about a quarter of the size of that of Earlshall and provided space only for a parterre of flower borders and miniature hedges, and Lorimer's first proposals for Earlshall show the central part of the garden to the east of the house treated in that way. He had set his close friend John Begg, who was also the best draughtsman he knew, to draw a fine bird's-eye view perspective of the whole layout, *Fig. 12*. It is entitled 'Work carried out at Earlshall between 1891 and 1894' but by the time it was exhibited at the R.S.A. in 1896 it had been overtaken by events and the parterre had been discarded in favour of a lawn set with yews clipped like heroic-scaled chessmen, *Pls. 9, 11, 14*. The yews were found in an abandoned garden in Edinburgh, probably by Lorimer, and after it was arranged to use them, the gardener at Earlshall was offered five pounds for every one which took. No failures are recorded!

Topiary had been introduced to Scotland from Holland in the fifteenth century but in the few examples which still exist the standards are usually set within borders, whereas at Earlshall they rise immediately from the lawn, echoing in minor key, the shapes of the house rising from the edge of this lawn. Nathaniel Lloyd who was to see it, so approved of this arrangement that he got Lutyens to use it for the garden when remodelling Great Dixter in Sussex for him.

Earlshall is approached by a drive, which turns off the road along the north of the policies (the grounds) through a covert of trees, passing then under an arched gatehouse, *Pl. 7*, into a wide meadow flanked to the left by a high garden wall, *Pl. 5*. An immediate contrast is struck between the seclusion of the garden, the house set midway along its wall, and the bare open space facing it along whose edge the drive traces its path. Just short of the house it ends in a turning circle and a narrow paved path crosses the turf to a large arched gateway set sideways to the drive. As the small pass-door within it is opened a rough cobbled yard (the former barmican or walled in courtyard around the well) comes to view crossed by smooth paving leading to the doors of the house and cottage at either side, and in front the massy shapes of the yew garden come into view over a low stone balustrade, to jostle, opening and closing ranks, as we move obliquely towards them.

The whole garden nestles beneath belts of sheltering trees set north, south, and on the east from where the cold winds of the North Sea come. A yew alley (walk), *Pls. 12, 15*, runs along the south of this pleasance overlooking the bowling green to its south from above a stone terrace. Delphiniums, hollyhocks, iris, lilies and phlox can be seen in the early photographs within the bays of this yew hedge, suggesting that although Lorimer was interested in plants for their historical associations, he was content to rely mainly on the old favourites he found in the gardens he visited nearby.

Immediately south of the cottages is now a small paved garden with rock plants, which is the only part of the garden to have been much changed. Originally it was laid out as another topiary garden echoing the topiary garden at miniature scale. South again of this part of the garden is the orchard, *Pl. 13*, laid out as simple rectangular borders with the straggly fruit trees separated by grass paths which lead to a small mount at the centre surmounted by a sun-dial. Vegetables and espaliered fruit trees are set north of the house and pleasance.

The various compartments of this garden have been laid out to open from each other with cunning spatial effects and changes of level. Axes have been used a great deal not so as to give one immediate all revealing single climax, but as a series of minor axes informally interwoven in their effects. The spirit of the first scheme has been retained but many changes of detail have been made in execution. One small garden shelter replaces two large corner pavilions to the south, and a sewing pavilion, *Pl. 10*, has been added in the north-west corner. A later bird's-eye view drawn by Rome Guthrie in 1901 after the garden had been completed shows a large sundial in the centre of the topiary garden for which no other evidence exists. He also gives details of a charming wood and iron trellis along the south of the bowling green which has probably decayed. The carved birds which topped it were probably carved by the Clow Bros, an example of whose work still exists in Skirling Peeblesshire, *Pl. 16*.

The family legend has it that Mackenzie was walking with Lorimer over Tentsmuir when he first stumbled across this dilapidated mansion. It is more likely that in those days before

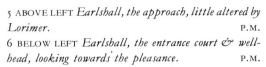

9 ABOVE LEFT *Earlshall, the topiary garden today from the house.* P.M.

10 BELOW LEFT *Earlshall, interior of the sewing pavilion.* R.S.L.

11 RIGHT *Earlshall, the topiary garden today.* P.M.

12–15 *Earlshall*, ABOVE LEFT *yew alley today*, P.M.; BELOW LEFT *orchard with mount & sundial*, P.M.; TOP RIGHT *topiary garden* C. *1910*, C.L.; MIDDLE RIGHT *yew alley* C. *1910*, C.L.

16 BELOW RIGHT *Skirling, toucan carved by the Brothers Clow.* J. SHEARER

17–20 *Earlshall*, ABOVE LEFT *painted gallery*, C.L.; BELOW LEFT *window*, P.M.; ABOVE RIGHT *hall & Falkland screen*; BELOW RIGHT *cottage kitchen*, C.L.

the car, they had come over from Kellie by train especially to see it, and that Mackenzie who was a family friend of the Lorimers had decided to give young Robin his chance. His own father was a Perth lawyer who sent him to the University of Edinburgh where he matriculated at the age of sixteen but is not recorded on any class list. He entered his father's firm but then gave up the law to enter a bleaching firm near Perth, of which he became senior partner. He was generally interested in fabrics and in particular tapestries. Lorimer turned to him for advice when a tapestry was sought for Kellie, but was critical later when Mackenzie ran a summer school on tapestry weaving, believing it only encouraged people to think they could learn techniques in weeks that the old craftsmen had taken decades to acquire, but he and Mackenzie continued to attend sales together. If Lorimer was already designing embroideries to be executed by his relatives, Mackenzie also made designs for woven linen tea towels based on patterns of rooks and rookeries derived from those at Earlshall. He ran garden fêtes at Earlshall and had pottery fairings with the same motif made by the Wemyss Pottery which also used other designs by him.

Mackenzie, it is clear, had a leaning to the Arts and Crafts which attracted Lorimer. In later years, Mackenzie, eleven years older than Lorimer, developed a severe expression and sported a large walrus moustache. Even his dress revealed his eccentricities of character: he usually wore a Mackenzie tartan waistcoat with pockets that had flaps in which he carried watch and snuff, and a Perth hat, like a squat top hat, made out of cloth of various shades of brown, black or grey. His greatest interest was in breeding Shetland ponies, for which he won many prizes, and his wife bred bloodhounds. They had no children. He was a freemason who considered tea and coffee to be poisons and seldom drank anything but whisky. This was the bohemian character to whom Lorimer always referred as 'the laird' and who introduced him at Earlshall to William Burrell, another art lover who was to be influential in Lorimer's career.

The earliest drawings of Earlshall can be recognised as being from Lorimer's own hand. Some of the garden drawings are Begg's, other immature sketches seem to be those of Lorimer's first apprentice J. F. Matthew who entered his office in May 1893 when it opened. John Matthew over his first five years with Lorimer was successively apprentice, improver and assistant, before taking over as office manager, in which post he remained for over a quarter of a century before being made a partner in 1926. He was to play a vital part in the firm's success. His father was a military tailor in Queen Street whose keen interest in all forms of ceremony and pageant he shared. After John left school he acted as a page in the retinue of the Lord High Commissioner at Holyrood, when in his spare time he made a model of the building which he gave to another page. Lorimer's sister Louise was visiting the house to collect the rent when she saw the model on the mantelpiece and she was so impressed by it that she borrowed it to show her brother. He went to Stevenson's, the bookseller on the Mound where John was working, and giving Mr Stevenson a week's wages in place of John's notice, he took him into his office there and then.

John, then an alert lad of seventeen, had had some previous experience in drawing,

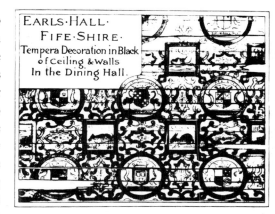

[13] *Earlshall, the painted gallery, tempera on plastered walls & boarded ceiling.*
E.A.A., S. Bk 1887–1894.

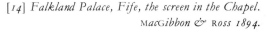

[14] *Falkland Palace, Fife, the screen in the Chapel.*
MacGibbon & Ross 1894.

having won a prize for it at James Gillespie's School, and he began immediately on the drawings for alterations at Aberlour House in Banff for J. R. Finlay of the *Scotsman*. The work entailed a new gateway, *Fig. 15*, and remodelling the drawing room, and when Alfred Waterhouse later told the client 'that he thought my [Lorimer's] drawing room there was the prettiest room he had ever seen', Lorimer was prompted to write, 'Just think of it. Thirty two years old and to have sunk so low as that already. Pity your poor friend.' If Lorimer's views on the London 'establishment' were already exceedingly critical, this had been Matthew's first job and he later pencilled 'our first job' on the back of one of the drawings. Lorimer always acted as if he knew just what he wanted to do but his drawings include many examples of schemes which changed entirely in character from the early to the final drawings, and the considerable number of slightly changed but incomplete drawings still existing suggests many switches of intention by Lorimer himself. He believed that one must always try to design on the spur of the moment, so once detailing had begun he always set great store by his assistants getting into the spirit of a job by frequent visits to the site. When he set about educating John architecturally, he put suitable books his way and soon gave him a copy of *Plain Handicrafts* edited by MackMurdo, followed at Christmas by *The Lamp of Architecture*. The Christmas of 1894 was marked by *Arts and Crafts Essays*, prefaced by William Morris, and that following by *Art and Handicraft* by Sedding. The choice of these books shows also Lorimer's pre-occupation with the methods of the arts and crafts movement.

As Lorimer settled back into Edinburgh life, other small commissions began to come in. He began remodelling 8 Buckingham Terrace for a relative, he extended Westbrook near Balerno with a wing for bathrooms and other offices, as well as two new houses for Colinton and North Berwick, close to Edinburgh, after which his practice settled at a modest but steady five commissions a year, as well as all the minor alterations which come the way of any young architect starting in practice. He worked at Minto House in 1894, remodelling a bridge across the burn, and adding some interior plasterwork. It was his first job for the county set. He made extensive alterations to St Marnocks, a country house near Dublin, *Fig. 16*, for which he extended the east end in a manner which foreshadows the Hill of Tarvit of ten years later, and planted palm trees to flank the entrance, as well as remodelling the existing garden. He built a medium-sized house in Argyll, Stronachullin Lodge, and reconstructed Ellary, a house nearby, after a fire, *Fig. 22*. He began designing a hotel for fishermen at Clousta on Shetland.

In 1895 he worked on some uninteresting alterations for Ormidale 'a beastly looking house' in Murrayfield, gates for Grandtully Castle, and Roxobel, a new house in Colinton. The following year he did some alterations for a Scottish Academician a few doors from the family house in Bruntsfield Crescent and extensions to Torduff, a house in Juniper Green. Nothing else came in and he wrote in the summer, 'Am beginning to feel in the deepest gloom about "My practice" and looking forward to a winter on the streets when yesterday up comes a bloke called Major Seton saying he has been much charmed with my Earlshall

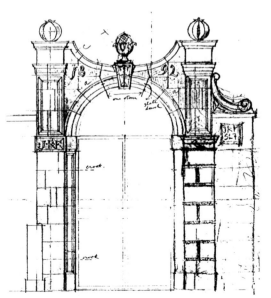

[*15*] *Aberlour House, Banff, gateway.*   O.D.

drawing in the R.S.A. and thought I was the man to restore an old place he had recently succeeded to in Aberdeenshire.' Mounie, an existing seventeenth century house, was a simple rectangular block of three floors set over a vaulted undercroft with a turnpike staircase rising from the first floor in a circular tower at the middle of the block, *Fig. 17*. The attic floor had dormer windows. An ambitious scheme was drawn up, to show a large new house planned with a narrow link to the old house and a long terraced garden planned to the south. Seton was something of a spendthrift, however, who was to mortgage the estate more than once until he finally retired to East Anglia to become a minister, and the estate had to be broken up. Almost nothing of Lorimer's fine scheme was carried out, but the old house was remodelled to give two floors of rooms which are too high for their breadth and with unfortunate results for the proportions. The attic floor and the dormers were removed and the only work in the garden which remains is an old dovecote from which Lorimer formed a small but charming pavilion. Nor did anything come from an ambitious scheme for Hall-yards in Peeblesshire (Exhibited at the R.S.A. in 1900), *Fig. 19*.

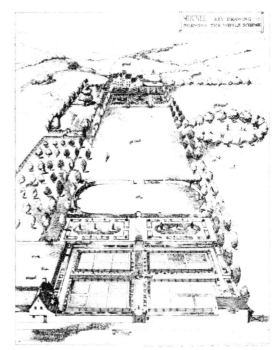

[17] *Mounie Castle, an ambitious garden scheme for Aberdeenshire.*   R.C.A.M.

Lorimer's country house work was still proceeding very slowly, largely on minor works, but his smaller houses were beginning to attract attention. *The Builder* had begun to publish illustrations of them in 1895, along with drawings of Earlshall, and in September a pull-out spread of four designs for modern Scottish houses built in local style was included. The Grange, North Berwick was for a law-lord, Lord Trayner, to whom Lorimer later became related through his wife. The perspective shows plain harled walls and a composition crowded with incidents mostly Scottish in character, *Fig. 20*. The house is set like a lookout on the brow of the hill which overlooks North Berwick from the south, and the public rooms were faced north with wide views over the Firth of Forth to the distant shores of Fife. As the site was exposed, so the drive was brought in from the south along the foot of a sheltering bank, and the kitchen garden within walls is set to the south in the lea of the house. The coachman's living quarters are set above the coach-house beside the entrance

[18] LEFT *Roxobel, Colinton.*   R.C.A.M.

[19] RIGHT *Hallyards, Peeblesshire, another unrealised scheme.*   N.L.S.

gates in a simple rectangular building with a red pantiled roof. The informally shaped gable is an early example of Lorimer's delight in such flourishes, *Pls. 24, 25.*

Two further perspective sketches showed west coast houses. After a fire he restored Ellary, a late Victorian Baronial house by Bryce, by merely adding a billiard room and heightening the tower. The plainness of the interiors, however did not give pleasure. 'I got most of it painted before the bride came on the scene,' he lamented, 'but she insisted on having her own way with the billiard room, my nice billiard room and do you know what this pig headed idiot has done, painted all the woodwork and the plaster dado imitation burr walnut with the most putrid yellow paper on the walls of my poor fireplace recess, my five sided window oriel. I simply burst out laughing.' Orr, the site agent with whom he was going round for the last time, told him, 'It's the only room in the house they like.' Lorimer's reply was, 'It's like a brothel in Pimlico. I'll spare you the furniture.'

Stronachullin Lodge, a few miles away to the east across the Mull of Kintyre, was received better, *Fig. 25.* It is set on the lower slopes of a moor overlooking Loch Fyne. The site was chosen for the view and such shelter as there is has been provided by thickets of rhododendrons. A sheltered court for harnessing the horses has been contrived by wrapping the house around the court in a U, and by placing the stable block across the other side, *Fig. 23.* This composition, like that of the two earlier houses, is full of incident yet knit together with an increasing mastery. The openings are placed very carefully in the simple wall surfaces and carefully proportioned, and the scale and massing have been manipulated

21 ABOVE *Roxobel, the off-beat symmetry of the* S. *elevation.* P.M.

22–23 BELOW *Roxobel, details of the coping.* P.M.

24 LEFT *The Grange, North Berwick, detail of gates & lodge.* P.M.

25 RIGHT *The Grange, North Berwick, lodge & stables.* P.M.

by changes in the eaves level, so that features are advanced or recessed to give a great variety of effect within a unity of overall impression. The drive arrives at the south west side of the house, so as to meet the main entrance, *Fig. 25*, at the end of one of the wings of the U-planned house and the stable court is found to the left, with the house extending to the right. On the far right in counterpoise, and designed to turn the corner to the main facade, is a pavilion, the main feature of which is a catslide gable oversailed by a few inches at the first

[20] *The Grange, as built in 1893.*   R.C.A.M.

[21] *The Grange, the 1904 extensions.*   R.C.A.M.

[22] ABOVE RIGHT *Ellary, Argyllshire, after restor-*
ation. N.L.S.

[23]–[25] *Stronachullin lodge, Argyllshire,* ABOVE
LEFT *the plan;* BELOW LEFT *the entrance;* MIDDLE
RIGHT *the* S. *approach;* BELOW RIGHT *view from* E.
N.L.S.

THE FRONT DOOR.

floor. The south-east face, in contrast, is advanced below in a large bay window which juts towards the south-west and the long view across Loch Fyne, and the line of the eaves swept low above is cut by one off-centre dormerhead. The rest of the accommodation lying beyond is set back subordinately with the service quarters lying across the back of the stable court. It was a fine piece of massing spoilt later in the thirties when Matthew was asked to add another wing.

The fourth perspective in *The Builder* showed a design for a manse at West Wemyss, *Fig. 26*. The coastal plain of Fife is dotted with small towns and for this more domestic landscape Lorimer chose a traditionally common L shaped block, its simple mass only enlivened by its details. The caption to the group of drawings read: 'These modern Scottish houses built in the local style illustrate the principle of employing in all cases local material and local workmanship and thus producing houses characteristic of a stonebuilding district.' The words were either Lorimer's or the editor's paraphrase of them.

[26] *West Wemyss Manse, two views.*   N.L.S.

It may seem contrary of Lorimer to have used harling to express the qualities of stone, yet experience of using granite in random rubble walls, in Aberdeenshire in particular, has shown that harling is the only way to make them weather tight in exposed situations. The granite being entirely impermeable, water begins to run down any granite wall face in all but the slightest of showers, while a wind will push the water through the slightest fissures in it, and it is no accident that harling came to be widely used in Scotland. It so happened, also, that a fashion for white walls adopted by Lorimer's contemporaries like Ernest Newton occasionally, or by art nouveau architects like Voysey universally, brought Lorimer's houses additional attention and Heathcote Statham, the editor of *The Builder*, in writing a book on modern houses two years later, remarked that Lorimer's designs had 'attracted a good deal of attention and admiration among the more artistic section of architects.

The designs were noteworthy for their fine sense of proportion and careful massing and this publicity established Lorimer as an up-and-coming Arts and Crafts designer of cottages derived from the vernacular. He had returned from London imbued with the ideals of William Morris and with the example of George Bodley, best known for his churches, whose success was due no more to his sensitive design than to his careful orchestration of his artists and craftsmen. The structural possibilities of any church in the Gothic offer wider opportunities for practising the great gospel of materials than a house, yet from his first days in practice Lorimer had found opportunities for the craftsmen who were to work with him, in many cases, for the rest of his life. Sam Wilson and Thomas Beattie were moulding enriched ceilings for him within his first year in practice and the Clow brothers, according to Hussey, had begun wood carving for him. They became as imbued with the spirit of the old work as he was, and, like him, they took holidays in Europe to sketch and to visit museums. Lorimer wrote in 1896 of spending, 'a few hours cooling one's hands in the grey twilight of *Gothic* things in Amiens', the first of many such references in his letters.

His first Gothic job was remodelling the Chapel of Wemyss Castle in Fife.[4] He told Dods now back in Australia, 'I was at Wemyss today and it always affects me the same as Earlshall.

I want to be left alone to dream and dream by the hour about the "right kind of stuff to do and the right kind of life to live" as you put it. There was nobody there today and after looking over the stonework of my chapel which is really not going to look so bad, a good Norman crypt, I went and strolled about the delicious rooms. It's not that there's anything wonderful about them but they have an atmosphere. Something you can't describe and that a mug can't feel, that you feel yourself thinking, you don't know why, about everything that is most precious in life and design, fancy that has taken fair shapes, children's laughter and the never to be discovered girl. The ideal life in the ideal old, traditional "un-hurrying" Scotland, and outside right below the windows, the great sad moving sea, and ships tacking for the Baltic. I think it's the sea that does it, and then you feel that you simply must keep on doing things your way, and that please God, if you don't altogether lose the place, that you may perhaps someday produce one or two jobs that have the "little more" about them, that to have done would be to have done something, but that if one allows oneself to be drawn into the ordinary rush of things, when you have the other temperament, you'd make life a simple hell for yourself.

His letters tell of the artists he was using. Phoebe Traquair, a painter and enamellist, had been staying at Kellie, 'I don't think I know *anyone* who is as sympathetic to me artistically. She's so *sane*, such a lover of simplicity, and the things that give real lasting pleasure are the simplest things of nature. The singing of birds, the bleating of sheep in the distance, morning and evening, everything and everyone she finds interesting and all this without a trace of self consciousness!' Louis Davis, the stained glass artist from London, came to stay at Kellie soon after. 'He's a ripper, a chap of about 40 but as keen as a boy. Such a lovable chap, he and I became great pals at Oxford last year', and 'he's going to do my altar piece at Wemyss and I wired to him to try to get on the job while *Randolph* is still keen about it. And *Phoebe* is going to paint a series of fourteen station of the Cross probably. Going to do a sample one first, and she and I devised such a nice piece on Sunday, *comme ça* . . . . a spray with a wee crown worked in at the top . . . last week we arranged a shrine to our Lady. It's in a deep recess there in at one side', and, 'on the other side there's to be an altar to Saint Margaret of Scotland'. The altar was to be a stone shelf supported by 'one twisty column without cap or base! Oh, we're a going of it.'

This early work is not so well integrated as his later Gothic work but this same letter comments on the theme which is central to all his work, the sense of place. 'The other day I started what I really think is rather a "romantic" idea. You know the house [Wemyss Castle] stands on a great cliff over the sea. Well, up to now they've never had access down to the beach but he's now devised a steep stair and then a steep winding path with a few steps there and here, down to the sea, this is to be the way for the public and what we're going to do is this, out of the face of God's solid rock, we're going to carve a niche with a figure of the titular saint, "St Mary Star of the Sea", I'd trouble your early Christians to beat *that*. Talbot is doing a large silver panel to be let into the window jamb with an inscription Randolph wrote and the full title of the chapel is "St Mary Star of the Sea at Wemyss" on the panel in raised letters with a simple border round of . . . good old square flowers' set between, 'two little beads, nice to hear of a *fresh* idea like that, isn't it?'

Lorimer used to write regularly to Dods as he travelled between those jobs which offered him plenty of time. The letters are often terse and jerky from the motion of the train, but imbued deeply with Lorimer's sense of poetry in life. The next Gothic job of any consequence was to be in Murrayfield, an Edinburgh suburb of stone-terraced houses. He began work on the Church of the Good Shepherd in 1897, *Fig. 27*. It has a long, low nave only twenty-five feet wide built of stone from the Hailes Quarry⁵ some four miles away, with a cusped wood ceiling under a simple slate roof, *Pl. 32*. Room for a north aisle was allowed but like the squat tower shown on the drawing illustrated in an *Architectural Review* in 1902, it has never been built. The result is a simple unassuming exterior of a scale similar to Walter Brierley's Goathland Church built a few years earlier. The interior, however, has been modelled in a way that is anything but sparsely rural and is a complex interplay of form. The piers of the chancel arch rise vertically until they terminate against the cusped roof in triangular caps, and the arch itself springs from brackets set about two thirds of their height above the floor. Similarly the east window has vertical jambs with a very flat arch bridging it. The glass is by Oscar Paterson and Thomas of Glasgow. A reredos screen, a feature found in so many of Bodley's churches, is placed across the entry to the chancel, and its emphasis is vertical. The cusped ceilings of nave and chancel rise from strongly horizontal cornices.

The collecting of antiques continued to be another all-important influence from which Lorimer began to derive furniture designs which he exhibited at the Arts and Crafts exhibitions. His blossoming friendship with William Burrell, destined to be Scotland's greatest and most extensive collector, drew him to collecting for its own sake. They were almost the same age, with similar interests in art, and were both bachelors. Lorimer wrote to Dods telling him that Burrell was 'dying to get hold of an old castle, and would turn me loose on one tomorrow if I could find one for him but I can't, but he's a rare good chap to be in with and I'll land him in for something yet. He travels pretty well all over Europe two or three times a year visiting their agents and is a great buyer of furniture etc., and really has very fine taste (God knows where he got it and his knowledge from). I went through to spend a night with them a few weeks ago, lives with his mother and two rather engaging sisters. Had a card last night fr[om] the Mama asking me through to dine on the 28th. You bet I'll go. I should think a big dinner there w[oul]d be great, and he wants to talk more about the old castle after the guests go.'

When the Burrells took a holiday in Europe later in the year Lorimer went with them. 'The party consisted of Burrell, my Glasgow client, his mother, a fine old Trojan of 64, his two sisters and a friend of B's called Mitchell.' They saw Rotterdam, Amsterdam and the Hague and he found that 'it was very interesting going round all the shops with Burrell, and I think I can say that I know the ropes in the way of antique shops', *Pl. 76*. Burrell meanwhile had been looking over Newark Castle on the cliffs near Elie in Fife. He came to stay at Kellie and they went over to see it together, after which Lorimer produced a scheme with 'a nailing

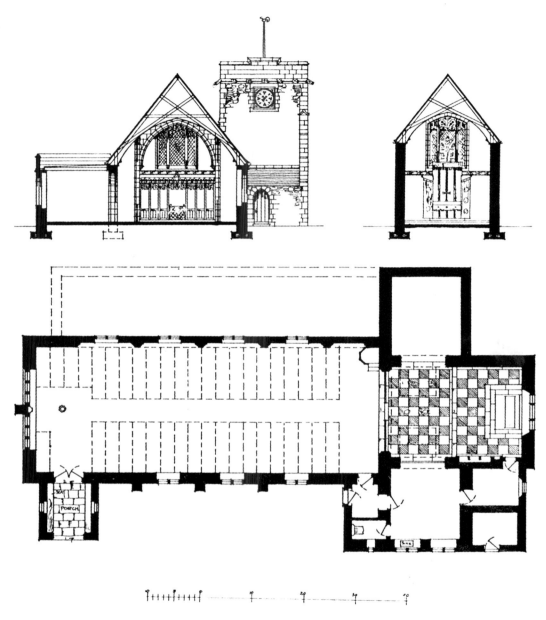

plan, look at my great vista, with the end window of the dining room looking right out to sea'. It was not to be, however, because the owner refused to sell, *Fig. 28*. There is extant another slightly different scheme by Lorimer made for the owner, Mr Baird, which suggests that he considered remodelling it for himself, but it was not carried out either. Both schemes foreshadowed the grand Baronial manner which Lorimer was to develop later.

If Lorimer worked from the example of the traditional buildings of his country, he was

NEWARK CASTLE FIFE

[28] *Newark Castle, Elie, a remodelling scheme for William Burrell.*   R.C.A.M.

not given to making direct quotations of them. An exception is the gatehouse for Balcarres, of which he wrote that his design was 'rather snippy in the Scots-French style à la Queen Mary's baths'. This small two-storey pavilion beneath its pyramidal roof set close by Holyrood Palace was ideal for the purpose. It lacked bulk and could be stood like a large sentry box near the gates without overshadowing them. The design appeared in *The Builder* in 1898 and was reworked a number of times in later years, in each case showing Lorimer's great skill in weaving the unsubstantial elements of the gateway with the freely massed but bulkier lodges.

Bardrochat, was a small house in Ayrshire designed by George Mackie Watson. Set well up a hillside with a wide view, R. F. McEwan commissioned Lorimer to design a much larger house, enlarging it five or six times much in the manner of Stronachullin. He made some minor alterations to the church in the neighbouring village of Colmonell in 1899. A gallery and a stained glass window by Louis Davis were added and the work was supervised by Lorimer himself. 'Was up at five and down to Ayrshire to a little alteration to a church. Ten hours on the going and coming and forty minutes on the job.' Many of his church jobs were even smaller, involving a commemorative panel or a piece of furniture, and seven years passed before he got another new church to do, at Morningside in Edinburgh.

He had begun to remodel Briglands by 1899. It comprised a long Georgian house of which the roof had been lowered to about 30°. A new wing, *Fig. 29*, was added and a new, steeper roof installed with steep corbie (crow stepped) gables and stone dormer heads, and an attractive garden court, *Fig. 30*, was laid out, with steps leading up the high terraced bank to its south. Lorimer was to excel in placing his buildings within the spirit of the place in which he built. At Briglands he took an old but spoilt building and gave it new life. The

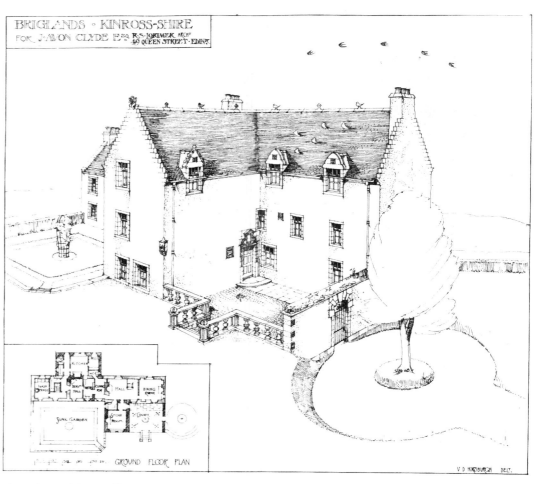

BRIGLANDS · KINROSS-SHIRE
FOR J·AVON CLYDE ESQ. R·S·LORIMER ARCHT
40 QUEEN STREET · EDINR

GROUND FLOOR PLAN

V·D·HORSBURGH DELT.

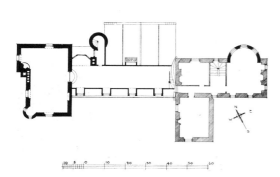

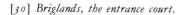

[29] *Briglands, 'Scotch' house grafted to a classical trunk, plan.* R.C.A.M.

[30] *Briglands, the entrance court.* R.C.A.M.

gleaming white walls, stone trim, and its garden all foreshadow the work for which he became particularly well known. The design had provided for a billiard room and other accommodation in a new wing to be extended on the west. This was deferred until 1907, *Pl. 26.*

Lorimer began to get a small but regular number of commissions outside Scotland, and he tells how one client, a Mr Benson, bought twelve acres in Surrey and then instructed him 'to build him a sort of overgrown cottage. I naturally said "All right" and when he was passing through Edinburgh six weeks ago took him out to see my Colinton houses, with which he was rather impressed'. The house which was to be called Whinfold was planned in an L-shaped block, the main entrance (since altered) set Scots fashion in the angle between the wings, and obscured from view to the drive by a large shrubbery set in the middle of the turning circle. The tile-hung upper floor and the windows set almost flush with the outer face of the walls give it a southern look. Lorimer thought the design had 'turned out rather well' or, 'as English as they can stick'.

26 ABOVE *Briglands*, S. *view showing later extensions on left.* P.M.
27 BELOW LEFT *Briglands, the farm buildings.* P.M.
28 BELOW MIDDLE *Briglands, battered quoins and ogives on the pavilion.* P.M.
29 BELOW RIGHT *Briglands, the gateway to the entrance court.* R.C.A.M.

30 ABOVE LEFT *Church of the Good Shepherd, Murrayfield, font.*   R.S.L.

31 BELOW LEFT *S. African war memorial, Alloa.*

32 ABOVE RIGHT *Church of the Good Shepherd, interior.*   R.S.L.

33 BELOW RIGHT *House in Elizabetsgaten, Helsinki for Ossian Donner.*   Sir P. Donner

Benson had introduced Lorimer to Gertrude Jekyll some years before, and six days after, when she moved into her new house near Hascombe Lorimer went to see her. He was enthralled by what he saw, and wrote a long description: 'She's a great authority on gardening and arts and crafts, and a great character generally.' She had bought, he continued, 'Twenty to thirty acres of a copse across the road, and laid out a complete place there, paths, gardens, bought a barn that was being demolished and re-erected it, and some other buildings about the garden, and left a hole in the centre of the ground for the house and now it's built . . . . . It looks so reasonable, so kindly, so perfectly beautiful that you feel that people might have been making love and living and dying there, and dear little children running about for the last – I was going to say, thousand years, anyway six hundred. They've used old tiles which of course helps, but the proportion, the way the thing's built (very long coursed rubble with thick joints and no corners) in fact it has been built by the old people of the old materials in the old "unhurrying" way but at the same time "sweet to all modern uses"'. He liked the decoration also, 'the whole house is whitewashed inside, from attic to basement and I think this is half the charm.' He concluded, 'Who do you think did this for her, a young chap called Lutyens, twenty-seven he is, and I've heard him described by the (Weir) Schultz school as a "Society" architect. Miss J. has pretty well run him.'

Although Lorimer continued to meet Miss Jekyll, the only garden she did with him for which records survive is that of Barton Hartshorn in Oxfordshire. He first made extensions to this Cotswold house in 1903, and followed by adding a large wing in 1908 when large scale alterations to the village were made to allow an extensive garden to be laid out with her advice. She is reputed to have helped also with the grounds of Whinfold but these have been greatly altered. The house in pinewoods on the crest of a hill was given a woodland garden with a series of glades and informal clearings. An avenue of Wellingtonias planted to the east of the house had grown to more than three times the height of the house when they were taken down some ten years ago and it is now difficult to separate the old from the new planting.

The Arts and Crafts cottage with its low ceilings and proportions was a reaction to the overscaled earlier Victorian villa and though some relief and contrast was often contrived by an entrance hall taken up through two stories some of his clients continued to demand dwellings with higher rooms throughout and of a more formal character. St Andrews is one such house designed for Elizabetsgarten in Helsinki. Its perspective which appeared in *The Builder* shows a Scots Jacobean building of the kind favoured by Lorimer's friend and rival John Kinross. High rooms, fair sized windows and tall roofs were combined with Flemish touches, all elegant enough but not characteristic of Lorimer, nor in anyway Finnish, *Pl. 33*.

Complaints arose on the final cost of this house but since Lorimer had supplied only drawings and specification and was not apparently asked to make any adjustments, he can hardly be blamed. The fisherman's hotel at Clousta in Shetlands was one job which he had to redesign completely to meet local conditions. His first design in 1894, *Fig. 31*, was for a

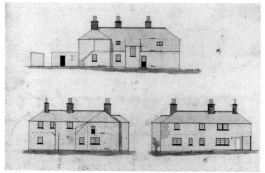

[31]–[32] *Clousta Hotel, Shetland,* ABOVE *first scheme in stone;* BELOW *second scheme in wood.*

R.C.A.M.

harled stone building with a slated roof, in character not unlike Stronachullin of the year before. The low profile, a practical benefit in its windy situation, led to low combe-ceilinged bedrooms which were made higher in the second design of 1895, *Fig. 32*, in which eaves had been raised and the pitch of the roof reduced. The remoteness of the site and lack of labour close by were probably what led to its final construction being in wood and a building curiously flat in effect for a Lorimer design.

The practice was going well, and Lorimer's name was becoming widely known but although he was earning more than enough to live very comfortably as a bachelor, with his parents' town and country houses to stay in, he was impatient for grander things. The prodigious worker he was, may be seen from one of his letters. 'Oh what a happy weekend I had last week, had sketched out the plan for another Colinton house, but never seemed to be getting at it . . . . Started Sat[urday] afternoon about three, worked till twelve-thirty, Sunday morning, came down unscraped and sans collar and worked from ten a.m. till twelve-thirty p.m. . . . finished the whole thing and got approval the next afternoon and its the best plan yet . . . . You know it's a real score having had a lot of these houses to do one after the other.'

His staff was still confined to three or four people. Lorimer had mentioned finding it impossible to pay Matthew the £15 due him in 1897 at the end of his apprenticeship but as he always invested his fees in shares or antiques he was constantly having problems of liquidity. The shoestring office Lorimer habitually ran may have been a result of his difficulty in obtaining much large-scale work, but other letters he wrote suggest that he saw it also as the only sure way of keeping his overheads to their very minimum. Yet even so small a staff, which would hardly expand over the next decade, was to develop its hierarchy. There were usually two apprentices and an improver or two, and during busy periods drawings would be farmed out rather than any further staff engaged. As manager, Matthew was always very friendly and jollied everyone along but Lorimer himself remained austere and kept his subordinates at a distance. The late James Richardson, who became Inspector of Ancient Monuments, worked alongside Reginald Fairlie in Lorimer's office at the turn of the century, concluding, 'I can't say we were Lorimer's friends any more than Ramsay Traquair was'. Traquair and Nobbs were early pupils. Nobbs, a particularly forceful assistant, won the R.I.B.A. Tite prize in 1902 for a design which Lorimer found 'uncommon good' and the R.I.B.A. Owen Jones prize in 1903, but even so Lorimer treated him with similar reserve and wrote later to Dods that, 'Nobby [is] back for a few weeks previous to taking London by storm. Don't know how he'll end, that boy, for all his go and ability I don't value his services very highly', [I] 'always feel that there's just as good a chance of his drawings being wrong as right, you know what I mean.'

Lorimer always showed signs of distrusting too much initiative in his staff, but Nobbs and Traquair went to McGill University to become professors and Nobbs to run a substantial practice as well with Hyde. Lorimer continued to farm out work to Victor Horsburgh, a former colleague at Rowand Anderson's, and to J. J. Joass who was then at the Edinburgh School of Applied Art before moving to London and becoming Belcher's partner. By 1900 Matthew had been office manager for a while but as a reserve officer with the Edinburgh Volunteers was called up when the Boer War began, and he left the office together with an apprentice, Lawrence, who had finished his time with Lorimer but was not being kept as an improver. 'Luckily', said Lorimer, 'I've been able to get a good deal of help from outlander Begg but it's not a paying business giving Matthew half-pay all the time he's away and paying Begg 2/6 an hour to do his work, however its a blessing to get hold of a chap that's any use.' Begg was back in Edinburgh after working some years in South Africa. Ten commissions had been gained the year before and the office was still working on them since no new work was got during the war, after which Matthew came back 'twice the man physically he was when he went. He had a fortnight's holiday, to see his friends etc., I handed him forty pounds being the half pay for the year and he started work on Monday, as if he's only been away for a week in place of fifteen months hard campaigning. He's a rare useful sort of man and I'm glad to have an office boss again' as, he continued, 'I wanted one badly. The others are a thirty bob a weeker, and a quid a weeker, and the pupil and boy'. Eight years had passed since Matthew had entered the office, and if the design inspiration still came mainly from Lorimer the office organisation which brought its realisation was Matthew's particular strength. Known thereafter as 'The Military Man' he was good with the staff, going round and chaffing them to defuse the tension after one of Lorimer's temperamental outbursts. They complemented each other's failings and the excellence of Lorimer's later work in the Gothic as well as in country houses rests almost as much on the support provided by Matthew as in Lorimer's vision.

Detail from bedspread.

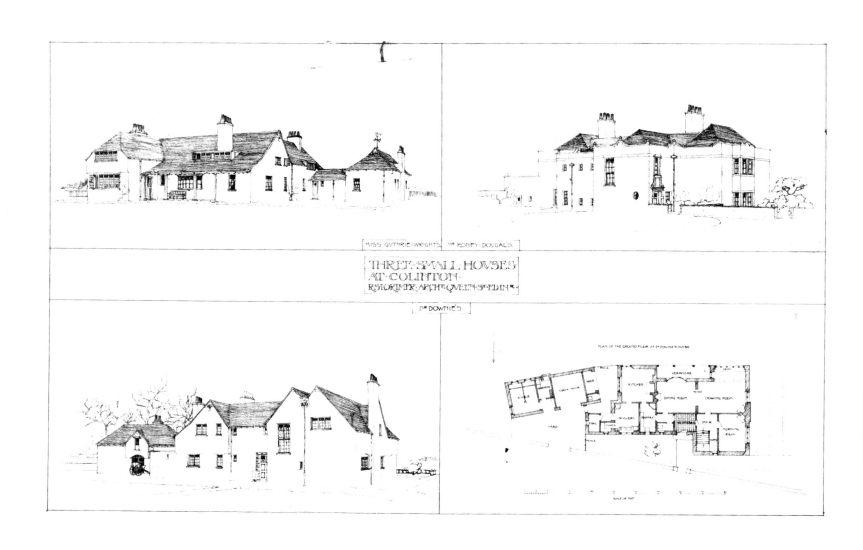

MISS GVTHRIE-WRIGHT'S.   Mʳ RONEY-DOVGAL'S.

THREE·SMALL·HOVSES
AT·COLINTON·
R·LORIMER·ARCHᵗ·QVEEN·Sᵗ·EDINᵇ·

Dʳ DOWNIE'S

PLAN·OF·THE·GROVND·FLOOR·OF·Dʳ·DOWNIE'S·HOVSE·

SCALE·OF·FEET·

[33] *The 'Colony' of Colinton Cottages, Edinburgh,*
ABOVE LEFT *Colinton Cottage;* BELOW *Pentland
Cottage & plan;* ABOVE RIGHT *Roxobel.*   R.C.A.M.

28

3

Harled Houses and the Colinton Manner

Most of the smaller houses of Lorimer have never been written up and they received almost no attention in Hussey's book. H. S. Goodhart Rendel, while speaking at Oxford of the domestic design of Lorimer's period, remarked that what Norman Shaw's architectural descendants were doing in England was being done, with a difference, in Scotland by a small band of architects whose Shaw was Rowand Anderson and whose Lutyens Sir Robert Lorimer. In this he drew attention correctly to the pioneer work of Norman Shaw in England and Rowand Anderson in Scotland in fostering the revival of interest in the traditional architectural forms of each country, as well as to the fact that Lutyens had built upon Shaw's work as Lorimer had upon Anderson's. His further conclusions were less sound when he found that by 1914 the 'formal Georgian Character' had percolated down to the smallest suburban house and that 'houses whose character was intentionally picturesque aspired to that quality by means rather of style and surface texture than of any romantic or irregular composition'. If this conclusion fitted Lutyen's work as a whole it fitted only a very small part of Lorimer's because the romantic tradition in the land of Sir Walter Scott and in the hands of Burn, Bryce and Gillespie Graham, and many architects who followed them, had remained strongly Baronial if mixed with Gothic allusions. Lorimer's earliest cottages have much in common with the simplicity and informality of Voysey's cottages, and later when he designed buildings with a fine Georgian formality, it was to order, and there are few signs that he – or Anderson – did so on personal inclinations.

Lorimer had begun designing his first low rambling houses in 1893 when his links with the arts and crafts movement were purely informal. He knew some of its leading designers, most of whom were in London, but he was back working among architects in Edinburgh whose chief preoccupation, if the talks reported in the transactions of the Edinburgh Architectural Association are anything to go by, was with the past building traditions of their own country – Scotland. The Grange and Stronachullin Lodge were medium sized houses, both designed for exposed country sites near the sea. Their picturesque massing arises from the site and the views afforded from it, yet those houses were not self-consciously pretty or eye sweet as Lorimer clearly felt most new art building to be. If features like the occasional bay window only recall John Ruskin's dictum that no drawing room is complete without one, nevertheless the houses' character had achieved something very close in spirit to the buildings of the Baronial period.

Colinton Cottage, another of his first clutch of new houses, posed problems of a different order, being the first of a colony of more than twenty suburban dwellings built to his design

[34] *The 'Colony' of Colinton Cottages,* ABOVE *Westfield;* MIDDLE *Binley Cottage;* BELOW *Acharra.*
R.C.A.M.

in Colinton near Edinburgh, *Fig. 33*. It was then a small village, nestling in a deep wooded dell through which a single track of the Caledonian Railway had been threaded. It was conveniently placed for commuting from Edinburgh and when Lorimer entered Wardrop's office in 1884, Anderson had already begun to build the dozen or so houses he put up there as developments. Their architectural treatment varies. He had built himself a house there in the seventies, Torduff, a Gothic house with a Norman Shaw balcony on the second floor to give tree-top views to the Pentland Hills. It is a tall tower-like house which Stirling Maxwell remembered as 'a small house with two really good rooms approached by an ample staircase and corridor.' Allermuir, built next door for Lady Anderson in the eighteen eighties (rumour has it because she had rebelled against living with so many stairs) is lower and more extended horizontally to take advantage of a well planted and secluded garden, and perhaps in recognition also that wide outlooks were increasingly irreconcilable with the houses around it being set on plots as small as a quarter of an acre. The house, which is a mixture of Jacobean and Baronial, is dignified if informal. His other houses nearby were plainer and more like villas in effect.

Lorimer's first Colinton design carried no startling changes even though it is placed on a most dramatic site set on the northern edge of the plunging ravine through which flows the Water of Leith, which rises in the hills a few miles off to the south. He again used simple white harled walls built solidly of stone, a traditional idiom which, if not popularly widespread in Victorian times in Scotland, could nevertheless show a long lineage and was then coming back to fashion. The carved stone surround to the front door and the deep stone chimney copes echo traditional forms and the pressed red clay roofing tiles, which he had used already for the Grange, were also in fashion and were used in preference to the cheaper but irregular Peeblesshire slates from Stobo. J. J. Stevenson had put the case in 1880 (in his book *House Architecture*) that slates in general were too often of bad colour. Scots slates, he said, were particularly dark of colour and could only provide a 'shaggy' looking roof. It may be that tiles do provide a tighter and closer finish to a roof but his argument in their favour was that they 'brighten the dinginess of our towns and if they do get black, black and red make a good contrast of colour'. There was an echo of earlier Victorian polychromy in this, and his own house was, like William Morris's, called The Red House, showing a liking for red which was shared by many of his contemporaries in Edinburgh who began to bring in Dumfriesshire red sandstone to spot the predominantly grey city of Edinburgh, built of stone from Craigleith, Ravelstone or Hailes, and roofed with blue-grey local slates. Anderson and Browne were among them and Stirling Maxwell[1] who commented unfavourably on Anderson's use of red sandstone columns on grey stone buildings has told how the red tiles he put on Lord Strathcona's house in the Highland fastness of Glencoe, looked so 'glaringly foreign' that they had to be stripped off and replaced by slates from the neighbouring quarry of Ballachulish. Lorimer used red tiles for nearly every house he did in Colinton, but as time went on he turned to slates elsewhere, sometimes using the dark local slates, and at other times the lighter toned slates from Easdale

[35] *Plan of Colinton Cottage.*   P.S.

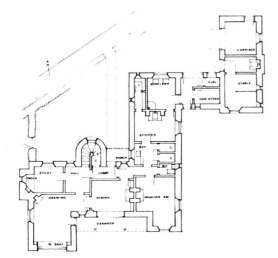

in Argyllshire or the pale, thicker, larger stabs of stone from the quarries of Caithness.

The site for Colinton Cottage was generous although much of it sloped too steeply to build on. The house, consequently, was planned as a Z, *Fig. 35*, set at an angle but close to the road on its north. The small triangular yard-like garden in front is crossed by the path to the front door so that the long arm of the kitchen wing extending towards the road is not seen full face, and the central arm of the Z is broken into areas of vertical emphasis by the projecting staircase tower, set, Scots fashion, within a curved tower, near its middle. The main entrance beside it is sheltered by an open porch and balcony above. The overall character of this almost sunless side is strong and northern, *Pl. 35*.

The south side overlooking the ravine, *Pl. 34* is dominated by long receding roof planes which echo the steep slopes below the house, and the general proportions are too long and low to recall anything but Devey's or Shaw's work, as does the hipped gable which also appears in the early cottages of Lutyens, and which recurs in most of Lorimer's Colinton houses before 1900. The drawing room and the bedroom above it set under this gable at the southern end of the Z are advanced to the brow of the slope, whereas the dining room is set back a little behind a long open verandah, the roof sloping back from the low line of the eaves to the ridge above checked only by a long, wide, dormer window of many mullions (and since remodelled). Various stores, the stables and a coach house are attached to the east side.

Colinton Cottage was the first of a number of designs in which he developed tall shadowy approach facades, many with Scots rounded staircase towers, which he combined with cottage facades on the south, casually composed and low in emphasis. Even so the character of this house overall was remarkably simple and restrained for 1893 (by which time Voysey had built very little). However Roxobel, *Pls. 21, 22, 23, Fig. 33*, the next house to be built by him in Colinton is a house apart, and although it is in no way a classical house the massing has a carefully balanced irregularity, except for its symmetrical south front, the simple unbroken wall faces of which rise through two floors to give it a formality unique among Lorimer's Colinton work. The slated roof is set behind parapets (for the first and last time on one of his Colinton houses) and the eaves only show above an open porch on the south side, a cottagey touch set symmetrically between the much higher two storey wings with parapets. The details within this uncharacteristic formality show his usual sense of fun. The flat wooden heads of the dormers are peaked centrally by mini-pediments to echo the hipped apexes of the roofs to the wings at either side, and a step up in the parapet, at a corner change of level on the other side of the house, is made the occasion for a syncopated play of quadrants.

Miss Guthrie Wright had entrusted Lorimer with the garden for Colinton Cottage, a simple affair, and also with some of the purchasing of furniture, which he did in Oxford. She then took steps to protect the outlook from her property, which was a corner site, by buying the site adjacent as well as the two sites immediately across the road on the north. First, however, Lorimer was given Pentland Cottage to design on a site diagonally across the road

[*36*] *Plan of Pentland Cottage.*   R.C.A.M.

to the south and a little further west, *Fig. 33*. This site was triangular also and on the edge of the ravine but smaller and more confined. The L-shaped block, *Fig. 36*, which was adopted fills most of the available space but leaves the widest part of the site as a small garden at the west side of the house. The shape of the plan of the house is simple enough but the eaves have been placed so low that the upper floor bedrooms can only be lit by windows placed in gables. The approach facade is a counterbalance of triangular shapes in which the two symmetrically opposed catslide roofs are inflected towards the main entrance beside them by the emphasis of the tall staircase window. Another gable further to the left is pushed out a few inches from first floor level, and the roof pitch is bent upwards towards yet another projecting gable over the stable, before the theme is transferred to the side elevation on the west.

If this house, like Colinton Cottage, appears higher and more formal in character on the north side of approach, and at first sight invites comparisons with Voysey's work, the rhythms are entirely different with the exception of the vertical emphasis of the stair window, and the wing in which it is set, which has both quoins (or coins, that is corners) running straight from eaves to ground. This emphasis was unusual and rarely used again by Lorimer. Indeed if one thing characterises his early house designs, it is his treatment of their quoins. The baronial buildings of Aberdeenshire had often made great play with corbels and stepped corbelling to introduce horizontal or diagonal checks to the upwards progress of their forms, and their corner quoins might be slightly rounded, sloping (or slightly battered). Lorimer, had learned from this rarely to let his quoins drop vertically straight from eaves to ground. He might splay the quoin at the ground floor and then step the quoin of the upper floor out on corner corbel courses, or a whole side of a room might be corbelled out a few inches. When neither thing was convenient a projecting stone sundial might be set diagonally projecting from a quoin to break up the line which he found too emphatic – as he was soon to do at Acharra. Continuous quoins were used by him rarely and at this period only within compositions where they would not obtrude.

The same preference for broken rhythms can be seen in the way he designed chimney stacks, for example, in the emphasis of the line of the stack across the plainly rectangular west facade of Pentland Cottage, *Pl. 37*. First, our attention is directed on the left to a window which has been given a segmental archway to emphasise it and give it a certain visual independence so that it contrasts with the corresponding window to the right, which is subordinated to the stack by being tucked hard up to it as well as to the overhung first floor brought out to the right from the chimney. Then the eaves' line is swung upwards, obliquely across and back to the stack, to allow another window to be inserted for the (sloping) combe-ceilinged bedroom overhead. Such playful composition was not uncommon in Scotland. The Fortingall cottages by James Maclaren, which he would have known, are a slightly earlier example and the Hill House at Helensburgh by Charles Rennie Mackintosh a slightly later example. Lorimer, however, was not using it consistently on this house and the back is arranged symmetrically: the roof comes down to the open porch

34 OPPOSITE ABOVE *Colinton Cottage from the s., perspective for the R.S.A. exhibition.* R.C.A.M.

35 OPPOSITE BELOW *Colinton Cottage from the w. side, from Pentland Avenue.* P.M.

which is a feature of all Colinton houses, set in this case between two two storey wings with opposed lop-sided hipped roofs over them.

Drawings of the first Colinton Cottages were exhibited at the Royal Scottish Academy in 1896 after which two more were begun for Miss Guthrie Wright, Binley Cottage and Westfield, and because Acharra, *Figs. 34, 40*, for Major Mears was to be built next to them, a group contract for all three was signed by the builder Nathaniel Grieves. As a result, he allowed a reduction of one and half per cent on the cost of each. The houses were to be more compact than the first three Lorimer had built. Binley Cottage, which cost just under £1,600, has a ground floor area of one thousand seven hundred square feet and is square in plan. The bedrooms were arranged on the upper floor under an H-shaped roof with the hipped ends pitched at fifty degrees to the horizontal, and the roof in the centre swept down to the first floor level over the open porch, *Pl. 39*.

Lorimer had very few set rules in planning houses. He felt that ideally they should be approached from the north and if, as at Binley Cottage or Westfield, the access was from the south, the approach would be brought in near the side boundary and a screen planted along it. Within the house, the one absolute rule was that neither service areas nor servants' quarters should look on to the main garden. The main reception rooms were always grouped on the ground floor for these houses but the kitchen might be at some distance from the dining room with a serving pantry set between them.

The interiors of all his designs show his complete preoccupation with contriving constantly varying inflexions in planning to give every room and every part of each building its own unique sense of place. Arnold Mitchell remarked on this in Binley Cottage and that 'the vestibule leads into a corridor that appears to be narrow; but around the corner on one side, the stairs are recessed, and when we turn the corridor on the other side, we find a deep square bay that gives quite a noble air of spaciousness to the well planned little building.' Acharra shows many similarities in planning but is approached from the west and is larger, the ground floor area being 2,300 square feet.

The earliest Colinton houses had been fitted to awkwardly shaped sites, but some of the later ones were on rectangular plots which led Lorimer to think that, 'In the case of the modest suburban house it is quite unnecessary to plump it down – four square to the winds – and right in the centre of the plot of ground.' He had this thought in mind when he planned Westfield, *Fig. 38*, as another almost square house, and he put it at thirty degrees to the road and across the right hand back corner of the site. Then he had second thoughts and pushed it further round to forty five degrees to face diagonally across the site and give the largest possible area of lawn in front of it. The entrance path leads straight to the front entrance, which, set in a curved tower, provides the pivot to sweep us smoothly through one hundred and thirty five degrees into the main corridor. This was one of Lorimer's simplest designs, a play of verticality by tower and gable against the reiterated horizontality of the main facade, the clutter of offices and stores hidden in the corner of the site around at the back.

Five years had passed since Lorimer began operations in Colinton, and in February 1898

36 OPPOSITE ABOVE *Pentland Cottage from the* N., *perspective drawing for the R.S.A. exhibition.*

R.C.A.M.

37 OPPOSITE BELOW *Pentland Cottage,* W. *sundial garden.*

P.M.

he wrote to Dods that he had fifteen thousand pounds worth of work in hand, and 'a huge boom coming out in *The Builder* – 3 double plates (I made it a special condition with Statham', [the editor] 'to publish them all in one number, and I'm going to send this round to about a hundred people or more. Which I think is a rare good thing to do. It just keeps people in mind of one's existence and I am in hopes that as the year is yet young this may fruit in the way of some jobs.' However, seven months later he was complaining that again he had 'nothing whatever in prospect for this winter but this one house', which he described as just 'another Colinton House and stable for about £2,600'. It was to be called Huntly, *Pl. 47.* The last of the compact Colinton houses, l'Ermitage, was under way for Charles Sarolea, a friend who was later to become Professor of French at the University, as well as Corner Cottage, a house for Stuart Silver, which was to be designed completely before being abandoned. Huntly, Almora, which came in soon after, and The Rowans, the fourth and last house for Miss Guthrie Wright and next door to her own, have cottagey touches but Lorimer had reached a point in his career after which he could be called upon to design many real cottages, but his houses would outgrow any sense of the term.

Lorimer had begun to refer to his Colinton Manner in design by 1900 but the only surviving letter which tells what he meant by this is on Foxcovert, a Victorian house which his sister Lady Chalmers had bought on the western slopes of Corstorphine Hill in Edinburgh, *Fig. 39.* He was to add a new entrance wing on the north with an irregular play of the subordinate elements set within an overall symmetry of outline, and he replanned the existing house also. 'I made a design', he wrote, 'then my brother came down and whenever he saw it said I hadn't grasped the right idea, and that all the public rooms ought to be upstairs to get the benefit of the splendid view over to the Forth. He was quite right, I hadn't

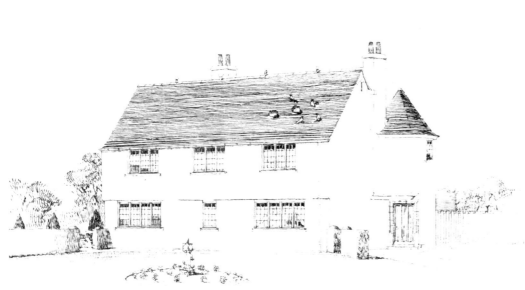

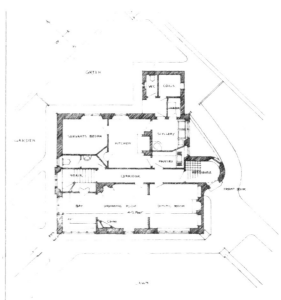

[38] *Westfield, a simple mass at an angle to the road.*
R.C.A.M.

[39] *Foxcovert, Corstorphine, Edinburgh.* R.C.A.M.

grasped the right idea, had arranged everything on the ground floor for cheapness and treated in the Colinton manner so I did a new design and have made a regular Scotch house with a ripping upstairs drawing room . . . with the devil's own high coved ceiling with plaster ends, her [Coat of] arms in a lozenge at one end and a spanking vine at the other ceiling of the oriel flat, stair with rough pavement cope leading down to the garden, won't that make rather an A.I. room – only other job that I'm keen about – is a Colinton Cottage with an upstairs living room.'

The Colinton houses, in their modest way, had been an attempt at a new approach, yet his letters had revealed his feelings on new things more clearly in furniture design. He had written to Dods asking whether it was not 'much more satisfactory to get sweet smelling new stuff made', and he told how he was trying more and more to get off buying old furniture. 'Don't you think to collect the typical products of *one's own times* would be a far more interesting thing to do than this of collecting the flotsam and jetsam of the so called good "old days". How interesting it would all become even after a few years, and things go so fast now, to have things really typical of the curious backing and fore-ing of "taste" that is always going on, cabbage wall papers to plain stripes and then back again.' It is clear that, for all his preference for white interiors, he saw them as he saw the fabric of the building, as a collective effort of craftsmen and artists, of cabinet makers, tapestry weavers, copper beaters, wrought iron workers, stained glass artists, joiners, masons and carvers.

The impetus of the arts and crafts cottage movement was waning by 1901 and Lorimer's enthusiasm for such design with it. Matthew was still in South Africa fighting and he was left to manage the office single handed. Work was scarce and he felt that unless some work came in he might 'as well put up the shutters as I have nothing to put me through the winter.

I want badly some jobs with a little money in them, I'm tired of these starved whitewashed houses. Wish I could get Willie B[urrell] started off with his pots of money he would be something like a client'.

His practice improved after the war had ended when he got his first commission for an entirely new mansion, Brackenburgh, in Cumberland. The commission for Rowallan, his first new mansion in Scotland, soon followed, with large extensions to four others, Craigmyle, Pitkerro, Barton Hartshorn and Hallyburton. Meanwhile he was finishing off the five Colinton houses. Almora, shows the same variety in planning remarked on in Binley Cottage and this is even taken further with each room being shaped quite differently within what is, in principle, a rectangular house planned on two storeys. The roof is swept low in places and there is no attic floor. Huntly, begun at about the same time, is planned mostly within a plainly rectangular block orientated east and west. The effect is taller and grander and an attic range of bedrooms is included. The entrance facade on the west features a corbelled bay at first floor which is carried up as a full height dormer with a Mansard gable over it. There are no cottage features in this house, apart from this new inflection given to the corbelled feature. A chauffeur's house and garage were added by a later owner, and a west wing with a rounded end added in the twenties.

Dilkusha which was begun a little later was intended to be harled like the other houses but was not, *Pl. 49*. The plan basically is a T of which the first phase, the eastern L, was built in 1901. The subsequent owner renamed the house Hartfell and added the western arm in 1906, more or less to the original plan. This is another tall house with some attic rooms, and includes quotations from many of his earlier houses. The opposed cat-slide roofs of Pentland Cottage are used over the main entrance, the dormer from Roxobel, a mansard dormer from Huntly, as well as baronial touches like a round corner tower with half dormers, and a chimney gable half crowstepped and half steeply pitched, all add up to another vigorous but restless composition. Glenlyon, another design from 1901, is equally

[40] *Acharra, entrance on the* N.   R.C.A.M.

38 ABOVE LEFT *Westfield, simple proportions & a slight overhang.* P.M.

39 BELOW LEFT *Acharra from the* S.*, aerials & glass house later additions.* P.M.

40 BELOW MIDDLE *Westfield, detail of doorway.* P.M.

41 ABOVE RIGHT *Westfield, the approach.* TOM SCOTT

42 BELOW RIGHT *Westfield, front entrance.* P.M.

43 OPPOSITE LEFT *Glenlyon, staircase.*   P.M.
44 OPPOSITE RIGHT *Glenlyon, from the* S.   P.M.
45 ABOVE *Glenlyon, from the* W.   P.M.
46 BELOW *Glenlyon, the drawing room outlook.*   P.M.

47 ABOVE LEFT *Huntly, Colinton, the wing to the left was added to Lorimer's design.* P.M.

48 BELOW *The Rowans, W. view of entrance.* P.M.

49 ABOVE RIGHT *Hartfell, the entrance from the* N.

TOM SCOTT

busy but the overall emphasis is lower and longer and calmer, *Pls. 43–46*. It was planned in a rough Z and placed close to the road on the north leaving narrow yard like spaces in front. The south of the house, *Pl. 44*, which looks over one of the longest gardens in Colinton is much like earlier cottages like Binley but features full height gables. The last of these houses, The Rowans, is also Z shaped in plan but taller having two pokey and dark bedrooms in the roof space. The dispositions of this house are the most private and secluded of his Colinton houses. The north facade presents an almost blank face to the road which it follows closely beneath a lively play of roof shapes. The path to the house is brought in alongside the west of the house until, having passed a projecting round tower, the entrance door is discovered on its far side facing away from the road, so that the line of approach is swung back on itself, and then this happens again in the hall, so that one completes a large S before the drawing room is reached, *Pl. 48*.

The interior spaces are, as usual with Lorimer, exquisitely proportioned and varied with alcoves of various shapes, and the master bedroom is an L-shaped room with a ceiling angled high into the roof space in contrast to the low flat ceiling of the deep bay directed to a tree top view of the Pentland Hills. The exterior has been carefully modelled too, and the west gable with a central chimney stack is recessed on both sides at the ground floor with the upper floor corbelled out above and on either side of the stack. A projecting shelf at one quoin at the sill level of the upper floor appears to be for pigeons to rest on. The main feature of the south facade, which overlooks a rose garden, is a deep square bay window with a continuous strip of windows, but this feature has had to be linked to a square tower at the south-east corner. The tower has been placed expressly to give oblique views through an angled outlook window of a small dell-like sunken garden. Apart from the crowding of too many features on this south facade and also on the east where they merely overlook the kitchen garden, the house is well modulated towards the garden which is still much as Lorimer laid it out. It may be that Lorimer was trying to do too much in these charming but relatively modest houses and after he married in 1903 his wife was to become a restraining influence which he readily acknowledged. 'I thought my own taste was rather severe but she's constantly pulling me up and telling me that I'm overdoing this and that and she was always right', and soon he was telling Dods that he felt he was becoming 'simpler and broader'.

The 1901 special number of *The Studio* had included nothing whatever by Lutyens or by Lorimer. The magazine which was the voice of the arts and crafts movement had illustrated and even commended the earlier furniture and embroidery designs by Lorimer, but its editor, Charles Holmes, preferred the new art architecture to the craft based architecture then being produced. Lorimer had met Herman Muthesius, the German cultural attaché, who was in London to study British architectural developments and who was the first critic to recognise the true worth of Lorimer's early achievements. He invited Lorimer to dinner and he wrote to Dods of his experience. 'He lives in a delightful little Queen Anne house on the Mall at Hammersmith not far from Wm. Morris's old home. He gave me a beautiful dinner with white wine and black coffee, and after he showed me a huge collection of photos of up to date domestic work, which on the first blush looked interesting but after a good steady 2nd look – D-n – it, how little there really was that one can feel keen about. However, it's always interesting to see what others are doing, and sometimes one derives a horrid satisfaction from feeling that they're not doing anything very excruciating. I don't think in viewing the whole collection that I once said to myself, now *there's* a thing I must *use up* straight.'

Muthesius, in return, wrote of Lorimer as the only architect in Scotland practising within the arts and crafts tradition, and in fact Lorimer and Oscar Paterson, the glass painter from Glasgow, were then the only two members of the society in the whole of Scotland. Lorimer's contribution, Muthesius wrote, was that he – 'first of all, saw the virtues of the unostentatious old Scottish buildings with their true hearted simplicity, and plain almost rugged moderation. For him, no longer was it a necessity to imitate the old Scottish rooms, wrapped in towers with corbelled corners, he had become sufficiently imbued in the old art, to know its more intimate charms and to put them to new uses. In a word, Lorimer has begun the same thing in Scotland, which had been done in London 35 years before by Norman Shaw's group. Today Lorimer's achievements in house building are the most interesting to compare to those of the Mackintosh group. He has erected a whole row of smaller houses in the Edinburgh suburb of Colinton, in the charming unostentatious old Scottish vernacular. The restoration of old manor houses, for example, Earlshall in Fife, were to him rich opportunities for remodelling. As works they afforded opportunities for his sensitivity and for his distinguished good taste and his interior design includes furniture in which he has given of his best. He has laid out a new garden also, in the idiom of the old Scots geometrical gardens, and generally he has given his greatest attention to the Scottish garden. Scotland will attain also a national perfection by his efforts, as England already has done on the foundations of the old folk arts of building.'

Walter Shaw Sparrow was the next critic to comment on Lorimer's work, which he did in a number of books which he edited from 1904 on modern British architecture. He had come into close contact with the arts and crafts movement when Charles Holmes asked him to help prepare a special number on the Arts and Crafts Exhibition of 1899. 'When I joined his staff,' he related, 'the Morris movement was fading away in England, but not in Germany where it was passing through many interesting transformations by which German industries were gaining a great and sinister advantage over our own. Apathy was descending once more on our country.' Shaw Sparrow felt that the Craft Architecture deserved more attention than it got and his books include a lot of Lorimer's, Lutyens's and Norman Shaw's work.

Lorimer was very conscious of the benefits of publicity, and when he got the commission for Brackenburgh he had told Dods that 'This must have been entirely due to seeing my work illustrated. I want a whole *Builder* to myself but Statham will only give me 3 double plates, so I've refused to send him any. When he sees my stuff in the hated rival he'll probably come to the place.' *The Builder* was a magazine with a technical emphasis and very little critical comment, and if he did get almost a whole number of the *Architectural Review* to himself, it was not until 1911.

We have become accustomed to such a faceless anonymity in the architecture of our day that the unending variety of Lorimer's work has become difficult to comprehend. This variety arose in the first place from applying an Arts and Crafts tenet of building faith that, 'a building if it is to be worth anything must have a quite definite proportion. Must be either definitely high or definitely low. The natural proportion for a cottage is the low proportion, low ceilings and large low windows.' Few of his Colinton houses were as long and none as emphatically low as Voysey's, but every effort was made by him to keep them compact and the bedrooms were usually squeezed up into the roof under combe (sloping) ceilings, partly for economy, but also to allow the low eaves-line.

The effect of Norman Shaw has also to be considered in this. Lorimer knew him well and had a deep respect for him and his work. Shaw had synthesised Baronial elements with English idioms as at Scotland Yard on the Embankment, but this was in no way a predominant trait in his work because their differences were not merely in form but more of the spirit behind them. It took Muthesius to see this clearly and to appreciate the part that Baronial in its own right as a national style played in Lorimer's work. Robert Kerr in 1856 in his book *The Gentleman's House* had put the view that Baronial revival houses bedecked with pepper-pot bartisans were merely the product of that 'dreary northern kingdom'. Later J. J. Stevenson pointed out in 1880 if there were 'no lack of towers and turrets and great projections of corbels...somehow these fail to reproduce the sternness of the old buildings', and herein lay the roots of the difference. If Lorimer was not aiming at sternness for its own sake, he had to reach it if he was to recapture the old sense of proportion of the Baronial style.

As Lorimer struggled towards a purer synthesis of these competing elements in his design, he was thinking, he said, 'More and more that there's a lot in what dear Hewy Wardrop told me years ago, that there are three things of *vital* importance in architecture, and that the first is proportion, the second is proportion and the third is – proportion'. Yet proportion, however good, does not always transcend national tastes and if Statham felt Lorimer's early houses in the local style were 'pushed too far in this instance', it is easy to conclude from his own work that he found their character too severe. For Lorimer, steeped in the Baronial tradition, the converse was true. He found all too many English buildings too 'pretty', and when he visited Cambridge he complained of the 'beastly prettyness of all the best modern work. Magdalen, Champney's College, etc. How sick one gets of these cuspings and crestings and stuff', and he went on to say that he thought that 'Scott's Pembroke College building is the only one of these things that shows real genius and grasp, the others are all just prettily imitative except a little of Jackson's stuff here and there.'

Beyond the Gothic work little seems to have interested Lorimer in England, apart from the domestic work of Lutyens. He told Dods that Muthesius had 'too unqualified an

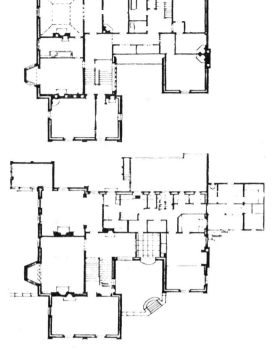

[41] *Weaponess House, Scarborough, ground & first floor plans.* Studio Y. Bk Dec. Art 1907.
[42] *Balcarres Lodge & gates, Fife, plan.* C.L.

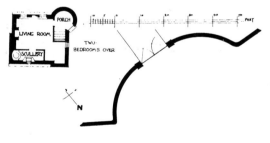

50–51 OPPOSITE LEFT *Weaponess House, views from* S.E. *and* S.W. R.S.L.
52 OPPOSITE ABOVE RIGHT *Linlithgow Bridge, flatted cottages.* R.S.L.
53–54 OPPOSITE MIDDLE RIGHT *Linlithgow Bridge, hall, 'Scotch' slates & a touch of Voysey.* R.S.L.
55 OPPOSITE BELOW RIGHT *High Barn, Surrey & Lorimer working in Lutyens territory.* R.S.L.

admiration' for Mackintosh, and of Voysey, that he had heard that 'Sturgess has been having a simple H-ll of a row with Voysey over his home, and no wonder, I'd lock the man up in the coal hole and keep him there', but he didn't say why. *The Studio,* which had regularly published Voysey's work finally published an article in 1905 on Artisans' Cottages which included Lorimer's Rustic Cottages, and their second *Year Book of Decorative Art* in 1907 included a lodge house by Lorimer at Pitkerro for Lord Avon Clyde, and his second ever brick house design, Weaponess near Scarborough. It was begun while Matthew was in South Africa and all the drawings were farmed out to John Begg. The main block is of three floors, including the attic bedrooms, with lower two storey wings, attached either side and bent round to form a U in plan, *Fig. 41.* The roof is a complicated array of gables and hips, valleys and dormers, *Pls. 50, 51.* Construction was begun in the summer of 1900, at an estimated cost of £4,000 and he made his last visit of inspection to this 'somewhat troublesome' job towards the end of 1901.

As his country house practice began to expand Lorimer received more commissions for the small lodges to be set at their gates. His first one for Balcarres in Fife was published by *The Builder* in 1900. It combines Colinton harled compactness with the delightfully free modelling of the Queen Mary's bath house close by Holyrood, *Pl. 57,* and is set behind the low walls flanking the rusticated stone gate pillars with their iron heraldic beasts on top. This compactly square gatehouse has two attic bedrooms, a scullery and a living room downstairs, and is placed at forty five degrees to the drive to give a direct line of view from living room to gate, *Fig. 42.* This functional arrangement has plastic similarities with Westfield where such an angling was adapted for privacy.

The profiles of all his lodges are carefully harmonised with the forms of the gateways. At Balcarres, the two quoins of the lodge nearest the gate are both taken straight up to echo the verticality of its pillars whereas the other quoin in view from the gate is corbelled out at first floor level as a horizontal note to echo the lines of the wall across which it is seen. The dormer, the stone figure at the apex of the pyramidal roof in what Lorimer called Aberdeenshire fashion, and the eaves of the tower set higher than on the rest of the lodge all direct attention upwards in a rhythmic group of verticals.

One of the next gatehouses to be built was for Earlshall. Lorimer had designed first a long low severely plain building, *Fig. 11,* athwart the drive which was carried through under a simple archway. J. J. Joass drew the perspective which was exhibited at the R.S.A. in 1893. Begg's perspective of the whole layout does not show it, and the new design which was built is shorter and taller and is set in the trees near the end of the drive, *Pl. 7.* The first design was stronger but the later design matches the rhythms of the existing building better, and the later gate house Lorimer designed for Rowallan in Ayrshire follows its general lines.

The next Holyrood type gatehouse was built for Pitkerro around 1902, *Pl. 58.* It is a mixture of Colinton planning with Lorimer's increasing play with curvilinear effects. The tall rusticated pillars of the gateway are surmounted by broken pediments with almost plain iron gates beneath an ornamental overthrow of late Renaissance inspiration. The lodge, as at

56 LEFT *Briglands Lodge, Kinross.* P.M.
57 ABOVE RIGHT *Balcarres Lodge, Fife.* R.S.L.
58 BELOW RIGHT *Pitkerro Lodge, Forfar.* R.S.L.

Balcarres, is set at an angle to the drive, *Fig. 43*, and has a continuous quoin nearest the gate, whereas the further one in view is splayed to take a lookout window pointed towards the main road. The hipped roof was a new departure for this kind of building. Shaw Sparrow was to assert in 1904 that wide eaves were needed on all roofs to provide deep cool shadows. If Voysey, Lutyens and most English architects followed this precept, the Scottish building tradition by contrast has preferred to use roof surfaces brought down to end at the edge of the wall head, to which the rhones (gutters) would be clipped directly. The shorn eaves thus produced expose no woodwork or slates to be fretted away by the wind, and may even derive from those unsettled days when as little combustible material as possible was left exposed. Whether or not Lorimer deemed a more southern form to fit this design better, he has used a hipped roof over the rectangular plan pitched ogivally so that its curved slated surfaces pick up light with delightfully varying effects, but so as also to push the eaves well out from the wall. The effects fit another of Shaw Sparrow's remarks that in design 'the very first quality to be shown is unity of impression. Dame Nature has always that quality in her coned fungi and domed mushrooms and I cannot but help thinking that the present day masters of roof construction like E. L. Lutyens and Mr Lorimer have taken hints from nature's art in coverlids'.

A year later Lorimer produced another entirely different Holyrood gatehouse for Briglands in Kinrossshire, *Fig. 45*. The gate is a very modest affair flanked by rubble farmyard walls, and the lodge is both more domestic in its lines like Pitkerro's and more baronial in detail like Balcarres'. The look-out window set in the corner to overlook the gate is the only feature not parallel to road or drive, *Pl. 56*. This design with minor variations was proposed for the Knoll at North Berwick, and used at Craigmyle in Aberdeenshire with Dutch gables, and it appeared also some years later in a catalogue of Henry Hope, *Fig. 44*, the window manufacturer, with cottages by Lutyens, Blow and other arts and crafts architects.

The first group of artisans' cottages which Lorimer was asked to design was at Inveralmond near Perth, *Fig. 46*. It is likely they were for a trust of which Mackenzie of Earlshall was a member, but they were not built. A plain terrace of four, on eighteen-feet frontages and each about eight hundred and eighty feet in area, offer a living room, a scullery with a minute bathroom off it, three upstairs bedrooms and an outside earth closet lavatory. Cusped dormers were proposed and a design for a pair of similar cottages was also made. When Galletly commissioned the first three Rustic Cottages in Colinton in 1901, Lorimer combined elements from Colinton Cottage with cusped dormers for their design and when he was asked later to add four more cottages, *Pls. 59–62*, he dusted down the Inveralmond design, including the chimney stacks topped by copings humped in a curve along their length, and merely changed the roof shape a little to give more head room for the slightly extended plan.

Slate hung dormers in all shapes and sizes abound in the New Town of Edinburgh. The cusped dormers which Lorimer favoured expose few edges to the wind and where the wall is

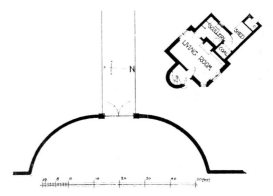

[43] *Pitkerro Lodge & gates, Forfar, plan.*   C.L.

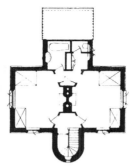
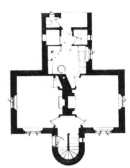

[44] Slate-hanging & harling for a design for a cottage with two rooms up & two down. Henry Hope.

taken up from the wall head around the windows in such dormers, he would have the leading edge built out about two inches in red tiles. This provided a stop on which to end the harling as well as a base upon which to bed the outer slates in cement. For the rest, apart from a small block of four tenements fitted within an exterior design very like the first three Rustic Cottages which he built a few years later at Linlithgow Bridge, *Pls. 52–54*, his later cottages were to be confined to those with large mansions.

If Lorimer built little in Colinton after 1901, he got a number of commissions for medium-sized houses around Edinburgh as well as one in Surrey, and those show an even greater degree of experiment than Colinton's. Teviotdale, a white harled house with something of Pentland Cottage in its design was a slightly earlier commission in North Berwick, *Fig. 47*. It is planned in an L to take advantage of the views to the North across the Forth, but the arrangement of the voids is stiff and apart from the corner tower has little Scots character.

High Barn at Hascombe in Surrey, *Pl. 55*, was built of Bargate stone, often used by the builder F. W. Troup, and in coursed rubble textured like that of the nearby house designed by Lutyens, The Orchards. Lorimer had met its owners, the Chances, and had seen over their house. Lorimer had used an open archway as an entrance porch at Teviotdale, but at High Barn five are scattered around. A Tudor bay window such as Lutyens liked was also incorporated, a hanging balcony probably improvised after one seen in France, and a bay window placed in Norman Shaw fashion to come out contrapuntally from the end of the side wall of a wing. Lorimer had lessened the confusion in direction to which this leads by recessing the bay within the thickness of the wall and then splaying the reveals inwards towards it, in a design like that of Whinfold nearby (where he had been trying to out-English the English). Back in Scotland he was producing simpler designs which were better knit together. The house at the Bridge of Teith is a simple T-shaped harled building relying mainly on its proportions for its effect. It was a plan which he used again for Whiteholm,

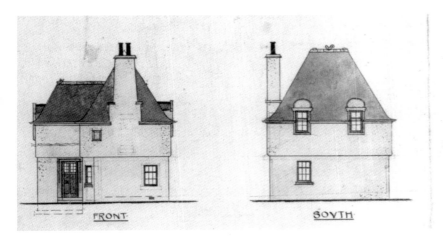

FRONT   SOVTH

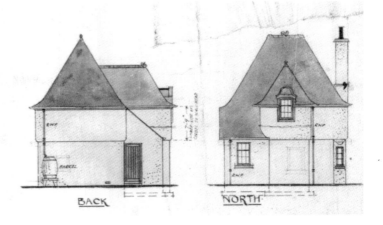

BACK   NORTH

[45] ABOVE *Compactness, variety & little head-room upstairs at Briglands lodge.*   R.C.A.M.
[46] LEFT *Inveralmond, Perth, part of an unrealised project.*   O.D.
[47] *Teviotdale, North Berwick,* BELOW LEFT *from the* W.; BELOW RIGHT *ground floor plan.*
          shaw sparrow 1904.

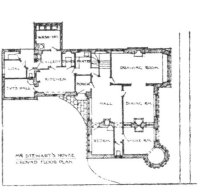

MR STEWART'S HOUSE
GROUND FLOOR PLAN

Fig. 48, a few years later at Gullane, which was slightly enlarged to give the public rooms in the top of the T two slate hung bay windows like those he had added to Lundie, a but and ben (two-roomed) cottage in Arncroach, close by Kellie, *Pl. 64*.

Marly Knowe, *Pl. 68*, is a larger house comparable in size to High Barn. It was built for an Edinburgh professor and is situated on the brow of a hill overlooking North Berwick. The approach drive which comes in from the north is taken along the east of the house before being swung around to a forecourt on its south. Professor Sharpey Schaeffer is known to have had very firm ideas of what he wanted and this layout certainly went against Lorimer's own ideas, but it did provide a more sheltered entrance to the house. The house itself has a central part on three floors with a range of three gables over, *Pl. 66*, as did the Grange which is nearby, but which here rises higher to contrast with the lower ridge of the roof which covers both the two storey wings of the house. Lorimer has used cusped dormers, slight curves to the roof surfaces and slate hanging to provide this house with a rustic effect, and to bring down the apparent scale of this large dramatic house set right on the ridge.

Lorimer began another of his most effective houses a year later. He spent a 'long day discussing a 3 thou[sand pound] house but found that the only thing that really seemed to fetch the wife was a large press [cupboard] off one of the bedrooms. However they passed the plans, *Fig. 49*, and swallowed the cost.' This house, Wayside, St Andrews, reverts to a

[48] *Whiteholm, Gullane,* LEFT *plans,* SHAW SPARROW *1906;* RIGHT *garden layout,* R.C.A.M.

BEDROOM PLAN

GROUND PLAN

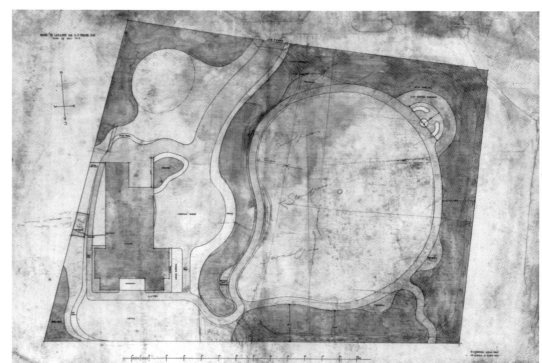

59 ABOVE LEFT *Rustic cottages, Colinton, in 1904.*
SHAW SPARROW, 1904.
60–62 BELOW LEFT *Rustic Cottages,* TOM SCOTT;
ABOVE RIGHT *a detail of window,* P.M.; BELOW RIGHT
an entrance detail, P.M.

63 LEFT *Brig of Teith, a Perthshire Cottage.* P.S.
64 ABOVE RIGHT *Whiteholm, Gullane,* C. *1908, from the* S. *overlooking the links.* R.S.L.
65 BELOW RIGHT *Robert Lorimer and family at Whiteholm in 1909.* R.S.L.

66 LEFT *Marly Knowe, North Berwick, the entrance from the* S. P.M.

67 ABOVE RIGHT *Marly Knowe, cusped dormer &*
slate hanging. P.M.

68 BELOW RIGHT *Marly Knowe, ground floor plan (* N.
is to the bottom of the page). SHAW SPARROW, 1906.

69 ABOVE *Wayside, St Andrews, from the garden on the* S.W.　　N.T.S.

70 BELOW *Wayside, from the* S.　　N.T.S.

Colinton formality on its north side combined with an informal south side dominated by his best ever play of roof surfaces, *Pls. 69, 70*. Slates from Easdale, Craiglea and Ballachulish mixed together, cover the subtly arranged and curved planes of the roof above walls of local stone textured like that of High Barn, and the tall curved windows of the two storey hall, placed within splayed reveals, respond in the vertical plane. It is almost as if Ramsay Traquair had taken all Lorimer's favourite themes and had knitted them harmoniously in the gentlest overall rhythm. Lorimer had, at this time, he told Dods, only Traquair and one other chap to help him and had three jobs at '3 thou[sand] or thereby, think I must farm out at least one of them to Horsburgh or I'll never get through.'

Dunderach at Craiglockhart, not far from Colinton, and of similar date is another stone and slated house. Plain walls, tall narrow windows, a corner tower and stone dormer heads make for a restrained and very Scottish design. The west (kitchen facade) however, recalls something of Wayside's ebb and flow of roof planes. Quite a different proposition was the house Lorimer gave Horsburgh to work on, being located at Mandal in Norway, for the Edinburgh family of Salvesen. When he had received a letter on a Wednesday morning about a wooden house they were to build in Norway and the local architect's delay of ten weeks before getting out plans, he went, 'over to tea and discussed the matter' and then that very evening produced a sketch design. He put in two eight and a half hour days working it up and was able to post 'complete plans, elevations and sections traced and coloured at 6 on Friday. Went to tea on Sunday and got the whole thing settled. Drew all the $\frac{1}{2}''$ [drawings] in about four days and Horsburgh is to start "washing" the $\frac{1}{8}''$ scale on Monday. Pretty slippy, don't you think?' Horsburgh also did the working drawings and the house was put up by out of work shipwrights. It has a U-shaped plan, and eaves and ridge running through at one level to contrast with the pine trees amid which it is situated. A large square bay as at the Rowans, and a series of oriel windows upstairs, a new feature for Lorimer, complete this crisp and simple design.

Shaw Sparrow in his book of 1906 illustrated a Lorimer design for a house in Peeblesshire and thereby hangs another tale. The commission may be said to have begun as a Baronial mansion for Lord Carmichael to be set on the hill above Skirling and to its north. The designs were made even though Lorimer had doubts whether it could be paid for, and its cancellation did not stop him exhibiting the drawings at the R.S.A. in 1908. Meanwhile Lorimer had designed the house Shaw Sparrow illustrated, *Fig. 50*, for the Maclehoses, printers to the University of Glasgow, to be put beside the green at Skirling, on another site belonging to Lord Carmichael (and which apparently he had been going to sell to them). The house is a modified L on plan, the ridge running continuously at one level. The eaves on the symmetrical garden elevation also follow through continuously. The line of the front elevation is broken up by a curved stair tower and there are several changes of level in the eaves. If this building had been built, its numerous breaks in plan would have broken down the horizontal emphasis suggested by the drawings but it is one of a number of Lorimer's designs of which Frank Deas, his lifelong architect friend, has said with some justice, 'All

[49] *Wayside, ground floor plan.*
shaw sparrow 1906.

were small' (but not as small as all that) and their design was based on English domestic tradition with a touch of Norman Shaw. They had however a definite Scots flavour and a fresh treatment of detail which stamped them with their designer's individuality.'

This design was also abandoned and then the Carmichaels decided to remodel the old cottages already on this site, and they brought in Ramsay Traquair who wrapped a largely wooden structure around the old cottages with a long low roof with wide bracketed eaves. Lorimer's correspondence has not yet revealed why these designs were abandoned but another potentially charming house for Banchory was also abandoned around this time. It was for a Mrs Fergusson and he described it as a 'sort of improved Colinton type, whitewash and slate roofs', *Fig. 51*. He was to design another dozen medium-sized houses of which half were to be harled or intended to be, but the last of them near Edinburgh was to be Harmeny for the Youngers at Balerno a village some three miles from Colinton, *Pl. 73*. White harled

[*50*] *Skirling, Peeblesshire, a design for a site beside a village green.* shaw sparrow 1906.

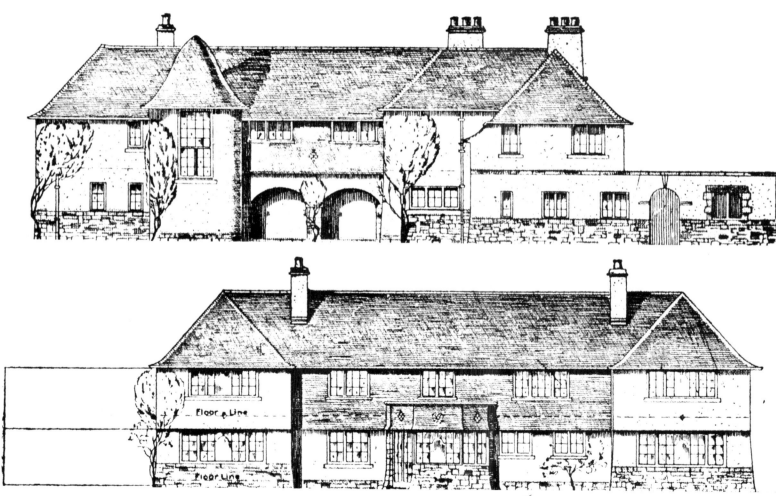

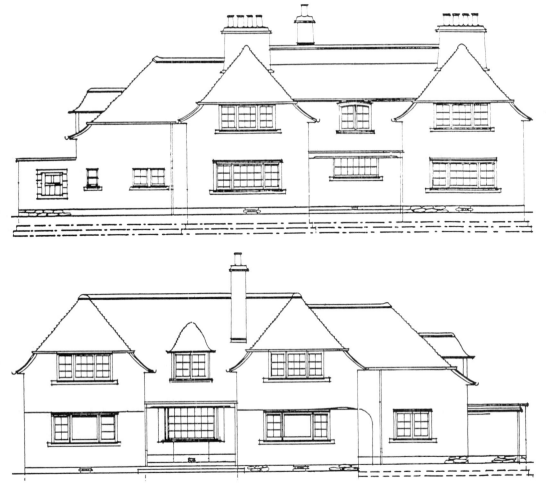

walls were used with stone trim for window surrounds, arches and doorways, as well as for the kneelers and apex stones for the gables to extend greatly and completely remodel an earlier small house. The deep stone copings for the chimneys revert to a sixteenth century traditional form and no cottage features were worked into this impressive but low key example of his developing grand Baronial manner in design. A new lodge and stable block was provided near the entrance gates, *Pls. 71, 72.*

Detail from bedspread.

Detail from bedspread.

71 ABOVE LEFT *Harmeny, lodge from entrance to drive, a westerly view.* P.M.

72 BELOW *Harmeny, Balerno, coach house & lodge from the* N. P.M.

73 ABOVE RIGHT *Harmeny, from the* S., *extension to left and some remodelling by Lorimer.* P.M.

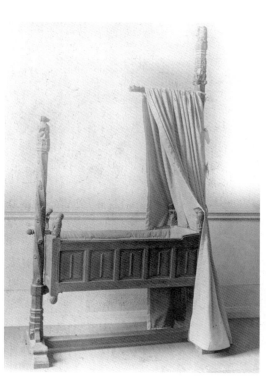

74 LEFT *Cradle design for William Burrell.* R.S.L.

75 RIGHT *Rowallan, Ayrshire, stair-well.* C.L.

4

The Grand Baronial Manner

Lorimer had reached the age of thirty six in 1901 and was complaining that he had hardly a 'single' friend left in the world. Begg and Dodds had married and now Burrell, *Pl. 52*, was engaged. Connie Mitchell, his betrothed, was a member of another influential commercial family in Glasgow and was 'sister of the chap his sister married a few months ago. Wants me to be his best man. I'm awfully pleased about it. He's rolling in money and 38 so its time he was spliced and she is extremely pretty, most refined girl, with a quite angelic temper. I should think it knocks our foreign trips on the head, these delightful three trips. I look back on them with such huge pleasure.'

Burrell began to search for a house. Lorimer had looked over a house in Ayrshire for him three years previously when he had been contemplating having a place in the country, and the scheme for remodelling Newark Castle in Fife had been abandoned. Burrell had continued to stay at his mother's house in Glasgow, until he finally chose a 'Greek' Thomson house near hers in Great Western Terrace. He wanted it remodelled, and Lorimer was told how it was to be made 'very simple as he has such lovely contents', and that Lorimer was to 'chip away the ginger bread'. Burrell had already laid the foundations for his collection of fifteenth century tapestries which was to become one of the best in the world, and the dining room walls were to be covered by them almost completely.

The woodwork throughout the house was replaced by oak. Walls were panelled in linen fold, new fire places were installed and an entirely new Gothic staircase, *Pl. 80*. The effect overall is more Jacobean than anything else. Much of the furniture was antique. Lorimer added an oak Gothic dining table with spirally fluted legs sloped outwards, *Pl. 81*, and he was soon asked to design a cradle, *Pl. 74*. 'Isn't he a record breaker? Think of going into the question of a cradle with such thoroughness, two or three months before the kid is due! Last Sunday was wet and drew the whole thing out full size. Have put a hound on top of the pillar at the foot, and the pelican in her piety on the one at the top. Won't it rather lift the bun? Brushed out with wire brushes and fumed. Its own mother won't know it from a piece of French Gothic, late fifteenth century as they always label this stuff at the SKM [South Kensington Museum].'

A double bed was designed with carved legs, in the same genre as the cradle and dining table, reflecting on one hand Burrell's deep interest at that time in fifteenth century art, and on the other hand Lorimer's wide experience in furniture design backed by Matthew's interest in and special knowledge of the language of symbols. It represents also a widening of Lorimer's use of Gothic forms from church furnishings to the secular in search of a

[52] *William Burrell from 'The Baillie', 5 November 1902.*

B.C.

49

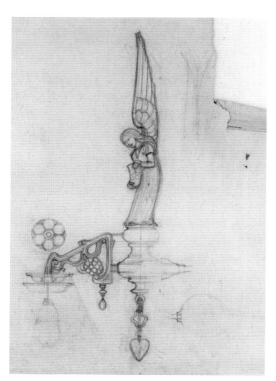

[53]–[54] *Designs for William Burrell,* ABOVE *light
fitting;* BELOW *carved newel posts.* R.C.A.M.

grandeur which became increasingly Baronial in the years following.

Burrell was making a great deal of money in shipping and Lorimer had been hoping for another commission like Earlshall from him, but collecting always took first place and it was not until 1916 that Burrell finally bought Hutton Castle. On this occasion he was holding back and six weeks after moving in had 'hardly hung up anything, got it too bare in fact, but its on the right side to err on. The dining room looks very fine. The whole place hung with the finest Gothic tapestries, and in the centre a Gothic table by yours truly. Some good chairs and that's all. He dines off the bare board and I must say I am old fashioned enough not to like it. I think there is something almost sacramental about the cloth'.

Lorimer came to know most of the people in Glasgow's art circles. He knew the Director of the College of Art well and he exhibited regularly at the Institute. He, Burrell and Lord Carmichael, to whom Burrell first introduced him and for whom he undertook several small commissions, all contributed to the International Exhibition held there in 1901. But apart from two churches, one of which was won in competition, the only commissions from his Glasgow connections were two mansion houses, one of which was for John Holms, a stockbroker who had also contributed to the exhibition, and for him Lorimer later designed a large mansion in Renfrewshire.

The commission for his first new mansion came from Fife connections. The Playfairs[1], who lived in St Andrews in Fife, were distant cousins and like Mackenzie of Earlshall, friends of the family. Lorimer designed a large memorial to Dr Playfair, *Pl. 92,* which was illustrated in the *Architectural Review* in 1899, and in 1900 after the family had moved to Hampshire their lengthy efforts on his behalf gained him the commission for Brackenburgh from Mr Joseph Harris. The accommodation required, as well as the Border Peel Tower already on the site, and even the site itself amid flattish rolling hills near Penrith in Cumberland, were all of a kind with which he was familiar, and he went to work to plan a long low two-storey building stretched out like Tilliefour, *Fig. 55.*

This was Lorimer's first excursion into Tudor design. Several years earlier he had told the Edinburgh Architectural Association that 'Morris says "If you have a building to put up in a countryside go to the place, study the district, see how the old buildings were done. Build your walls of the local stone in the way the stone suggests. Use all the local materials and ways of doing things so far as you can. In fact try to make your building look at home like a bit of the countryside",' *Pls. 82–90.* He designed a long low building in keeping with the many such Tudor buildings in the more northerly parts of England. There is no record from where he might have taken the details although he refers to a 'Kirby' bay window. Roofs had been commonly set behind parapets for protection and to provide walkways from which to watch the surrounding country, and Lorimer had flirted with them for Roxobel and the unbuilt tower of the Church of the Good Shepherd. Brackenburgh is very much longer than either and despite the numerous checks and switches in direction in its length the effect of the label mould which crowns it is so strongly horizontal that Hussey has complained that at this time, 'These linear instrusions are characteristic of Lorimer's work', and that when he had outgrown them, his work became both more personal and more plastically effective.

A house which had particularly impressed Lorimer was by Norman Shaw, and a few years earlier (in 1897) he had made a pilgrimage to Neston overlooking the River Dee to see the tall three storeyed building, which was perhaps more Elizabethan than Tudor. He told Dods 'Dawpool – yes – there wasn't a rear [W.C.] or a H.M.C. [House maid's closet] in the whole place that I hadn't my nose into . . . . I told Frankie Deas that if he got an order for it he was to let me know'. He had done so and they both went to Liverpool by train, stopping the night there, before crossing the Mersey, to take a hansom cab in Birkenhead for the last seven miles across the Wirral. Mrs Ismay received them and provided a 'rattling good lunch' after which the butler showed them round, and 'everything was worth seeing. I never saw *any* job that had been so perfectly worked out, not a bungle from beginning to end and everywhere most careful elaborate detail. How that old man ever got through all his work with the staff he had is a mystery. I called on him next Sunday at Hampstead and said it looked as if it must have been very carefully done and slowly done, and that I supposed he must have had lots of time over it. "Oh know [Lorimer wrote it thus] on the contrary it was done fast, just as fast as possible", he said, and of course belittled the whole thing as if any suckling infant might have done the same'.

This elder architect, highly respected by Lorimer, had been chaffing a well-kent junior colleague, but Lorimer was to have further thoughts, as was his wont, particularly on the interior of Dawpool. 'The front entrance and staircase are the most interesting things, and a modelled *in situ* ceiling worked out in the most delightful way, real plaster. About some of the rooms I confess I felt a want. I think when you go into a room first it ought to give you a sort of *Total impression*, if you know what I mean, of colour or light and shade, or of charm and lucid order. Now these rooms hadn't that. You started to finger away at the "bits" at once, in fact it all comes back to the old thing, simplicity, simplicity, simplicity and proportion. I mean if you have a suite of rooms, treat them in *the main* all the same, *all* white, or *all* oak, or else they'll never have the right kind of style.' The sentiments were impeccable and the tone of these remarks is characteristic of Lorimer's perfectionism, especially when considering the work of others. In this he had earlier so alarmed his mother, that his brother John had to reassure her after she had written despairing whether Robin would 'ever do anything but criticise my pictures and everyone about him'. In fact Lorimer's comments on Shaw's work at Dawpool, which has since been demolished, were high praise compared to the ferocity of those he passed habitually on so many other architects!

His small staff was struggling to push out all the drawings on Brackenburgh including 'the eighth s[cale] plans . . . which take an antiquarian sheet to hoe', that is to say that a sheet was fifty two inches by thirty one inches to accommodate a plan of this size. Horsburgh, a youth and Nobbs filling in temporarily for a few weeks were all fully occupied during January. The estimated cost was £27,000 and building was to begin in late summer, but he found time also for much social activity. If he was still unmarried it was in no way due

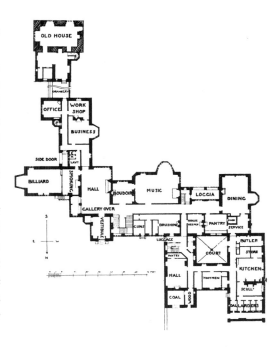

[55] *Brackenburgh, Cumberland, ground floor plan.*
C.L.

to lack of opportunity. He had told Dods in 1897 that he sometimes wished he 'could simply fall head and ears – with some girl – I suppose one is too b---dy dry, old and critical.' He had been on several Continental trips with Burrell who had two unmarried sisters. He found Mary particularly pleasant and intelligent but was put off by her Glasgow accent. On another occasion he had been 'awfully fetched by the seventeen and half year old daughter of Eustace Balfour', an architect friend who was A. J. Balfour's (the Prime Minister's) brother, and had worked with Champneys and designed the coffee house at Inveraray. She invited him to a house party at Whittinghame[2] for three nights two years later. He was back in East Lothian the following week for another two nights at Biel including a dance, and went on to Yester for another dance the following night. It came to nothing but he met an attractive girl at Burrell's wedding 'who is simply worth pots – 100 thou[sand] sort of thing. If one married a girl with 3 or 4 thou[sand] a year, I would be drinking from sheer boredom after a few months, and lapse into a sort of beery country gent – a long sleep every day after your too big lunch'. He had evidently given the whole matter a good deal of thought because he concluded, 'a working life for me and rather the penniless lass with a long pedigree than the daughter of an oofish wealthy bourgeois, and this particular one's girl looks like a hairdresser and drinks like a pike, so they tell me.'

Hall, of Galashiels, who was building Brackenburgh had the walls three feet out of the ground after eighteen months and thirty five hewers to work on it, partly because trade was slack elsewhere. Lorimer's next visit was not to be for another eight weeks, or so, when the huge Kirby window of the Hall would be taking shape. He felt he had 'rather a ripping plan' for this hall, with a flat oak ceiling, ribs and large carved bosses. The proportions of the music room, thirty six by twenty four feet were chosen for dancing, 'with a huge bay, this and an ante room arranged so that there can be proper communication, "Oh how I wish it was the ball night" exclaimed little Mrs Harris at dinner last night. She wants to engage Iff's band already'.

A charming garden, *Pl. 84*, completed the scheme but Lorimer professed himself not altogether satisfied with the 'scrappy' results, as he put it, of an interior not well enough knit together. He told Dods, 'My dining room has about an eleven foot ceiling . . . divided into bays with beams frieze etc and a crystal electrolier, and the adjoining boudoir is about the same, then the hall again is oak and tapestry with a wood ceiling with carved and gilded flowers in the rib intersections adjoining it. The ball-room oak of God knows what character! What a worm one feels when one thinks of it and goes through the sort of house I was through in the Hague a few days ago. An antique [building] friend Tuinisson has restored from a shop into a most beautiful Dutch House.'

One of Lorimer's circle of friends was a property agent, J. Galletly. The billiards room he got Lorimer to add to his Colinton house, Inchdrewer, had a '38 × 24, segmental plaster ceiling all modelled in position, big oriel and ingle, and oak panelled up to the springing with pilasters at intervals with inlay in them.' Afterwards he attended a dance given in it where he met James Dunn, a contemporary of his who was complaining that his partner

76 ABOVE LEFT *Lorimer (beneath flag) & Burrell family in Holland.* M. Mitchell
77–79 MIDDLE LEFT *Antique Dutch silver bowl*, B.C.; MIDDLE & BELOW LEFT *Lorimer's wedding present for Dods & detail.* SIR LORIMER DODS
80–81 *Great Western Terrace, Glasgow,* ABOVE RIGHT *staircase;* BELOW RIGHT *dining room,* R.S.L.

82 ABOVE LEFT *Brackenburgh & garden newly planted.* R.S.L.

83 *Brackenburgh, the forecourt as it was.* R.S.L.

84 *Brackenburgh, old Peel Tower at right (through the trees).* R.S.L.

85 BELOW RIGHT *Brackenburgh, garden detail.* R.S.L.

86 OPPOSITE ABOVE LEFT *Brackenburgh, the billiard room.* R.S.L.

87 OPPOSITE BELOW LEFT *Brackenburgh, the hall with minstrels' gallery.* R.S.L.

88 OPPOSITE ABOVE RIGHT *Brackenburgh, the drawing room.* R.S.L.

89 OPPOSITE BELOW RIGHT *Brackenburgh, the hall from beneath minstrels' gallery.* R.S.L.

90 ABOVE LEFT *Brackenburgh, East Lodge.*   P.S.
91 BELOW LEFT *54 Melville Street, remodelled.* L.S.
92 ABOVE MIDDLE *Playfair memorial, St Andrews.*
                                       R.S.L.
93 ABOVE RIGHT *Fettercairn, the library.*   R.S.L.
94 BELOW RIGHT *Lorimer's dining room at Melville
Street.*   R.S.L.

Finlay did little work (his father owned the *Scotsman* and Aberlour House) and who strongly recommended Lorimer against taking a partner because 'a small business that you look after yourself with a few fellows, is the best, he says, and I think from the practical point of view of making oof [money] its the best.'

The year after Matthew's return from South Africa Lorimer had increased his salary to three guineas a week on the understanding that 'the word screw wasn't to be mentioned for two years then the other night he came and asked me if it would in any way prejudice his position with me if he was getting married! Think that a how d'ye do, the blooming clerk getting married when his blooming boss can't afford it.' The 'blooming clerk' did marry after which he set up house in one of the Rustic Cottages in Colinton which Lorimer had just built for Galletly. If Lorimer had not found the right girl for himself, nevertheless he had been thinking about buying a house. 'It's been a scheme of mine for some years to buy a house or houses in the west end of Edin.[burgh] because the number of "pros" who have *got* to live within a given radius, is large, and the number of houses is small, and so is the given radius.' Communications were still primitive. His office correspondence had been all written out longhand and transferred directly into a copy book of onion skins until 1901 when a typewriter was bought. Cars were still rare, and Lorimer never learned to drive. He cycled out regularly the five miles to Colinton and for shorter journeys in town went on foot, by cab or tramcar.

Lorimer had Galletly watching the market for him and one day 'he sent me along about 11, a cutting of the *Scotsman* of that morning with advertisement of no 50 – Melville Street S[outh] side near Cathedral, *Pl. 91*. Was out the office in two two's, called for Hume the plumber, went all through the house, examined roof, found people buzzing all round the place but they weren't quick enough. Saw Galletly, directed him to see agent, did so, and we had our offer, three thou[sand] in by 1.30 to be binding till 12 o'clock next day, Friday. Got our acceptance, arranged house to let, Saturday's *Scotsman*, by Monday morning had eight applications and by Monday afternoon let it for £180. There's a feu duty of £21 [a kind of ground rent]. I've got to spend £350 on it, but still it will give a fair return, anyhow here's the solid house, a lot better than sticking your money in these d[amne]d companies. I'm putting a bond for £1,500 on it at $3\frac{1}{4}$, but if things go humming, will clear it off.'

The purchase of this house was the first stage of a larger scheme and Lorimer was soon 'in treaty for the one next door, and if I got it will be able some day to carry out my long cherished scheme of having house next door to office with a door through – twig? Use the whole of one house myself and the two ground floor rooms of the next house for office.' He evidently didn't foresee any great enlargement of his staff because he intended to let off the basement and the rest of the house to one or two spinsters whose rent would pay for the whole outlay, and in the process he would not only draw upon his experience of buildings but would also widen it.

He was going to put all his money into Edinburgh houses of this class, he said, and though he never did move his office to Melville Street, he bought number fifty four which he remodelled for his own town house. Like Burrell's house it was set in a three storey terrace of similar houses, but Burrell had contented himself with a thorough remodelling of the interior and had made little change to the outside apart from some leaded lights. Lorimer, however, was to remodel number fifty four inside and out with a contempt for what the New Town of Edinburgh stood for equalled only by Ruskin, who would have liked to replace all its rectangular windows with cusped, and its parapets with gables. Not only had the houses in Melville Street similar facades, they were grouped symmetrically about axes. All the windows in the range in which his house sits had nine-pane sashes. He took out all sixteen of his sashes and substituted sashes with sixteen panes. He took off the long cast iron balcony at the first floor which is repeated on each house all down the street, then slapped out the masonry below the sill of the middle window to provide French windows, in front of which he had a small stone balcony installed on brackets with a decorative wrought iron balustrade. Finally and perhaps worst of all, he had a mansard roof installed to give the house higher attic rooms, which broke up from the general roof line of the street, with tall segmentally headed dormers to light these rooms.

The original design may have been undistinguished but its repetitive neutrality made it a particularly effective foil for St Mary's Cathedral which Gilbert Scott had built as the terminating feature of the street. Lorimer was quite oblivious to this effect and as Stuart Matthew has observed dryly, 'Lorimer ruined one end of Melville Street and my father the other', meaning the alterations by J. F. Matthew to the old Melville College (since restored).

He completed the reconstruction of his house by relatively minor alterations inside. The dining room was given a bay window on the south away from the street, a panelled ceiling with carved bosses and double doors to the adjoining room, and the stairwell was remodelled. The furniture he chose shows a widening in his tastes if not a change. The interiors were not dominated by plain or veneered Louis Quinze pieces which he had preferred earlier but by Gothic pieces such as he had designed for Great Western Terrace. The dining room fireplace carved by Louis Deuchars is derived from early Gothic examples, the side table is seventeenth century and a Gothic table was made for him by Whytock and Reid on the lines of Burrell's, *Pl. 94*.

Fifty years had passed since Ruskin had laid his strictures on the classical regularity of the New Town in Edinburgh[3], and if Lorimer still thought of himself as basically a gothic man, no other architect had seen fit to make alterations of this scale on any other house in the New Town, and it may be that like Walter Scott, he regarded the New Town as being composed of 'English' houses. If so, he was rectifying his own house with features he deemed more suitable to Scotland, and his letters carry suggestions that he intended the grand manner which he had begun to adopt to evoke feelings for 'Bonnie Scotland,' as he had felt Louis Quinze to evoke 'la Gloire de France'.

Lorimer was at last in love. After long years discussing love by correspondence, Dods had finally asked him why he did not do something about it and he replied that he had been on the point of getting fixed up with two different girls, but 'Something – God knows what

– made me refrain'. He was, he admitted, getting long in the tooth and had bought two houses but what kept him off marriage on the last occasion was that 'the girl didn't know a note of music, and you know music means a marvellous lot to me. My idea of bliss is to get home dog-tired at about 6.30, to a beautiful white drawing room and find a beautiful svelt girl playing Brahms or Chopin on the piano and an infant crowing and gooing on the hearth rug.' He then swore Dods to secrecy telling him he mentioned such things only to him or to Burrell. He had met his future wife in 1902. Violet was one of the nine Wyld children living in the Tile House, near Denham in Buckinghamshire. The house had nineteen bedrooms, lodges to the park, a pleasure garden with croquet lawn and tennis courts, as well as pheasant, partridge and duck shooting nearby. Lorimer did not himself shoot but would disappear into the beech woods to listen to the birds, and he got a further insight into country house life from his frequent visits which was to stand him in good stead as his practice in country houses grew.

He took Miss Wyld to lunch at Fullers restaurant near Regent Circus in London, and they went on to evensong 'at the Abbey'; then to tea before going to her home and, later to a Housman play, 'Bethlehem', which left him with swimming eyes. They met next week to visit the South Kensington Museum and the week following he saw her off from Victoria Station for a three month's stay in Sicily. Later that year they married. He was thirty nine, the same age at which his own father had married.

Among the country house jobs which Lorimer had begun to receive was a fair sized extension to Hallyburton, a Baronial revival house designed by Andrew Heiton near Coupar Angus, and he was expecting the job to cost £1,400. The dining room, *Pl. 106*, is a square room on plan with a tall panelled ceiling, and a slightly lower bay to one side, and the oak panelling is worked round a series of very fine tapestries. He had been to Paris with Menzies and his wife to advise on their purchase: 'Think I'm using him very well as I'm only charging him 5 gs [guineas] a day and expenses'. They bought three tapestries costing two thousand two hundred pounds, including a hunting scene which they found later didn't quite go with the others which were Louis Douze. 'This piece as you see is pure Gothic. You will remember', he told Dods, 'the two woodland scenes in a corner of the tapestry court at SKM, we had seen another Louis Douze piece in Paris and I got it over on approval so ye brilliant idea struck me of getting my *valiant little girl*, to buy this Gothic piece for our dining room at Melville Street, *Pl. 94*. She rose to it like the little trump she is so I wrote to Menzies and said that if the other piece suited 'I'd take the hunting scene off his hands. I had to play my cards with the utmost nicety, not to let him see how dead keen I was to relieve him of it, as I had measured the spot in the dining room and found it just fitted!! I don't think you were ever so cracked on tapestry as I am, but this piece is the sort of thing that affords me the most violent joy. To live in the same room with it will be never ending pleasure.'

The alterations which Lorimer was making to his house in Melville Street showed where his own tastes were tending but also, as he told Dods, 'I regard it as being just as important for me to be in the centre of things as for a doctor to be in Charlotte Square! You want to keep in touch with all these pot-bellied W. S. [lawyers] and people, you know what human nature is, if you're prosperous they'll employ you, and if they think you're small beer, and live away at Murrayfield or Stockbridge or somewhere they'll let you severely alone.' Both these suburbs of Edinburgh are less than two miles out and only being able to return hospitality at his club may account for some of his lack of success in breaking earlier in to the country house market after such an auspicious start at Earlshall. After Aberlour, he had got only the bridge for Minto House, gates for Grandtully Castle, and a library alteration for Fettercairn in 1898, *Pl. 93*. Affairs had improved after the end of the Boer War and he was working on Pitkerro, a sixteenth century Baronial house in Angus, to which he was called back twice to make further extensions, on Craigmyle, a late sixteenth century Jacobean house in Aberdeenshire, a marvellous granite hill top house, now no more, to which he made large extensions, he was building his first mansion in England and about to start another in Scotland.

Lorimer's first commission for a new Scottish mansion was one which came in 1901 from his Glasgow connections. Cameron Corbett, his client, had had some training as a sculptor before taking over an uncle's land development business, and after successfully expanding its interests around London he entered parliament as the Liberal member for the Tradeston division of Glasgow. He had a house in Hans Place in London and leased a large house in Glasgow whose expansion threatened to engulf it. Mrs Corbett's mother then bought the six thousand acre Rowallan estate with a charming sixteenth century castle[4] set low in a valley with the waters of the Carmel tumbling past its walls. The situation was damp and the views restricted so a new house was decided upon to be sited on the hill to the west from which wide views extended to the coast, and to Ailsa Craig and the mountainous island of Arran still farther off.

The prospect of this mansion, for a Member of Parliament, intended to hold the large house parties of those days was exciting for Lorimer, who determined to plan it so that the service areas would be completely segregated from the public and private areas and, as this house was to be at least six times as large as any of Lorimer's previous new Scots houses, he planned it around three courts, *Fig. 56*. The approach drive which is taken straight past the house to the service court follows the line of the track which formerly led to Rowallan Mains, its farm buildings on what became the forecourt of the new house. A thicket of rhododendrons lines the drive until the forecourt *Pl. 97*, opens to the left, when the house, previously hidden, bursts upon the view from across it. The impression intended was of a line of roofs of varying heights ranged loosely across it, the lowest roofs on either side of the main entrance under its steep corbie gable, other roofs to either side rising higher, and the still higher roof of the H-shaped main block glimpsed beyond. Thus the arrangement was elliptical in effect, and bisected by the entrance gable, and partly gabled tower behind it, with a third gable to draw the attention across to the main block, *Fig. 57*.

The main apartments are placed on the first floor, for which the precedents are more truly Baronial (for reasons of safety) than revival Baronial, and the grand staircase, *Pl. 103*, rises

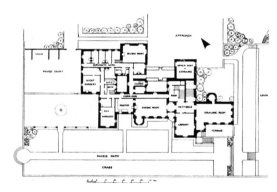

[56] *Rowallan, Ayrshire, plan of* piano nobile.
C.L.

95 LEFT *Alice Corbett by W.E. Lockhart.* C.L.

96 RIGHT *Rowallan, the Lodge.* C.L.

within the tower, with the main staircase, linking all floors, offset in the western part of the tower. The billiard, gun and garden rooms on the ground floor are all reached by it, and there are a number of doors giving directly to the garden. Thus the climax of the design was reserved for the south garden front with a tall central pavilion and high mullioned[5] windows flanked by a pair of steep gables, *Fig. 58*. It was to have housed the hall, an impressively lofty chamber which a surviving drawing suggests was intended to open straight from the upper vestibule without any intervening door. Such open planning offers the faintest echo of the hall houses which figure only in the early years of English influence on Scots history. Latterly, halls were squeezed into one floor of a tower house, although in L-shaped towers the solar might be provided in the jam (or wing) alongside. Almost the only buildings in Scotland with large halls set within ranges of first floor apartments were the palaces of James IV. So the effect of Lorimer's great hall may be called Royal rather than Baronial. It would have offered a meeting place grander than the drawing room, but less formal, and close enough to the dining room to allow refreshments to be served to shooting parties, or to members of the Eglinton Hunt as their mounts were assembling in the forecourt below.

The original plans for this scheme have been lost but it seems that the mansard roofs flanking the main entrance were intended to accommodate a service corridor linked across the entrance hall between them by a gallery. This would have allowed staff to pass over the hall to the east wings. The choice of this roof form which has no links with the Baronial can only be explained by a desire in Lorimer to reduce the scale of the blocks as much as possible in order to emphasise the height of the main block behind. Similarly the diminutive arcade that was proposed for the south side of the east court was scaled down to emphasise the full height of the confined but impressive court as seen through the French windows set halfway up the grand staircase.

The manipulation of form by Lorimer, as always, was primarily plastic but carried out within the practices of building and forms of the Baronial period, as far as he could. This intricate composition, in which both the main and subsidiary blocks employ many changes of scale and of roof height, *Pl. 99*, was to have been painted white, as Lorimer preferred harled to plain masonry walls at this time. The small scale drawings of Rowallan suggest a building with harling stopped against the stone dressings around the openings. Some of the details like the fillets which run around the profile of the crowsteps also look as though intended as stops for the harling, but it is nowhere mentioned. Probably, as at Ardkinglas a few years later, of which the sectional drawings show harling, Lorimer was talked out of it by clients who felt it looked a cheap material only suitable for covering the roughly built cottages and that dressed stonework was to be preferred for the main house.

The design of Rowallan had begun in November 1901, the working drawings were done in four months and were sent to the surveyors in March for quantities to be taken, and Lorimer wrote to a friend in August of the close of this first chapter of design: 'I had a note on Monday from Mrs Corbett saying why couldn't I hurry up, losing all the summer etc. On the *Wednesday evening* I wired them I'd call on them in London on Thursday morning with the

97 OPPOSITE *Rowallan, the forecourt.*　　C.L.

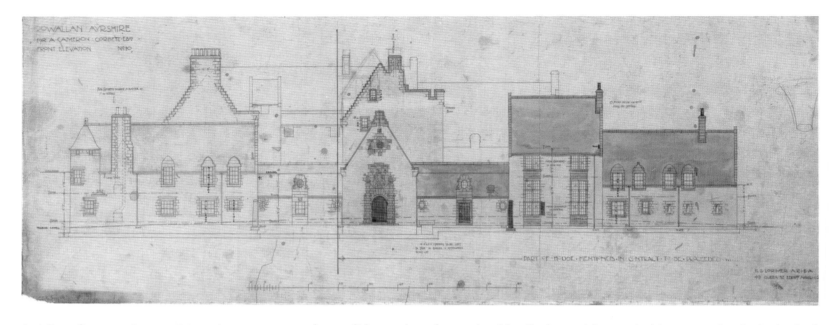

[57] *Rowallan*, N.E. *elevation of first scheme.*
R.C.A.M.

tenders – did so only to be received by Corbett with tears in his eyes saying he had wired trying to stop me as his wife had suddenly become very ill, and that he could discuss nothing.' Lorimer went on to Surrey where he had other work in progress. Returning to London he found a wire at his club asking him to call. He went to Hans Place to find that Corbett 'wanted to talk about the place where she [Alice] was to be buried as she had died the night before'. Lorimer gave up Rowallan as lost and quickly designed a simple memorial and she was laid to rest on the Windy Moor high above the Rowallan estate, an eerie place, loud with the whistling curlew.

Some weeks later Lorimer received fresh instructions that the project was to go ahead but that it would be necessary to 'reduce the house by about 100,000 cubit feet! one of these nice simple problems, just take one of these wires with the two handles and cut out a slab as if it was so much cheese and proceed! Nothing simpler. I've suggested omitting the whole bachelors wing pro tem.' However, the reasons why the scheme was proceeded with in any form lie further back in time. John Polson, Cameron Corbett's father-in-law and lord of the manors of Tranent and Cockenzie in East Lothian which he had acquired in 1871, was the driving force behind the rise of the firm of Brown and Polson of Paisley. His wife Mary (daughter of Mr Shanks a neighbouring manufacturer of earthenware) had taken over his public interests on his death in 1900. She endowed a ward in Paisley Hospital in his memory in 1904, and among other things, gave money to the eye hospital and for the improvement of Paisley Cross. She endowed also, in memory of her daughter, the Alice Mary Corbett home in Glasgow for which the late Lord Rowallan, then aged nine, laid the foundation stone. She received the freedom of Paisley in 1909, the year after Cameron Corbett had received that of Glasgow.

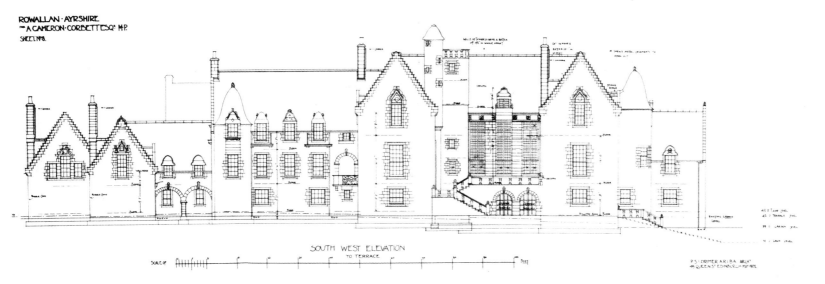

SOUTH WEST ELEVATION
TO TERRACE

SCALE OF

P. S. LORIMER A.R.I.B.A. ARCHᵗ
4 QUEEN Sᵗ EDINBURGH MAY 1902

[58] *Rowallan*, s.w. *elevation of first scheme.*
R.C.A.M.

The cramped and dark quarters of the old castle had been discarded to provide both accommodation for entertaining and the gift which Mrs Polson intended for her daughter. When the work resumed after Alice's death, cut down in scale, though with little diminution in cost, she was apt to remark to her son-in-law during the long years of building, 'I don't grudge the money, if it's for the children's good, but I want to know how much it will be!'

The tenders for the cut-down plans were submitted in 1902 and Lorimer wrote to the local firm, Boyd & Forest of Kilmarnock, to tell them that they were 'not the lowest but you're getting there'. The omission of whole wings of this house had necessitated some adjustments in the remainder. The Great Hall, the central climax of the original scheme was extended a little to become the drawing room, which now forming the end of the building, is provided with additional windows to overlook the garden on the east, *Pl. 98*. A few other adjustments were made and Boyd and Forest's all trades tender for £20,361/5/4d was provisionally accepted. Among economies discussed was the cost of bringing hewn stone dressings from the quarries of Prudham and Blackpasture in the north of England. A quarry was reopened on the estate to the north of the old castle but the stone proved to be so varied in quality that by mid 1904, despite a large bing of suitable stone rubble being ready, the question of importing dressings from further afield was again under discussion and a sharp correspondence was carried on as to who might bear the costs of opening further levels of stone should it become necessary. In the event more stone had to be fetched in from Edinburgh (Hailes Quarry) and used for the bridges on the drive among other work. As the walls rose the floors were poured in in concrete since Lorimer was very conscious of the risks of fire and it had become his custom to write offering his services whenever a mansion burned down in Scotland.

59

The simple rectangular blocks within which Rowallan is planned are contained by ten corbie stepped gables to interlock with such variety that there is no hint of a Tudor Manor in the building, some two hundred feet long, and Lorimer has had to add only a battlemented tower, and four bell capped turrets to evoke the full gravity of the Baronial. The general simplicity in treatment of surface is strengthened by the way most quoins run from eaves to ground without interruption, and it also provides a good foil for such embellishments as there are. Door surrounds, gablets and dormer heads have been enriched by the carvers habitually employed by Lorimer.

The Rowallan coat of arms which is set above the entrance and between the horns of an inverted arch over it flanked by massive rusticated columns, includes a crow, *Pl. 102*. The motto, *Deus Pascit Corvus*, God feeds the crows, was chosen for its play on Corvus, in Scotch Corbie, and the family name of Corbett. The accounts suggest that William Beveridge of Edinburgh carried it out. The decorated gate posts on the south front were done by William Stoddart of Edinburgh, who with two assistants at 1/4d per hour and one apprentice at $8\frac{1}{2}$d probably carried out the dormers and window gablets. Such details were culled from a variety of sources. Some window pediments are broadly modelled on sixteenth century examples, others over dormers are ogival, some plain and others enriched. If Lorimer demonstrated no art nouveau tendencies whatever, he was, nevertheless, showing an increased liking for curved details. The large additions he was making at this time to Craigmyle, an Aberdeenshire house which already had Dutch gables, shows its influence in several later houses. At Rowallan, he contents himself with round towers, bell capped turrets, as well as curving the hanging balcony to the south and the apex stones of the crowstepped gables.

Lorimer, like Lutyens, was asked on occasions, to undertake the entire design and choose everything for the house. Rowallan was not such a commission although it contains much furniture to his design. The general effects of the interior, however, are typical of the way he worked. If tower houses earlier in history had many dark corners because windows were kept as few and as small as possible for reasons of defence, Lorimer's use of strong contrasts of light and shade inside his houses – so in keeping with earlier traditions – is something which has become too sombre for modern tastes. However, the effect of underlighting some parts of a building is to produce a contrast by which other places gain apparent brightness. Such an interplay begins immediately on entering Rowallan. The lofty entrance which is brightly side – lit by high mullioned windows gives on to a broad range of stone stairs rising from its far side towards the *piano nobile*. The lighting from a window, intended to gaze upon a tall shadowy courtyard, which now looks into a mass of trees is completely adequate. A landing is reached at the head of the stairs from which a long corridor was to have led to the left to offer a sense of release before entering the strongly enclosing and shadowy upper vestibule, and from which doors open to the saloon and library. When the east wing was omitted, the corridor became unnecessary, and the opening to it was replaced by a small window, which has a view entirely blocked by nearby trees. It does not provide the release

98 ABOVE *Rowallan, easterly view.*   C.L.

99 BELOW *Rowallan, from* W.S.W.   R.S.L.

100 ABOVE *Rowallan, detail of tower.*   C.L.
101 BELOW LEFT *Rowallan, the stable court.*   C.L.
102 BELOW RIGHT *Rowallan, the entrance.*   R.S.L.

103 *Rowallan, the entrance hall.* C.L.

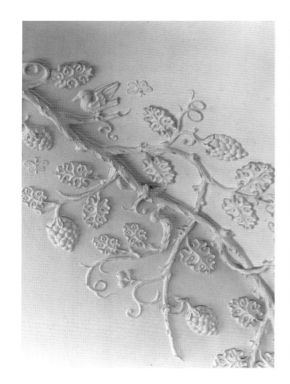

104 LEFT *Rowallan, detail of bedroom ceiling.* C.L.
105 RIGHT *Rowallan, a bedroom.* C.L.

so necessary to introduce the upper vestibule, deliberately underlit by indirect lighting from the lobby to the dining room and from even more distant windows to the west of the stair tower. If the effect has become slightly oppressive by these enforced changes, the saloon and the library seem – as was always intended – to be flooded with light, and this without recourse to anything but sash windows which if generous in size by Baronial standards, are not overlarge by present ones.

Large staircase windows are not any part of the original Baronial tradition and the main stairs of many nineteenth century revival mansions rise in large top lit wells, creating an oppressive sense of enclosure and of height. The Rowallan stair-well avoids both effects by being offset from the grand staircase and side lit by tall mullioned windows overlooking a courtyard. The rich wood finishings were carried out by Nathaniel Grieve, the carvers probably being the Clow brothers. A large Gobelins tapestry of Odysseus and Circe is an important part of the decoration, and a recess on an intermediate landing houses the portrait of John Polson painted by his friend W. E. Lockhart. The drawing room is about forty five feet long with a plain oval hollow in the ceiling. The marble fireplace incorporates dolphins by a contemporary Italian sculptor, and above it hangs a beautiful full-length portrait of Alice Corbett, *Pl. 95*, also by Lockhart. Although nothing so Gothic as a window bay or oriel is incorporated, both drawing room and dining room have recesses which open into adjoining turrets. The library has a Juliet balcony above the fireplace which is reached from the adjacent bookroom. This was to have provided a minstrels' gallery to the great hall (now remodelled as the drawing room). The balcony and curved decorated ceiling of the Library convey an animation sobered by the long lines of books in the built-in oak shelves along its walls.

The subcontractors on this job were mostly those from Edinburgh with whom Lorimer liked to work. As nominated contractors their estimates had to lie within the main contract figure. Scott Morton carried out the finishings in the library. The panelling in the dining room which this firm carried out to Lorimer's general directions, rises to full wall height, and is divided into a variety of sizes, some panels with linen folds. The small scale of this panelling reflects the early period of the furniture in wire brushed carved oak, which Lorimer says elsewhere the South Kensington (V & A) Museum would call 'fifteenth century French Gothic'. Whytock and Reid supplied the 'sideboard to design [of Lorimer] with 4 twisted legs, shaped stretcher and 3 deep drawers in frieze', for £22. They also supplied a sidetable £12.10s. oval table £13.8s, and telescopic dining table £42 and two dumb waiters in Spanish mahogany each £14.10s, two marble topped tables for the vestibule and two library tables all to Lorimer's design. Nathaniel Grieve, who carried out the drawing room floor in American Oak was the contractor for many of the Colinton cottages and also specialised in fine joinery. Lorimer also used carvers to model the decorated plaster ceilings. The certified accounts show that the bulk of the work at Rowallan was done by Sam Wilson of Edinburgh. G. P. Bankart, to whom this work has been wrongly attributed, signed a quotation by the Bromsgrove Guild of Applied Art for a lead tank, and the Guild supplied the enriched cornice and beam-casings in the dining room. This standard design, used also at Ardkinglas, has a repetitiveness which Lorimer goes to such pains elsewhere to avoid. The way the decorative tendrils flow all over the sides and bottom of the beam obscures the arrises, and the diminutive mouldings along the junction with the ceiling are too weak to contain their decorative movement. Lorimer's preliminary sketches for the ceiling of one of the west bedrooms exists. It is a rough sketch from which Wilson has modelled the ceiling loosely in the manner common in Scotland in the sixteenth century, *Pls. 104, 105*. Other features, like the wreath and pendant over the stairs hall are modelled crisply with sharp edges in the manner of the seventeenth century. The two modes can also be seen used together – as in the seventeenth century plaster of the vine room at Kellie Castle.

As the building neared completion Corbett's mother-in-law would move in as chatelaine during his frequent absences in London required in attending parliament. Invariably, so the story goes, Lorimer would arrive from Edinburgh to urge and cajole her into sanctioning the completion of the east wing, urging that 'the children will never forgive you if it is not built'. Certainly, a doorway was built into the east wall of the entrance hall ready for the extension, complete even to the pintels for the strap hinges, and then built up. The story, as it is told, suggests a one-sided concern by Lorimer, but the fact that the kitchen wing had been built unaltered and exactly as designed for the much larger house suggests that the completion of the east wing was not ruled out entirely until later on. The generous kitchen quarters are provided with a variety of stores, enough for a lengthy siege, and all lined immaculately with white glazed brick. The house staff in the early days comprised the butler, a footman, a head housemaid, three kitchen maids and four gardeners. However the children who have ultimately benefitted from this house were not so much Alice's, whom Mrs Polson had in mind, but her great-grandchildren whom she did not live to see playing in the echoing corridor and stairs on wet days and riding the policies with their mother in all weathers.

The layout of the grounds poised special problems of character. Traditionally, a Scots tower house (like Edzell) might have a walled garden attached to one side as a private arcadia into which the turnpike stair debouched. Open pastureland would stretch right up to the walls on the other side. These dispositions appealed to Lorimer strongly for reasons of history as much as of effect and he had been able to follow them closely in his garden layouts for Kellie and Earlshall. He found a similarly placed walled garden by the old Castle at Rowallan which was still in reasonable repair. A garden pavilion was added to the corner around which the drive to the new house turns, and espaliers were planted and paths layed out. A gardener's cottage was also built and with these changes, the garden became the kitchen garden for the new house. Thus in the fashion of the eighteenth century, the enclosed garden is at a remove from the new house, and the immediate surroundings freed thereby from its encumbrance, have been more broadly landscaped to provide a garden in the form of a long platform overlooking distant views from above a lengthy straight retaining wall. Unlike William Bruce's early garden at Balcaskie[6] in Fife, which Lorimer had long known, Rowallan has no steep slope to enable the house to be detached from the distant prospect by several strongly stepped terraces, and the lawns and paved walks which have been laid out do not offer more than an extensive outlook on a stroll along them. Indeed, the house was designed to be seen from the south only through the trees of a ride which starts at the stables (north of the house) and takes a rectangular course around the house, and in the middle distance from it. The garden itself is reached from the drawing room by an upper terrace and then by descending an open staircase (like those which led to the earlier town houses in the burghs set on the first floor above their undercrofts) or from the main bedroom by the turnpike stair, a blend of earlier traditional form with later ones, *Pl. 98*. The terrace to the east of the house closely follows the line of the outer face of the lost east wing, and provides a particularly charming view of the house. The lawn is wider than the lost bachelor's wing and extends further north than it, as though providing space for it when needed. If Lorimer had been certain that Rowallan was never to be completed I think that he would have swept the incoming drive leftwards across this lawn to approach the house obliquely. Advantage would have been taken by this of the aspect of the house which suffers least from incompleteness. Yet despite some sadness of a greater opportunity which was missed, this many gabled house which was begun as an elaborate pun on the name of its future occupants has achieved a grandeur which in its very incompleteness offers the truest memorial to Alice Corbett who never saw it, yet to whom ultimately it owes its being.

How successful a design was Rowallan to Lorimer? The surviving letters do not tell us, although many details are mentioned. When he had been occupied with the Colinton cottages in 1897 he had told Dods that he thought 'proportion and whitewash are good enough and *shadow* – a good deal of shadow'. He was probably overruled on the whitewash but his first scheme, in particular, had made much play with shadow, and in the middle of building Rowallan he told Dods, 'The older I grow, dear boy, the more I appreciate that proportion is the tremendously important thing in architecture. Everything else matters also, but if you haven't proportion to start with, nothing else is any good, and proportion, a knowledge and feeling for it, is a thing that only comes with practice and much observation and experience. Putting through job after job, and making mistakes and having rows and rough knocks generally. What a lot that teaches one', and as the job ended he wrote about 'the awful crab that I feel to *my* work as to everyone's domestic work at present is the want of rhythm. The old unconscious lads, struck a keynote – set a tune. Their tune, the only tune that existed for them and on this tune they played in room after room the most delicious variations.'

Whatever doubts remained in Lorimer's mind as to his own success in achieving constant variety within an overall unity of expression, Brackenburgh and Rowallan had assured his position as a leading country house architect. He discarded 'Rampart' as his telegraphic address in favour of 'Plinth' and the Royal Scottish Academy elected him associate.

Antique tile

Bedspread design.

106 Hallyburton, Coupar Angus, the dining room,
with panelling fitted to tapestries.   C.L.

107 *Davenham Memorial, figures of Courage &
Gentleness carved by the Clow Brothers.* R.S.L.

5

The Edinburgh Craft Designers

Lorimer's first love was the Baronial, he sided with the Goths and was in principle opposed to Classicism, and he had returned from London fired with a deep enthusiasm for William Morris and his teachings, and the way these threads are interwoven in his thinking is nowhere put more clearly than in the lecture on William Morris which he gave in 1897 to the Edinburgh Architectural Association. Morris had been 'little more than a name to him' only five or six years earlier, but Morris was a person, he told the Association, who had gone to Oxford University before entering the office of George Edmund Street where he would have learned to appreciate 'the value of a feeling for scale without which no design can ever do anything'. We need not be surprised, Lorimer continued, 'that he did not find all he sought for in Street's office. Though a Gothic man to the core, it was the spirit of Gothic he was after, not the letter, *Pl. 37*. The Gothic of the craftsmen, not the classical professional Gothic, – if I may so term it', and Morris had come to feel that all the paper design involved in working as an architect was the wrong way or that, 'the only real way to approach design was through a thorough knowledge and appreciation of the material in which your design was to be carried out.'

That was Morris's whole gospel as Lorimer saw it, and since Baronial craftsmanship and Gothic craftsmanship can be seen as branches from the same tree there was no problem of reconciliation for Lorimer. However, before he could follow Morris's example in designing the furniture and other artefacts which formed the mass of Morris's output, his first commission had come in for the restoration of Earlshall, and this too was the kind of work in which Morris had interested himself. Lorimer went on to tell of the despoliation of so many old Gothic churches at the hands of mid-Victorian restorers, and how Morris had come forward as the prime mover in forming a society to protect ancient buildings, to stay the hand of these so-called restorers. The society came to be popularly known as the 'Antiscrape'. 'I hope', Lorimer told his Edinburgh audience, 'you all agree with me that it is quite impossible to restore an old Gothic building. You can *mend* it. You can keep it in repair and prevent it from falling down but to restore it is, and always will be, absolutely impossible. The life and traditions that gave it being are gone and can never return – you might as well try to regalvanise a dead horse.'

The external state of Earlshall was such that it had only needed mending and he had been able to turn to Falkland Palace, not above a score of miles away, for a wood screen contemporary with Earlshall upon which to model one required there at the end of the hall. If so much medieval woodwork has been lost in the wars with England, as well as during the

Reformation, such that did remain had become the object of keen scrutiny in the revival in interest in Scots historical building which took place in the latter half of the nineteenth century. Much of the woodwork was measured up, and drawings made which were published as collections in the Architectural Association's Sketchbooks. Falkland's screen was among such work and had also appeared in MacGibbon and Ross's massive work on the castellated buildings of Scotland which had appeared a few years earlier. The screen was of sturdy construction, made up of wood members in parts turned, run with planed mouldings, and hand carved without any weakness arising. The painted ceiling, according to Weaver in the *Country Life* magazine, was so badly decayed that the surface had to be cut away in sections and then glued back piece by piece to new boards and it is likely in a house built in 1540 that all the floorboards elsewhere were left exposed and that plaster ceilings were added later. Those now existing have plain Georgian surfaces and are rimmed by simple cornice bands, and any further plaster work was probably done by Messrs Moxon and Carfrae, of which firm Mr Nixon and Mr Hamilton, *Pl. 108*, according to J. F. Matthew, 'did all the early work for us'. Thomas Beattie, who worked on all the earliest jobs, and became one of Lorimer's favourite modellers, claimed that he only executed the 'carving on dormer windows and other parts'. He had also worked on Lorimer's second commission where he had to 'form plain enrichments for Aberlour House'.

Lorimer's sketchbooks reveal his early interest in furniture, and the year he spent in London with Bodley, who was renowned for his woodwork designs, afforded him the time and opportunity for frequent visits to the furniture in the South Kensington Museum. Mackenzie of Earlshall, however, was a collector of the antique so that almost the only piece of furniture of any importance for the house which Lorimer was allowed to design was a hall table, *Pl. 141*. It is built solidly in oak to carry an inlaid marble top. The legs are grooved to emphasise their length and diminish the effect of their thickness and are curved forwards at the bottom to suggest feet. They join the platform of the table in ornamentally carved and curved terminations. It incorporates thereby a number of features which he was to repeat in following years within an overall Dutch influence.

In the years that followed, Lorimer's architectural work comprised mainly new houses including many Colinton cottages, and the furniture designed during this period was mostly at cottage scale. He exhibited two such pieces in 1893 at the Arts and Crafts Exhibition in London. The catalogue lists an oak bureau 'adapted from an old design' and made for him by William Wheeler, the village joiner at Arncroach near Kellie, *Pls. 109, 110*, as well as an inlaid walnut linen press which had been executed by A. Paterson of Morrison and Company in Edinburgh, *Pls. 111, 112*. The critic of *The Studio* magazine recalled this work three years later in reporting the next exhibition saying that, 'the furniture designed by R. S. Lorimer shown at the last exhibition was so good that this time one refers to his contributions with some degree of certainty that they will be admirable'. His entries to this later exhibition included an embroidered linen back, a wood inlay executed for him by Whytock and Reid of Edinburgh, and two pieces of furniture which *The Studio* illustrated.

Wheeler had made the oak chest which incorporated an inlaid panel recalling a landscape by Piero di Cosima and made up for him by Whytock and Reid. The correspondent of *The Builder* magazine criticised this panel for being an unhappy 'form of decoration, though it is a revival of an old fancy' and he found that, 'the knob handles to the drawer below are so small as to look paltry'. If this latter criticism seems justified, *The Studio* critic found the same piece to have been 'admirably managed' in its use of 'the natural marking of the various woods'. Yet another later piece made by Wheeler for Lorimer was an oak writing desk with a salmon pink Marble slab on top which failed to harmonise with the colour of the wood, according to *The Studio's* critic. As Lorimer was in no way a colourist and only used colour at all with great restraint, all we can judge of these early works from their photographs was that if they followed traditional forms and often showed a general Dutch influence, they were all very well made and proportioned, an achievement soon to be recognised when he heard early in 1897 that he had 'been elected a member of the Arts and Crafts[1], didn't know my name was down even, though Crane had told Jack [his brother] this some time ago. Suppose I ought to be proud to be associated with C. R. Ashbee, Voysey, etc. Anyway I accepted, as it only costs 10/- a year.'

Lorimer had met members of the Art Workers' Guild while working in London and he went down to the triennial exhibitions. He gave his own views of the 1896 show to Dods telling him, 'I went there three times or so and upon my soul, can I remember anything I really liked . . . . Yes, some really delightful simple jewellery and silver things from Ashbee's place, he's really coming at it now, a table electric lamp by Schultz – your enemy – but you'd have liked it', and he had taken the opportunity to buy a copy of William Morris's lecture on Gothic architecture for one and sixpence which he said later was his dearest possession. Whenever he was in London on business he would visit his friends, most of whom were associated with the Guild. He had tea with Mrs Tapper on this visit, while her husband was absent in Australia, and he met Schultz, Barnsley and Troup who had also been invited by her. When he passed through London the following year to visit his Surrey job, Whinfold, he said he spent the night enjoyably at Schultz's with 'a whole crowd up one night after the A.W.G. meeting', and he mentioned that Thomas, Dawber, Whall, Davis had all been at the meeting of the Art Workers' Guild.' He even took some holidays with associates of the Guild, and a foursome made up with his brother Jack, Weir Schultz and Louis Davis took a tour of northern France together. Davis was the stained glass artist with whom he was closest. They visited Brighton together in 1897 and both Davis and his daughter stayed at Kellie during a visit to Scotland in 1902. Christopher Whall was another English stained glass artist whom he knew well but did not much use.

He had reservations about some of the Guild's activity and he confided to Dods that 'The A.W.G. have been awfully agog over a masque they have just had. J. H. [his brother] has just sent me down the book about it, will get a copy and send to you. I know the rank feebleness of a lot of it, both poetry and drawing, will amuse you.' In 1899 he told him that 'The arts and crafts is back in London and I'm going up some day . . . . Its said to be worse

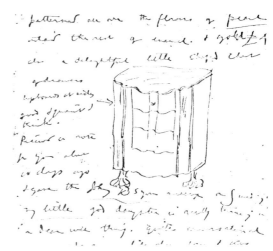

[59] 'A delightful little shaped chest of drawers' showing Lorimer's deep pleasure in curves.   E.F.

[60] *Tulips, sketch for a wood inlay.*   R.S.L.

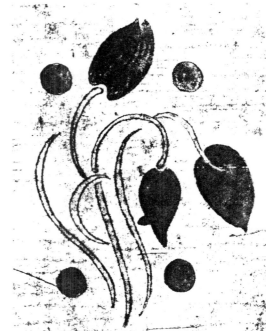

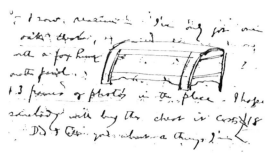

[61] *Chest exhibited at the Arts & Crafts Exhibition of 1899.* R.S.L.

than ever'. It seems the reservations were mutual because Lorimer reminded Dods of how 'he used to laugh over the artificial crudeness of some of the stuff at the A & C', and informed him that he had 'only got one oak chest with a fox hunt on the panel and three frames of photos in the place', *Fig. 61*, and he hoped 'somebody will buy the chest – it costs £18', *Pl. 119*. The last mention of the Guild in his letters was of going to the members' day in 1903 (an exhibition to which he had contributed four items), before going on to Aston Webb's At Home at the Institute in the evening. Although he sent nothing in 1906, 1910 or 1916, he more than made up for those omissions with a grand total of seventeen exhibits in 1912, and he remained loyal to the Society throughout his life, sending in two items in 1926, including a small oak bookcase costing seven guineas and a small oak table with a shaped and dished top at ten pounds.

These exhibitions had stimulated Lorimer to most of his early ventures into furniture design and the way in which, in typical Arts and Crafts fashion, he had evolved them by the closest collaboration with the craftsmen executing his designs is reflected by the advice he gave to Dods, who had asked him to get him some good furniture to ship out to Australia. He replied, 'I've always been on the lookout for a real good gate-leg table but have never yet seen one. Even when one has studied the subject as much as you and I have, you find it's very rarely that one comes across a piece with the real air of distinction about it, "the little more" and then one could always get it reproduced for less money, so my dear boy, what you ought to do is this. Make out a list with sketches of things you really want and if I can find old examples you'll have them, if not I can get them made, though at the same time I feel its an awful pity if you can't be coaching up some chap out there to make decent stuff.' This is exactly what Lorimer had been doing with Wheeler, Paterson and Gorie.

Such coaching required constant collaboration through every stage in the execution of each piece, and the piece would finally incorporate a great number of adjustments of detail as the design was refined on this interchange of views and experience of designer and craftsmen. The cabinet making firm of Whytock and Reid, which specialised in making furniture, came later to be entrusted with most of this work for Lorimer. The particular craftsmen would be given the briefest instructions and would often be required to make working details of the piece for approval before the work was begun. The same close collaboration would follow all through its execution and the earlier pieces which were made for him became the prototypes for later developments, until the craftsmen had put so much into their evolution that the firm was free to repeat those designs for its other clients when the need arose, and this makes the dating of many of the pieces impossible.

Reid had begun business in 1780 and Whytock in 1805 and, after a separate existence through three generations, they had amalgamated around 1870. Several prints of some undated sheets of drawings of furniture have turned up among Lorimer's office papers, *Figs. 62, 63*. The drawings are inaccurate in detail but convincing overall which suggests that they were traced quickly from Whytock and Reid's pattern book, probably for discussions on the furnishing of one of Lorimer's last great mansion remodellings, Marchmont in Ber-

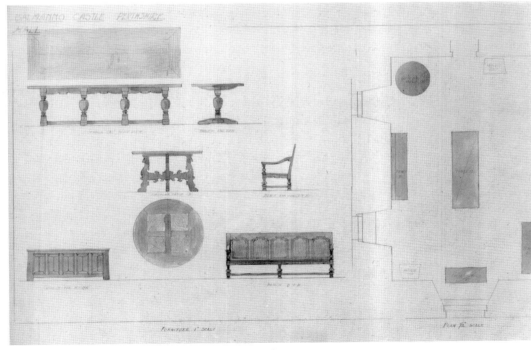

[62]–[63] *Gothic, Jacobean and Rococo pieces for Balmanno, probably traced from a pattern book of Lorimer designs.* R.C.A.M.

wickshire, begun in 1916. A number of the large Georgian pieces included were made for this house but the drawings also show a number of plain oak trestle tables made up of simple but beautifully shaped components held together by wood pegs. These designs echo the simple domesticity of Lorimer's cottage period from which they most certainly come, *Pl. 118*.

Morris had been preaching a functionalism based upon the nature of materials. Lorimer quoted him to his Edinburgh architectural audience, 'Suppose you have a piece of furniture to design, don't pretend to make it an imitation of French, or Scotch, or Jacobean, or anything else but ask yourself what is the thing for – make it the most convenient shape, then use the most beautiful wood you can get hold of and use it in such a way as to show its utmost beauty of grain and texture.' Lorimer designed a dresser which fits these exhortations closely and which was illustrated in two books by Shaw Sparrow, *Pl. 120*. He illustrated a modern dresser of traditional shape (designed for Mackenzie), detailed by Lorimer in a way all his own, in which great play is made between the advancing and receding planes possible in such a modest 'cottage' piece. Thick planks of elm form the sides, their forward edge grooved to emphasise their delicately curving profiles. The repeated horizontals in the shelves which they support are partly left open for the display of pewter plates and partly hidden behind wooden doors of a particularly rich waving grain to hide the inevitable array of small things which otherwise clutter a dining room. The working top below the shelves is emphasised by a full-width inlaid panel enclosing the top shelf, whereas the bottom shelf is left open to continue the open and shut theme downwards, and as to colour, what could be more effective than the silky sheen of pewter set against the rough richness of elm, enlivened by the small muted flecks of colour in the inlaid panel?

Lorimer was not content to limit himself to work of such direct simplicity but, in turning to other themes, he was hampered by how little old Scotch furniture there is, and a framed group of photographs of his furniture apparently prepared for exhibition, probably for the A.W.G. but not catalogued by it or the R.S.A., reflects this, and only one wooden arm chair (dated 1899 in Hussey) reveals any Scots influence. A bureau with a double arched pediment on top was based on an old Dutch piece owned by Dods to whom he wrote that he, 'was going to start the reproduction of your bureau in walnut', because he felt he had 'hit on a way of making it the finest thing in the world – listen when in Amsterdam, saw in a picture dealers, on top of a cloak, three most lovely brass figures, you know the sort of thing, Atlas and Fame and Justice, thinks I, "If these were on top of R. S. D[od]'s bureau, how A.1. it would be"', and he made a quick sketch noting also that he was getting someone to look for these figures for him. 'Amn't I right, it will make it as fine as that kind of thing you would see in the backyard of one of Vermeer's interiors.'

A similar piece of furniture with one much heavier figure above it is included in the framed photographs, as well as three tables from other Dutch models with delicately fragile legs and curved veneered surfaces. J. Gorie of Whytock and Reid is named as the maker of all eleven pieces. This did not prevent Lorimer having almost identical pieces made by other craftsmen because he told Dods of a pair of bookstands like those made by Gorie which he said were 'founded on old examples but with a tall narrow proportion with goat feet by the Clows for which I made studies of our own goat one Sunday morning! "Auld Stephen", Grieve's chap made them.' *Fig. 65.*

Lorimer justified his widening experiments in furniture design on the grounds that he was choosing the most convenient shape and then refining it. Morris would have said, he noted, that 'we should get rid of the idea that we can make a thing French by giving it a twist one way or English by giving it a twist another way'. Nevertheless, Lorimer did have his own prejudices. In 1896 he went over with Walter Tapper from Bodley's office to see Bodley's partner, Thomas Garner. They took their bicycles to Bicester by train and bicycled over the last six or seven miles to Fritwell. 'I don't know really whether I was delighted as I expected or not. The house itself is perfectly charming outside and in, but the garden of the place is without much charm and in looking through the furniture, I didn't see anything, you know what I mean, about which I said to myself "Well its a d----d mistake Garner having that because it simply ought to belong to me"'. They lunched pleasantly and afterwards sat in the garden under a cherry tree but he found the Garners, 'so desperately English and narrow, something awful. Of course nothing but English furniture in the house and all belonging to the date before inlay and veneer was dreamed of, though the things are beautiful examples of their own rather played out kind.'

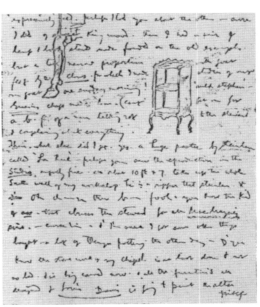

[64]–[65] *Sketches from letters to Dods.*   E.F.

The Dutch museums which he had visited on his frequent holidays there had left a marked influence on his furniture design and by 1900 he had designed a bench for his mother's home in Bruntsfield Crescent, *Pl. 126.* He told Dods of its 'legs and stretchers largely cribbed from some I saw in the Riks Museum at Amsterdam last year. The point about the things is the stretchers and the repeat'. He was delighted with their curvilinear form; 'You can imagine that these things swung about in the most beautiful spokeshave manner are A.1.'. He had also a particular liking for French furniture. He had brought several Norman oak pieces on other tours, including a wardrobe which was later built in to a recess in the hall at his house in Melville Street. Another wardrobe chosen by his brother was adapted for the north wall of the dining room at Kellie and their mutual friend D. Y. Cameron had an escritoire in this style which he gave to an Edinburgh Gallery. Lorimer was also very keen on Louis Quinze veneered furniture. He had begun to buy such pieces by 1896 when he told Dods of a shop which he had found with 'a lot of things in my fine severe style. *Still* think that Louis XV veneered furniture *when you can get it severe enough* (but only then) and looking as if it were *made* for use is the finest stuff that has ever been done.' *Pl. 129.* Queen Anne was yet another style he used at times. Hussey says he discovered it while in Bodley's office, and it was at that time that his links were at their closest with Norman Shaw who had much to do with its revival. He told Dods of a further project for 'a real "Queen Anne" tea table with a "well" for keeping the tea-cups etc. and so on I'll go, and gradually one will get a good many "worthy" possessions, of course its expensive but I don't think more so than buying the old stuff.'

[66] ABOVE *From a letter to Dods.* E.F.
[67] MIDDLE *Silver-mounted coconut shell from a letter to Dods 1896.* E.F.
[68] BELOW *Dutch 'Mothers' dish' from a letter to Dods.* E.F.

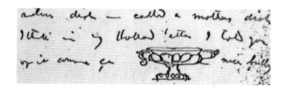

He was still as impetuous in choosing furniture as in making some of his designs, and he occasionally had regrets. 'I bought a lacquer dressing glass at Johnstone, Wigmore Street, well! When I got it to Kellie, I found it wasn't so nice as I had thought and besides, it didn't help to push the great gospel of material, that given a lovely wood, that lacquer and all that is superfluous, besides one of the pillars was loose and the whole thing not up to scratch so I sent it back to Johnstone and said I'd do a swap with him, but the stand was charming in design so I spent the whole Sunday designing a dressing glass for it. Took the mirror part fr[om] that beauty that I had reproduced some time ago, but made it larger, quite big enough for dear Mrs R. S. L. in the sweet bye and bye, and then took the motif of the stand, and really produced a clinker. Took it straight to Whytock's works on the Monday morning and spent an hour discussing the banding etc. with Philp[and] the very dear man who makes my things, Gorie.' *Fig. 66.* He went on to muse on how badly finished much of the old work was and how much better it was 'to take a fine model and do your own "comments" on it, and then you have a sound sweet smelling thing, fit to last for a few hundred years with careful usage. Mind, I think I'll just drop Philp a line now to make the drawers of pencil *cedar*, wouldn't that be nice?' *Pl. 143.*

Nothing was too small to attract his attention. He was on his way to St Marnock's when he saw in Grafton Street, Dublin, 'the sugar basin of my heart's desire, the one I've been on the "key vive" for ever since I saw R. E. Wemyss's one, *Fig. 67*, A coconut [shell] silver mounted, such a quaint shape and very dainty little feet'. He bought it for himself, and afterwards designed similar ones for which Whytock and Reids used to polish the shells after which decorations in silver were added, the later ones by Elizabeth Kirkwood. Margaret Swan recalled that 'special people were given bowls lined with silver and occasionally a lace pattern was worked in along the edge. The legs were nearly always silver, just the occasional one with wooden legs. A supply was kept in the office for use as wedding presents.

Dods had announced his engagement and Lorimer in reply wrote telling him that at first 'I couldn't think what to do for your present, so I've done this. When in Holland I bought a very jolly silver dish, called a mother's dish.'[2] *Fig. 68.* It was he continued, a 'nice bulby silvery thing. Well I took it to Talbot and said look here, you've got to make a pair of these things for £5. Said he'd count it up and let me know. Came along and said he'd do the pair for £5. 10s.' *Pls. 78, 79.*

For metal casting of light fittings, or memorial plates Lorimer went to Henshaw's of Edinburgh, *Fig. 53*, but he also used the Bromsgrove Guild of Craftsmen for cast lead tanks, garden figures and some light fittings. Such little cast plaster as he used was done by them. Metalwork of a different kind was involved in fireplaces, many of which were made up for him by the Well Fire Company in a variety of metals, tiles, stines and woods. Some were for ingles, other in corners, *Pl. 148*, some panelled all around and many had oil paintings installed by the joiners within the surrounding panelling, and over the mantel shelf. The raised hearths were usually plain and of stone but sometimes of brick or tiles, all with grilles

108 ABOVE LEFT *Moxon and Carfrae's Mr Hamilton, Modelling Earl Haig's insignia* C. *1920.*   R.S.L.

109–110 BELOW *An early chest,* C. *1893, exhibited at the Arts and Crafts Exhibition.*   R.S.L.

111–112 ABOVE RIGHT *Linen cupboard, probably for Lorimer's sister, Lady Chalmers, & detail of the inlay.*   steigal Antiques

113–114 ABOVE & MIDDLE LEFT *A chest, & on the reverse side of this early photo Lorimer has written* '"There is a refined simplicity in all that is perfectly beautiful which is incompatible with vulgar display though not with splendour or magnificence in their place". G. F. Watts!!! R.S.L. May 1894' R.S.L. 115–116 BELOW & ABOVE *Chest & detail.* P.M.

119 ABOVE RIGHT *Inlaid chest exhibited at the Arts & Crafts Exhibition in London in 1899.*
P.M. & L.S.

120 BELOW RIGHT *A 'modern' dresser in elmwood with a hunting scene inlaid panel, for R. W. R. Mackenzie of Earlshall.* SHAW SPARROW, 1904.

117 ABOVE LEFT *Kellie Castle dining room, chairs to Lorimer's design, the gateleg table not.* P.M. & L.S.
118 BELOW LEFT *Kellie Castle, trestle table by Lorimer.* P.M. & L.S.

121–122 ABOVE *Oak settle for R. W. R. Mackenzie & detail.* P.M. & L.S.

123 LEFT *'Modern' dresser in elmwood.* P.M. & L.S.

124 MIDDLE RIGHT *Detail of inlay on the 'modern' dresser.* P.M. & L.S.

125 BELOW RIGHT *Inlaid elmwood chest.* P.M. & L.S.

inset from which ducts took the draught directly into the fire well. The metal surrounds are flanked by tiles or marble, always with a gentle but satisfactory play of surface. He had advised the Edinburgh architects, 'Suppose you are drawing marble jambs for a fireplace – What one generally sees done is the marble moulded with wretched little ogees and fillets and quarter rounds, which quite contradict the material. Now seeing the material is very beautiful in itself, the way to show its beauty is by using it either in flat strips or with a simple waved moulding with no lines in it at all,' which is how he preferred to use it, *Pl. 149*.

Some of the fire irons and fenders he designed made use of iron and steel in their most ductile simplicity, *Pl. 155*, but he did not send any of this work to the Arts and Crafts Exhibitions, and of his extensive work in wrought iron he submitted only 'a gateway to [a] garden in Banffshire' to the Royal Scottish Academy, which he did in 1893. This was for Aberlour House. It was the first time he had exhibited at the Academy but perhaps he felt wrought iron did not offer good exhibits because it was no lack of enthusiasm for the material itself which prevented him from submitting further examples. He had taken up wrought iron design with his customary enthusiasm. As a student he had measured and drawn out the terrace stairs at Donibristle in Fife, including all the intricacies of its balustrades and archways. His first design was the well-head arch at Earlshall, *Pl. 6* a simple affair of twisted bar surmounted by a large flower in the manner of those on the old gates of Traquair House, and his later gate designs elsewhere show a variety of influences. An early example from 1897 at Balcarres shows him using a strongly linear pattern of vertical bars all of which are forged with a continuous array of twists and piercings by Houston and Stewart, *Pl. 57*. A crest is included in outline high up and flanked by thistles. Other decorative features include birds and plant forms, all small in scale, but contriving a rich heraldic effect as befits a baronial establishment of some size. Other early works in Fife were probably executed by the village blacksmith at Arncroach. James Bennet is known to have worked for him, but he soon came to rely on Thomas Hadden for almost all his wrought iron because Hadden was a rare bird, a working blacksmith with an imagination of his own. Hadden had trained at Howgate near Edinburgh, then he had worked in Abbeyhill in Edinburgh, as well as in London, before starting to collaborate with Lorimer. Hussey tells us that when Hadden and Lorimer were both young men, Hadden had sought Lorimer's advice about how to set up in business for himself, and Lorimer had advised him it was too risky commercially. Yet after Hadden had set himself up, despite this discouraging advice,, Lorimer entered into the same close collaboration with him as with all the other craftsmen he used.

This collaboration produced the ductile flowing shapes which Lorimer suggested and which Hadden experimented with and refined, *Pl. 151*. Pitkerro, a much smaller house than Balcarres, was given gates which have a crest in metal placed in the arched overthrow, which achieves a quietly baroque vitality of curves, allied with tulip and lily forms. The top of the gates, themselves a simple affair of verticals, is swept down to meet in a reversed arch in counterpoint to the overthrow. Traquair flower forms can also be seen on the gates for

Skirling Churchyard in Peeblesshire, along with the use of many tightly branched spirals. They are a recurrent feature in his work, still to be seen at the end of his career in the gates of the Shrine of the Scottish War Memorial. The gates have a simple vertical pattern of bars branching in many spirals, and the side panels are taken up to suggest Gothic pinnacles. Spiral forms of an almost Celtic grace can be seen at Monzie Castle, a restoration after fire, and one of his infrequent classical works (1908), *Pl. 220*. The sinuous curves are worked into an overall design for the balustrades for the grand staircase which is strongly modular and repeats within a firm framework of horizontals and vertical bars square in section. The grand stairs at Marchmont in Berwickshire, almost his last remodelling of a classical building in 1916, is a fruitier version of the same themes, with the odd rose and occasional spray of cherries grafted on to the spirals, *Pl. 250*. Elder Dickson, writing on the crafts in the *Statistical Account of Edinburgh (1966)*, claimed that under Lorimer's influence the blacksmith's craft suddenly took new life in Edinburgh, and it is true that it recaptured a certain Gothic vitality in form.

R. W. Mackenzie, his first client, had been very keen on the tapestries which were to become an all important element in Lorimer's grand manner in design. He was not keen or knowledgeable enough in his early days to venture into buying old tapestries himself, and it is possible that new tapestries were beyond his purse. He certainly appreciated them and in particular Morris's designs, and he told the Edinburgh Architects Association how Morris had started on tapestries with his usual energy, and had 'studied the finest Arras tapestry he could find, pulled some to bits, studied the wools, the thread, the method of dyeing – in fact thoroughly mastered the whole subject and in the course of a few years produced tapestry which it is no exaggeration to say is as fine as any that has ever been done'. He described the tapestry Morris and Burne Jones did for Exeter College in Oxford as not a large one, 'I daresay not more than 14 feet by 9 feet but it is not too much to say that you might hunt the world through, and you wouldn't find anything finer.'

Perhaps embroidery had to suffice instead, and this was among the interests of his close friend Phoebe Traquair, whose son Ramsay had been his pupil. Lorimer began to buy antique pieces of needlework, and he made designs for four large bedspreads for Kellie which he showed at the Arts and Crafts Exhibition of 1899 and which were illustrated in *The Studio, Figs. 6, 72*. The subject Lorimer preferred were beasts and birds, flowers and fruit taken from nature with a Pre-Raphaelite concern for detail *Fig. 69*. One of the Kellie bedspreads recalls a Persian painting and another medieval English patterns, as *The Studio* commented, 'A few bright colours are employed. The birds, too, are in gay variegated colours. As regards the general effect, it is as garden-like in colour as it is quaintly conventional in design.'

Lorimer's own views on such design were that 'The chief of the limitations that spring from the essence of the art is that the decorator's art cannot be imitative even to the limited extent that the picture painter's is'. This was no excuse, he went on to argue, for any 'want of observation of nature or laziness in drawing, on the contrary unless you know plenty about

[69] *Sketch for an embroidery design.*   R.C.A.M.

75

the natural form you are conventionalising you will not only feel it impossible to give people a satisfactory impression of what is in your own mind about it, but you will also be so hampered by your ignorance that you will not be able to make your conventionalised form ornamental. It will not fill a space properly.' Like Morris, he was a countryman at heart and it is his ornamental work which reveals it most clearly, *Fig. 73*.

It might seem that the cottage interiors of his Colinton houses, with their plain white walls and flowing sense of space, were a thing apart from the rich modelling and strong sense of enclosure of the Baronial interiors which he developed later, were it not that they derive from the same sense of place and from the same traditions. A Baronial scheme by him might well comprise an all white drawing room with plain walls and a simply enriched ceiling but the study, the library and sometimes the dining room as well would be richly busy rooms in which all the features were nevertheless highly integrated. The paintings or the tapestries were not just hung on the walls, they were built in with the panelling, adjusted to them and around them. This was nothing novel but the thoroughness with which it was carried through and the harmony of balance achieved were remarkable. A foretaste of the richness that was to be achieved at Hallyburton and Ardkinglas can be seen in his first steps to the fully integrated interior which he took in rehabilitating Ellary in 1894. Another early Baronial design was the library at Fettercairn in 1897 for which he used the woodwork to knit together the fireplace, the bookshelves and the family portraits into an all-embracing unity in which, meticulously, to avoid labels the titles of the portraits have been carved into the woodwork *Pl. 93*.

Brackenburgh, his first new mansion, is a long low house in Tudor style, the garden side of which Pevsner found to be 'splendidly composed' with charming touches 'betraying that historicism was no longer taken in deadly earnest'. Inside it includes some lofty double height rooms and much oak panelling, *Pls. 86–89*. The Harrises had tastes in furniture which differed from Lorimer's, however, and he decided when he visited the house after it had been occupied that 'the furniture they have put in the place is too putrid for words, and in spite of wanting to hang oneself from most of the ceilings, still one has a sort of comfortable feeling of "something accomplished something done"', and he strolled about as always highly perceptive to every nuance but contented as he later told Dods that, 'Here where there was lately hammering and chopping, were the kiddies racing up and down the corridors; and in the evening a man who was staying there discoursed Brahms' songs in my music room and Mrs Harris played a thing of Bach's most delightfully on her fiddle.'

If Lorimer's taste in furniture was catholic, and he had a keen eye for quality from wherever it might be drawn, he was difficult to please. He and Dods had been such inveterate museum-goers and they had come to know their favourite pieces of furniture so intimately that when the north east court of the South Kensington Museum was re-arranged he wrote to tell Dods that, 'Most of the best pieces of the Peyre woodwork are there . . . the dear little linen-fold settle, that table with the pierced scrolls, the lovely little cabinet with the circles.' He had visited Peyre to see all this furniture when it was still in his hands and he

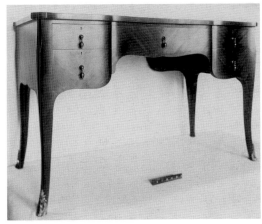

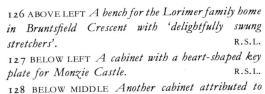

126 ABOVE LEFT *A bench for the Lorimer family home in Bruntsfield Crescent with 'delightfully swung stretchers'.* R.S.L.

127 BELOW LEFT *A cabinet with a heart-shaped key plate for Monzie Castle.* R.S.L.

128 BELOW MIDDLE *Another cabinet attributed to Lorimer.* R.S.L.

129 ABOVE RIGHT *A Louis Quinze-influenced table for Monzie Castle.* R.S.L.

130 BELOW RIGHT *Kellie Castle, another bookcase designed by Lorimer.* P.M. & L.S.

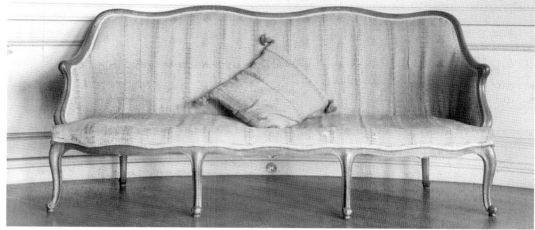

131 ABOVE LEFT *A cane drawing room chair for Monzie Castle.* P.M. & L.S.

132, 135–138 MIDDLE LEFT & MIDDLE *Handles.* P.M.

133 BELOW LEFT *A chest of drawers.* P.M. & L.S.

134 *A sofa for Monzie Castle.* P.M. & L.S.

139 BELOW RIGHT *Chest in burr-maple.* P.M. & L.S.

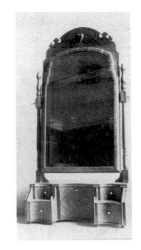

140 ABOVE LEFT *An oak sideboard, the drawers faced with walnut.* P.M. & L.S.
141 BELOW LEFT *Lady Lorimer's writing desk, a variation on the Earlshall table.* P.M. & L.S.
142–143 ABOVE RIGHT *Looking glasses.* R.S.L.
144 BELOW RIGHT *Another Lorimer chair evolved from traditional examples.* P.M. & L.S.

145–150 *Fireplaces*, ABOVE LEFT *Kellie Castle, with antique Dutch tiles*, P.M. & L.S.; BELOW LEFT *Monzie Castle, with antique tiles*, P.M. & L.S.; ABOVE MIDDLE *Lympne Castle, carved stone & brick*, R.S.L.; BELOW MIDDLE *corner fireplace*, R.S.L.; ABOVE RIGHT *Burrell's library*, R.S.L.; BELOW RIGHT *incorporating antique woodwork for Burrell*, R.S.L.

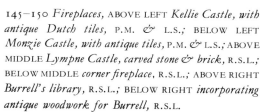

also knew Salting, another well known collector. Two years later he was up again to see Saltings' collection, which had been newly installed, when the 'bobby' guarding it told him it was worth £800,000. 'Well my brother has been meeting Sir John Carmichael lately', Lorimer wrote, 'at the Glasgow Exhibition where Sir J. was arranging his stuff in the loan section and told him that if you asked Salting to lunch he liked you to let him know several days before because if he knew he was going to get a good bellyful at lunch time he could *save on his breakfast*, needn't have *any* in fact!' The collector Lorimer knew best was still Burrell, who was a prodigious collector of art in all its forms, so that what his collection lacked in restraint was made up for by sheer opulence. Neither Lorimer's cottage pieces, nor the delicate pieces of furniture of French, Dutch or English derivation which he had been designing, would have been suitable for Burrell's house, nor could they have stood the juxtaposition with his large collection of tapestries, and something quite different was needed. Lorimer spent the night with the Burrells just six weeks after they had moved in. 'It's a mighty change from his former house which was a regular collector's house', commented Lorimer, whose first requirement was that a house should look like a home and not a museum. 'His dining room looks very fine. The whole place hung with the finest Gothic tapestries, and in the centre a Gothic table by yours truly, some good chairs, that's about all.' *Pl. 81*. Like Morris, he reasoned that 'The way you hang your walls with tapestry instead of whitewash or paper, or you may cover them with mosaic or have them frescoed by a great painter; all this is not luxury if it be done for beauty's sake and not for show. "Have nothing in your house that you do not know to be useful or believe to be beautiful".'

This much quoted aphorism contains the contradiction which lies not only in Lorimer's thinking but also in the theoretical basis of the whole arts and crafts movement. On the one hand the gospel of materials sets limits of truthful expression upon construction, whereas the subjective belief in beauty opens the door to unlimited decoration. The painted grand piano at Lympne Castle, *Pl. 169*, the decoration for which Lorimer brought in Phoebe Traquair, was a magnificently painted case upon Gothic trestles with spirally fluted legs. Burrell's dining room is equally rich in effect with walls which were hidden entirely by fifteenth century tapestries to show only briefly as small strips of panelling around the fireplace, achieving a hushed atmosphere by so much absorbent surface and by its softness an excellent foil for Lorimer's crisp Gothic oak furniture which is why, perhaps, Burrell always chose to dine off the bare boards.

The solidity of all this Gothic woodwork was relieved by the wide use of spirals. The legs of the table, which are like inclined columns, have been spirally fluted, as have all the balusters on the stairs and landings. He may have taken the motif from German furniture he had seen in Nuremberg, but an example of such a table for Stanmore Hall produced by William Morris's firm had appeared in *The Studio* early in the nineties. Morris's table was in effect made up of three tables with a total of eighteen legs, but Burrell's, with a mere eight, was also extendable. Lorimer was also called upon to produce the Gothic cradle and a massive double bed with ends solidly made up of linenfold panels, with the ends of the

77

bedposts carved as angels at the head and crouching lions at the foot, and the newel posts of the stairs were terminated by carved mastiffs.

The massive woodwork is keyed to the vigour of the tapestries to create a solemn note which was new in Lorimer's domestic work. James Richardson who was working for him at this time, or soon after (he could not remember which) and who was to specialise in medieval woodwork after he had become Inspector of Ancient Monuments, claimed that it was Burrell who focussed Lorimer's attentions so sharply on fifteenth century woodwork, and that without this spur Lorimer would not have developed the proficiency he was to demonstrate some years later in the Thistle Chapel design. This view is supported by the fact that Burrell is known to have given Lorimer detailed instructions, *Pl. 150*, and was given to ordering all manner of changes on the spot as he visited his commissions, and this whether accompanied by Lorimer or not. It indicates also that at least some of Lorimer's switches in style derived from the need to meet the particular needs of particular clients. However, more Gothic furniture was soon required. Whereas Burrell had preferred a Jacobean side table for his dining room, the Corbetts asked Lorimer to design Gothic side tables for the dining room at Rowallan, *Pl. 166*, which is a much larger and higher room than Burrell's and panelled throughout in oak without tapestries. Their table is less massive and has only five legs including one at the very centre. The horizontal struts, the stretchers, are curved inwards and away from the feet of the diners, but curved also to avoid any tramelling effect on the appearance of the legs. All these tables were made by Whytock and Reid.

The effect of designing these pieces was almost immediate upon Lorimer, as he followed Burrell's lead by designing a little Gothic bed for the spare room in Melville Street, *Pl. 167*, with 'two little octagon posts finished at top with little seated animals, with this and our own Caen oak armoires and everything else pretty well in harmony, the room looked no sae hielant' that is to say rudely Highland, 'leastways, better than the room one gets in the average house you stay in. A fearful and wonderful bed is at present being constructed for Vi.' He described this bed for his wife as having 'twisted pillars about as tall as fishing rods with angels on top. She went up to the Clows with her friend on Saturday to see them, and is awfully excited about it. Says it *must* be done for her to sleep in on Xmas night. Then there is a dining table in half Gothic and half Dutch manner being made with twisted legs and ends that pull out to make it longer. This master piece to be delivered next Saturday D.V. and we've got the prettiest girl in Edinburgh and her husband coming to lunch on Sunday.'

Dods did not wholly share these Gothic enthusiasms but Lorimer, undaunted, wrote back, telling Dods that he and his wife had 'laughed over your remarks about "the Gothic foolishness"', and told him with obscure logic, 'wait till you see the photo of the Gothic dining table, my boy . . . bacon and eggs tastes tip top off it. Had a plateful this morning and its comfortable to sit at too.' The ends of this table slid out in Dutch manner to seat twelve, and at only twenty seven and a half inches wide 'there's grand opportunities for a little innocent foot flirtation as things are apt to get a bit mixed.' *Fig. 70.*

Lorimer had fined down the proportions of all these pieces of furniture for himself. His

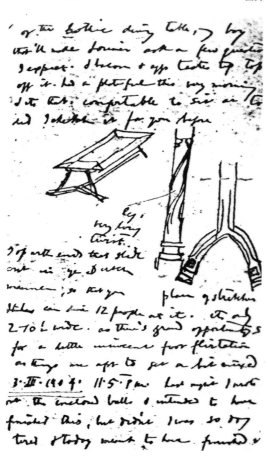

[70] *Sketch of Lorimer's own dining table, from a letter to Dods.*   E.F.

78

first son Christopher was born and his *epoque gotique* cradle was ready prepared and 'much simpler than Willie B's, an angel at the foot and pelican at the head post and the cradle part shaped a little, and just plain boards dovetailed at the corners', *Fig. 71*. Yet the ponderousness of Burrell's furniture was nothing new in Scotland, and an interesting side light on Victorian interior design in the closing decades of the nineteenth century is provided by Scott Morton and Co, one of the two firms which executed most of Lorimer's joinery and architectural woodwork. It had worked earlier for the architects Wardrop and Reid, and very probably Lorimer first had contact with it as Hew Wardrop's apprentice. The firm was founded by William Scott Morton, an architect who set up with his brother in Edinburgh in 1870 to manufacture 'art furniture' and to provide all manner of furnishings for the household as William Morris had begun to do at Merton. Their father had been a village joiner in Ayrshire, and William had been apprenticed to a Glasgow architect James Smith, in whose office William Leiper and William Forrest Salmon were also working. He became particularly interested in both furniture and interior design and when his family removed to London, he went to work there for Johnston and Jeans, a furnishing firm. He used his spare time in designing carpets and curtains for Messrs Templeton, a well known Glasgow firm of carpet manufacturers, and W. P. Frith, the painter of Victorian genre paintings, employed him to draw the elaborate architectural backgrounds of such pictures as 'The Railway Station'.

He and his brother returned to Scotland in 1867 and followed their father into the joinery business by setting up as cabinetmakers in 1870. William's earlier activities as a freelance designer soon led him to broaden the firm's activities to include a variety of furnishings. He even found time for some architecture and to contribute a sketch design he had made in 1868 for a block of mansions (Flats) in Mayfair, to the Royal Scottish Academy exhibition of 1874. The firm found a ready market for its products and after little more than a year in business he had produced a new canvas-based material for covering walls which he called Tynecastle Tapestry. He was much more interested in colour than Lorimer and he began also to design wallpapers. The firm contracted for the design and execution of complete building interiors, and all kinds of carpeting and upholstery materials were stocked for this as well as imported oriental carpets. Tiles were made for them and hand-painted stained glass was produced by Shrigley and Hunt of Manchester, fireplaces and grates by Boyds of London and the Falkirk iron company, all to the designs of William Scott Morton.

The business became so varied and brisk that it had to move to larger premises which William designed for them in Murieston Road, Tynecastle. Nevertheless he retained links with his original profession and was elected a member of the E.A.A. Sketchbook Committee, upon which he served from 1883 to 1886, and as he was for ever on the look out for decorative motives to apply in the work, he was able to contribute a number of his own sketches, *Fig. 74*. They do not bear comparison with his work for Frith, and their complete lack of finesse suggests someone too hurried by the pressure of business to have the time or inclination for the fine draughtsmanship of which he was capable. He was, like Lorimer,

[71] *A cot for Lorimer's first child, from a letter to Dods.* E.F.

[72] *A bedspread to Lorimer's design.* R.C.A.M.

79

very strongly influenced by Morris's example and it is difficult to know whether his work took him, in the seventies and eighties, outside Scotland more than Lorimer's was to do in the nineties. The Bishop's parlour he fitted up for the 1888 Glasgow Exhibition was, like so much of Lorimer's work, developed from old Scottish patterns of frieze, panelled ceiling, dado and chairs, and the upper walls were covered with moulded leather, *Fig. 73*. The parlour was part of a wood and canvas mock-up of an old Baronial building which formerly had stood on part of the exhibition site and it was erected to house a collection of archaeological exhibits. W. Raffles Davidson who wrote and illustrated a book on the exhibition, and who was one of Rowand Anderson's associates at the Edinburgh School of Applied Art, found that the 'whole tone' of the parlour was good but that the dim religious light made the contents difficult to view.

The processes of embossing and colouring wall fabrics in ways similar to early gesso work became William's main interest and a number of talks he gave on this subject including one to the Royal Scottish Society of Arts[3] were reported in the magazines during the eighteen nineties. He continued to manage the firm in Edinburgh and its branch in London. He had sent his son Stewart to America in 1889 to establish agencies for the firm and as the London branch was engrossing more and more of his time he moved there to live, remaining senior partner but delegating responsibility for the Edinburgh establishment to Stewart and the London branch to Robert. Templetons had come in as partners for the manufacture of the Tynecastle wall coverings and the woodwork and furniture business was continued separately during which time private design commissions were gradually being discontinued in favour of joinery sub-contracting (including carved woodwork) to architects, the railways and shipbuilders.

Scott Morton was still a firm very much orientated towards design when Lorimer began to practise, which allowed him to make the merest outline of his intentions, before going to discuss them with the foreman and designers who were to work it up. Preliminary models

[73] *Sketch for an embroidery design.*   R.C.A.M.

151–155 *Details of wrot iron*, ABOVE LEFT *Pitkerro, overthrow*, P.M.; BELOW LEFT *The Grange, finial*, P.M.; BELOW MIDDLE *gates*, Berwickshire, R.S.L.; ABOVE MIDDLE *Ardkinglas, handrail*, P.M.; ABOVE RIGHT *fire-irons*, P.M.
156 BELOW RIGHT *Ardkinglas, steps down to the terrace.* P.M.

157–162 *The Thistle Chapel*, ABOVE LEFT *under construction*, R.S.L.; BELOW FAR LEFT *stalls in workshop*, R.S.L.; ABOVE RIGHT *vaulting under construction*, R.S.L.; BELOW LEFT *window by Louis Davis*, R.S.L.; BELOW RIGHT *detail of carvings*, S.C.L.; BELOW FAR RIGHT *shrine entrance doorway*, S.C.L.

163 LEFT *Looking* E. *in the Thistle Chapel to the Monarch's Throne.* R.S.L.

164 ABOVE RIGHT *Carved bosses of the Thistle Chapel by Joseph Hayes.* R.S.L.

165 BELOW RIGHT *Woodwork in Dunblane Cathedral to Lorimer's design.* R.S.L.

166 ABOVE LEFT *Side-table for Rowallan.* R.S.L.
167 ABOVE MIDDLE *Bed for Melville Street.* R.S.L.
168 BELOW LEFT *Davenham Memorial in carver's workshop.* R.S.L.
169 ABOVE RIGHT *Lympne Castle piano, with panels painted by Phoebe Traquair.* S.R.M.
170 BELOW RIGHT *Gothic table, Kellie.* P.M. & L.S.

were often made but, even so, much of the decorative detail might be left to be worked out fully as the work proceeded. Lorimer would look in to the workshop from time to time to 'boss the job' as he put it and all large works like a reredos would be assembled in the shop before being shipped to the site in pieces. He might suggest further minor adjustments of detail, and he always took the opportunity to have his penknife sharpened by one of the craftsmen.

[74] *The Bishop's parlour for the 1888 Glasgow Exhibition, a baronial design by W. Scott Morton, drawn by Raffles Davidson.* Virtue, London, 1888.

Wood-carvers tended to move from firm to firm with the work but Lorimer habitually delegated a variety of work to the few he favoured, some of whom were among the more than sixty employed by the firm in 1905. The design service begun by William was continued to some extent in later years. The five ton granite lintel across the drawing room fireplace at Ardkinglas was designed by Scott Morton (probably by David Ramsay who had succeeded Trail as the chief designer) to Lorimer's instructions before being given to the carvers. Their skill was such that when Lorimer sent only sixteenth scale drawings to Ardkinglas for the two external staircases which were to rise to the first floor like forestairs, the masons found it impossible to set them out from such small scale drawings and it was Willy Sharon, Scott Morton's man, who not only made the large scale detailed drawings for the different steps, each segmentally curved in plan, but also set out the complex geometry of their spiral for the masons to begin work, *Pl. 156*. This reliance upon Scott Morton's craftsmen, and the trust he showed them was to survive in Edinburgh through the twenties as David Ramsay, their chief designer, made hundreds of drawings for the angels and other devices needed for the innumerable war memorials which then formed so large a part of Lorimer's work.

The greater part of Lorimer's joinery was undertaken either by Grieves or by Scott Morton but he gave the occasional job to J. and G. Scott, and Morrison's of Charlotte Square, whose designer Andrew Ednie taught furniture design at the College of Art. He also gave work to Watherstons of Queensferry Street and J. F. Forrest who did much of his work in the West, and to D. Macandrew and Company for his work in the north.

The grand piano for Lympne, which has been mentioned earlier, shows a marriage of ideas. Lorimer, like his brother John, believed a picture should tell a story, and as he was passionately fond of music, what more suitable object than an instrument. Phoebe Traquair, painter, enamellist and colourist, developed and executed the decorative themes, *Pl. 169*. Lawrence Weaver has related how the outside of the lid of this grand piano is a freely-treated Arabesque tree, rising from a world full of flowers with Cupid sleeping in the centre. Among the branches of the tree are fauns, angels, centaurs, dragons and birds, while behind the world is a sea full of fishes. All these delightful conceits are depicted in transparent oil-colours on a ground of gilt toned to a greenish tint, the natural wood not showing anywhere. It is a form of technique which demands great certainty of touch, because the work is finished as done, and it is impossible to make any alteration without a fresh ground.

Weaver was as impressed by the arrangements of ideas in the decoration as in the execution, for which Lorimer must be given some credit. On the inside of the lid Psyche is shown meeting Pan, who symbolises the music of nature. 'The god,' wrote Weaver, 'is seated on the round green world, surrounded by water, on which Psyche stands, looking at him with a gaze instinct with wonder, Pan, however, is absorbed in the music of his pipes and does not observe her, but Eros with his bow surveys them both. Round the outside of the case on its vertical surfaces is a series of nine panels which illustrate – the Song of Solomon! The Shulamite is brought before Solomon in the first panel, then she is with him in his banquetting hall, then in the Women's rooms and at last asleep. The fifth shows Solomon returning from War, in the sixth he presses his suit, then her shepherd lover returns, she is released and returns home with him to the wedding feast in the final panel. The sequence incorporates various features of Scottish scenery and changes in light from dawn to midday to night and the long panel over the keyboard represents three subjects from Rossetti's sonnets 'I sat with love beside the wayside well.' Phoebe, who could be a very good painter, was patchy in performance, but for Lympne, under Lorimer's leadership, she created a minor masterpiece.

The designs of the plaster ceilings for his country house designs he derived from historical examples, as well he might since it is a material which has almost no visual characteristics of its own. He had grown up beneath the late seventeenth century work at Kellie Castle, and Laurence Turner,[4] whom Lorimer knew describes them as plasteresque or of an earlier manner but 'typical of the work of local plasterers' of about 1676, and says that as the same patterns appear at Balcaskie, Craigievar, Muchalls, Cawdor and Wemyss, they are probably by the same craftsmen. Lorimer in turn was to use patterns derived in particular from its vine room, *Fig. 7*, and to a lesser extent from the earl's bedroom. He had begun to use another modeller than Beattie by 1899 because he told Dods that John Kinross had 'got my tame modeller Sam Wilson who gave him a feeble imitation of the vine trees he had been doing for me at Briglands a few months before', and Wilson it was, who was to do the vine bedroom ceiling at Ardkinglas.

As a Gothic man Lorimer loved variety in effect as giving a vitality of impression and he used direct modelling wherever he was allowed to. As Turner suggests, 'It must have required considerable skill to "run" the mouldings by hand and eye only to a line marked on the ceiling. The modern plasterer is quite unaccustomed to doing this without the help and guidance of some firm edge against which he can move the mould backwards and forwards. This enabled him to pass it accurately over the same place each time. Had the Elizabethan plasterer used a shaped board or template against which the mould could be worked, the curve of the moulding formed from it would have been exactly the same in every repeat and this is by no means so. It is just this irregularity that is so charming and interesting in all Elizabethan and Jacobean ceilings', and in most of Lorimer's houses, it may be added.

Lorimer's attitude might be summed up as 'No repeats' and Beattie spent 'nearly two months' on work at Ardkinglas 'being modelled direct on the ceiling' and it was a job on which Sam Wilson also was employed. Such rough layout drawings for ceilings as still exist show how much he relied on these two modellers to interpret what he had in mind. Yet his letters which reveal so much about the way he went about things make almost no mention of the modellers and carvers upon whom he relied so much. One exception in 1896 was when he told Dods, 'My Balcarres lodge is done, and that nice carver Beveridge has carved the dormers A1, especially the one with an ostrich on it with a key in its mouth. Think Balcarres will be pleased with this and the sundial. I hope to God it will "fruit" in the way of some jobs coming out of it. The sundial was an old pillar they had and I did steps for it with, "I wish the

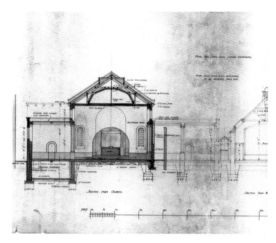

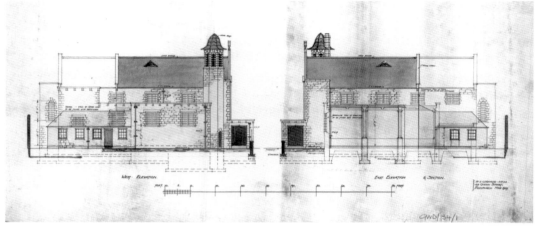

[75]–[76] *St Mark's Church, Glasgow, section &*
elevations.   R.C.A.M.

sun should shine on all my fruits and flowers as well as mind" on the lowest of the steps and this carver I've struck is a real dear, gets the 'feelin".' *Pl. 57.*

There was a sacramental element to most of the decoration used by Lorimer. The decorations on his domestic work have an underlying worship of nature whereas the ecclesiastical work employs its own Gothic idioms also derived from nature in part, but also from the structural forms of masonry which are the very basis of the Gothic mode. St John Evangelist begun in 1907 was a simple country church designed for Joseph Harris at Plumpton near Brackenburgh, and it shows Lorimer at his simplest and most English in design. Austerely plain stone walls inside and out allied with a simple roof of Westmorland slates, a vaulted timber ceiling of square panels within ribs, clear glass in windows which are 'admittedly conventional' says Sir Nikolaus Pevsner and the 'south tower, with its pronounced batter and its bell openings as a stone screen of reticulation, the south porch also with a batter and the bare windowless east wall are features not easily forgotten.' St John, Evangelist, has more than a hint of the border peel in its sparse strength; St Marks, Glasgow, begun the following year was nothing remarkable although its panelled wood ceiling was detailed with Lorimer's usual finesse, *Figs. 75, 76.* In 1909 he began the Thistle Chapel in Edinburgh. Only a small building was needed, but the ceremonial splendour that attends the meetings of the Knights of the Thistle who were to use it allowed Lorimer and his craftsmen to evolve the most richly Gothic building of its time. An earlier scheme for a side chapel for this purpose at St Giles in Edinburgh had been drawn up by William Hay but attention had then switched to Holyrood Abbey as a better site. This project was supported by Lord Leven and Melville who left £40,000 for this purpose in 1906. Thomas Ross was named the architect but before the scheme could begin a dispute[5] arose about whether the walls of the Abbey which had long been in ruins were strong enough to support a new roof. Professor Lethaby who was called in to advise pronounced against it, and the money reverted to the Leven family, until one of the sons offered his portion again and was joined by his brothers. The Knights were convened and the suggestion of a chapel attached to St

84

Giles was considered again, public feeling according to D. Y. Cameron favouring it as the ancient resting place of Scottish kings, and at this point Lorimer was brought in. He was very well known to Lethaby and the executors of Lord Leven, one of whom had patronised him before.

The Chapel was to be secluded rather than open to the nave as was the previous scheme but this could not be achieved without interfering with the Cathedral's use by general congregations. The existing Cathedral could not have been extended on the north where it already jutted out to narrow the High Street but its south overlooked Parliament Square and it was decided to put the new Chapel on the side beside the choir to avoid depriving the main body of the kirk of its south light. This ancient building had been completely recased in stone by William Burn (in 1829-33) so that a chapel at its south-east corner only thirty eight feet long and eighteen feet wide did not intrude upon any ancient miracle of harmony, *Pl. 157*.

The line of the parapet coping of the new chapel was kept subordinately a little lower than the main building, and behind it a vault in the perpendicular style of the late fifteenth century was proposed, Hussey says, because Lorimer felt that this was Gothic expression at its finest. Even more pertinent was the fact that the flat arches of this period allowed Lorimer to set the springing of the vault as high as possible within the confined space available, and even then he found it necessary to add a further five feet to the walls when they were 'all but finished', to make the height to the apex of the vaulting forty two feet, and thus the greatest internal dimension. It is clear, too, that Lorimer chose perpendicular vaulting because it allowed him to incorporate a riot of ornamentally carved bosses richly painted, but sufficiently detached in effect to float well above the spiky ring of oak canopies set over the stalls and carved as richly as Lorimer and the Clows knew how. The exterior of the chapel is treated more simply. A strong base is provided, repeatedly emphasised by the re-iteration of horizontal mouldings, above which rises a series of miniaturised buttresses with many set backs providing a strong vertical emphasis. The east window is lancet, *Pl. 163*, the rest perpendicular with dropped arches to harmonise rather with the nave windows by Burn rather than with the vaulting within, but beneath them are set the crests of the Knights in a broad horizontal band.

The Chapel provides the place where Monarch and Scottish Knights may meet, where investitures could be held, and the Knight's banners hung. The low antechapel is set between the Chapel and the Choir. It is twenty five feet long and fourteen feet wide and roofed by a vault in two bays also richly encrusted with carved bosses, *Pl. 164*. The entrance to the Chapel itself is by a doorway offset to the left of the vaulted bay to provide wall space beside it for the arms of the donor and an inscription to him in a irregular arrangement of symmetrical components within an overall symmetrical arch. This was a favourite Lorimer ploy, here used also to keep the path for circulation which enters near the west wall far enough from it to provide space for the stalls along the wall, *Pl. 162*.

Both stalls and windows are arranged to express precedence. The Monarch's stall set centrally on a dais against the west wall has the tallest canopy, its pinnacle rising to thirty three feet, topped by a crown which itself rises above the sill of the window behind so that it is silhouetted against the light. This west window is set higher than all the other windows, and the stalls on either side of the Monarch's have canopies which step down to meet those of the Knights' along the side walls which rise only to twenty five feet in height.

The Thistle Chapel has no altar at its east end which is occupied for investitures by a throne, the canopy of which is linked horizontally by the woodwork to those of the Knights' since this is a Presbyterian Chapel where all are considered equal in the eyes of the Lord. If Lorimer has shown the greatest skill in orchestrating the symbolism and heraldry required of him as well as so much detail within so small a building, the overwhelming grandeur of effect is as much due to the magnificent wood carving by the brothers Clow, *Pl. 158*, as it is to the multitude of bosses overhead carved heraldically or to motives from nature by Joseph Hayes. *The Builder* had reported on the way the design was evolved, 'partly from drawings and partly from models, a large shed being erected in the building yard where models were prepared – the design growing and changing as possibilities and limitations became apparent to the architect and the carvers, with whom he has worked continuously for the last fifteen years'. As Hussey notes, 'Though the work was theirs and was often varied by them from his original design, they had as he [Lorimer] once put it, "to get their cue from him".'

The woodwork had been carried out by Nathaniel Grieves' craftsmen, with the two Clows to undertake all the finest carving, and it was perhaps this loose association which made it unnecessary for Grieves to employ carvers directly. William Laing recalls that his father who managed Grieves before him was urged many times by Lorimer to employ carvers as Scott Morton did, but that he always replied, 'Never! They're artists and you don't pay artists by the hour.' The Clows, however, would come to him for advice on what to charge Lorimer for the jobs he brought them, and they ordered their wood through the firm. Margaret Brown recalled how Lorimer would send her along to them with his instructions. 'I used to go along to Hanover Street where the Clows had a single room. They were funny little men, in high rubber collars. [Probably celluloid in those days.] They were so polite. If the first one said something, the other would repeat it in exactly the same words. They lived on very little and during the trade holidays, they went to Belgium to look at and measure up old work.' They were so engrossed by their work that neither married, 'They had become part of Lorimer and worked for no-one else,' according to James Richardson. 'He utilised these men's carvings and he guided them to the right way. If you look at the work of the Thistle Chapel, you see a combination of rough work and fine 15th century work. It was all from full size details, and when a part was to be carved it was very roughly outlined in chalk by Lorimer, when they took up the tune as it were and they filled it in.'

Richardson had tried to use the Clows on a memorial he had designed for St Baldred's Church in North Berwick. He took the drawings to Grieves and the Clows, and got estimates from them. 'The drawings were full size. You could carve straight from my drawings. I went round to the Clows when I heard the wood was ready. I asked them when they would be started. They told me Sir Robert had been in, and that they had told him it was for me. He said that on no account were they to do the carving for me. So I went round to Lorimer's office. Matthew was like a bird keeping something away from its young. He put himself between me and Lorimer's door. I asked him if Lorimer was in. "No" he said, but I could hear sounds in the room and steps going away and so I refused to go away. Matthew got in a great state of dither. There were steps coming in again, the door opened and there was Lorimer pushing towards me. I walked him back in the office. I told him what the Clows had said. I looked at him and told him he should go to their workshop and put up a sign saying R. S. Lorimer.'

Lorimer did feel proprietary about his craftsmen, and in particular those like the Clows whom he had coached in his own way of thinking, but the implacable self-righteousness which sometimes he exhibited made him enemies. According to Richardson, Fairlie took over the work at Kilmany, after Anstruther Gray had objected to being told by Lorimer what he was to have, and it was Fairlie who took over Hutton Castle after Burrell terminated Lorimer's commission, not with good results for the job, however.

There are a number of churches like Beverly Minster which have stalls the lines of which are generally followed by those of the Thistle Chapel and there are others like Carlisle and St George's Chapel Windsor, which bear a very general resemblance, yet these were all much higher and broader buildings so that by grouping such stalls closely about a small area of Ailsa granite inset with Iona marble Lorimer created the effect of a pool amid 'a fantastic forest flaming upwards' in Hussey's words. The joint efforts of the Clows and Lorimer had matched the work of the fifteenth century in vigour.

The glass in the windows is pale with splashes of colour for the armorial decorations inset, *Pl. 160*. The east window is by Douglas Strachan whom Lorimer had newly discovered, the others are by his old friend Louis Davis with whom, Hussey tells us without saying why, he had so severe a disagreement that he nearly took the job away from him. Was it that Davis wanted to use much more colour which would have produced a dimmer light inside, and that Lorimer insisted on his pale glass to give sufficient light for all the details of this interior to be seen clearly? Miss Brown remembered her first visit to Strachan's studio in Balcarres Street. We went 'by tramcar, there were no buses at that time. When we got there Sir Robert said to him, "she doesn't know anything about glass" so Douglas came across the studio, he was a kindly man, bringing two pieces of glass. "What's the difference" he asked and I said "One's thick and one's thin". "Yes" he said "It's a question of light and letting it through or blocking it"'. Lorimer was getting Strachan to coach his secretary in the right way of things.

His own preference in stained glass was revealed in the article he wrote on the subject in *Country Life* in 1915. He begun by enthusing about the kind of stained glass 'that sings and sparkles and vibrates with pure and gleaming colour' but far from thinking of bright generous colour, he went on to single out the north clerestory windows of Saint Martin's in

Coney Street, York, for their 'pale luminous tones of clear or almost clear glass. . . . the effect remaining that of a pale translucent, glimmering thing, whose loveliness by its very simplicity holds the spectator spellbound.'

Few stories have reached us of disputes with his craftsmen but his relations with the artists who were his social equals made them the more difficult to resolve when they did arise. Although he used Scottish craftsmen for most of the work, Lorimer had become very keen at that time on the enamel work of an Englishman, Mr Soper, whom he wanted to execute the crests for the stalls. He wrote to a member of the committee, Sir Herbert Maxwell who is said to have replied, 'Keep your ain fish guts for your ain sea maws [seagulls]', and the work was given to Phoebe Traquair. It is difficult to see why he should not have wished to give the work to Phoebe who was a very close friend, whose dances he attended, and whose enamelled pendants he gave as wedding presents on more than one occasion. He and Strachan, on the other hand, differed strongly in that Strachan was foremost a colourist but they did share an intense love for music. They would meet at the Lamplighters' Club in Edinburgh at about nine o'clock in the evening where the entertainment was conversation and a glass of whisky and where they might meet their friend D. Y. Cameron, before going on to listen to the longer playing records which Strachan was one of the first in Edinburgh to have.

It would be remarkable were no differences of opinion to arise on a design not only so intricate in itself with its closely related arts and crafts, but also one so intimately connected with the High Kirk of Edinburgh. All was resolved and well resolved and after the Chapel was opened in 1911, when appropriately enough, Lorimer was rewarded for his services to Monarch and the Knights of the Thistle by being knighted himself at Holyrood Palace. The work had established securely the reputation of the Edinburgh School of Craft Design and he was asked to extend the Chancel and Nave of St Mary's church at Broughty Ferry near Dundee, an unrewarding job of matching the original. Though he was never again to receive a commission for a small jewel of a chapel by which to rival the riches of Rosslyn, he was asked to continue the restoration of Dunblane Cathedral in 1912, the first of a number of commissions in which he and the Clows would again show their capabilities in woodwork for larger buildings closer in scale to those which had provided the original inspiration.

Antique tile

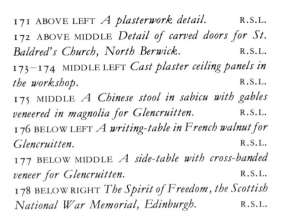

171 ABOVE LEFT *A plasterwork detail.* R.S.L.

172 ABOVE MIDDLE *Detail of carved doors for St. Baldred's Church, North Berwick.* R.S.L.

173–174 MIDDLE LEFT *Cast plaster ceiling panels in the workshop.* R.S.L.

175 MIDDLE *A Chinese stool in sabicu with gables veneered in magnolia for Glencruitten.* R.S.L.

176 BELOW LEFT *A writing-table in French walnut for Glencruitten.* R.S.L.

177 BELOW MIDDLE *A side-table with cross-banded veneer for Glencruitten.* R.S.L.

178 BELOW RIGHT *The Spirit of Freedom, the Scottish National War Memorial, Edinburgh.* R.S.L.

179 *Dunderave, a west coast restoration beside Loch Fyne, Argyll, a southerly view.* P.M.

6

Lorimer in Mid Career

The turn of the century brought an improvement in Lorimer's fortunes as a country house architect and he began to receive regular commissions, both for small alterations and large extensions as well as the occasional commission for the entirely new mansion. Much of this work was in or around the central belt of Scotland. He had begun to remodel Briglands by 1899. It was a modest classical house set in the flatly rolling farmlands of Perthshire and Kinross. The second floor in the attics was given new dormer windows, a large northern bay-window was added to the drawing room, and a courtyard on the south made within the two arms of the house, with steps leading up the high terraced bank to its south. The garden treatment, the crisp white harled walls and the carved stone trim were all in harmony with the sixteenth century work.

He got other work situated in the depths of the Borders as well as in picturesque stretches of the Highlands. Craigmyle in Aberdeenshire was probably his next remodelling job for which considerable extensions were also required. The main block existing was rectangular in form, built of granite and topped by a Dutch gable, a house which stood like a lookout on the brow of the foothills of the Cairngorm Mountains looking far out across the Dee. A large lower wing on two floors was added to the west of the house and the existing lower east wing with corbie gables was left untouched but for a small addition to its north. The curved enrichments of the new main entrance, almost the only part of the building now standing, were carved with the broad touch which suits the hard intractable granite of Aberdeen, *Pl. 180*. The Dutch gables which he added were dressed with granite in a series of flowing S curves, the easterly gable swept up from half way to meet a chimney stack set within it. These new gables, although more interesting in shape, harmonised perfectly with the earlier gables made up of quadrants, *Fig. 77*. Lorimer was using such baroque gables with a liking for curves but always, as he had already done at St Andrews in Helsinki or High Barn in Surrey, as points of emphasis rather than the major theme. A similar gable but smaller still adorns the small lodge set at the front of the west drive of Craigmyle.

Some terracing was added south of the house to tie in this enlarged house with its site, *Pl. 182*, and the stable yard along the ridge and a little higher than the house was completely remodelled and large parts of the roof lifted up to improve the profile. The exposure of a hill top which provided such magnificent views had led to the house having to be harled but this provided a greater crispness of form. The interior, however, was to be yet another disappointment, and on his last tour of inspection he pronounced it 'hopeless as the woman has made the most painful mess of the place inside'.

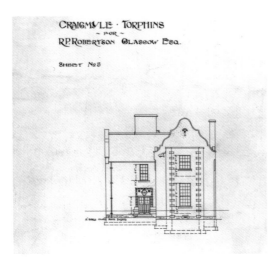

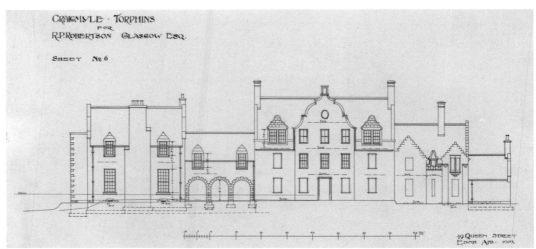

49 QUEEN STREET
EDINR APR· 1903

[77] *Craigmyle, a remodelling in Aberdeenshire granite,* ABOVE LEFT *entrance;* ABOVE RIGHT S. *elevation.*
                                                    R.C.A.M.

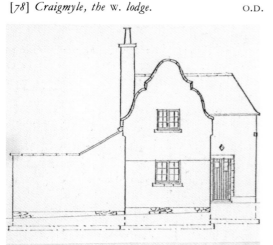

[78] *Craigmyle, the* W. *lodge.*   O.D.

Lorimer began to remodel yet another East of Scotland house near Broughty Ferry in 1902. Pitkerro was another sixteenth century house, rectangular in plan with three floors which had already been once remodelled, according to Hussey, with flatter roofs for economy, *Pl. 183*. The turret roofs also had been removed. Lorimer reinstated the steep roof and inserted dormers to make this block the service quarters for the new house which he then attached as a new wing at right angles to it in a play of form which shows him at his best, *Fig. 79*. The entrance is put at the far end of the long rectangular facade of the new wing along which the entrance is approached, *Pl. 185*, and it is emphasised by the strong cornice over it which reiterates the line of the eaves above, after which the whole design is given a turning rhythm in counter-point, and to the right, towards the main facade on the other side of this block. The roughly triangular form of the enrichment over the door, the first theme, is transferred to the single dormer head breaking upwards through the eaves, and then taken back to the enriched window in the gable of the service quarters, which being projected forwards provides a stop beyond the turning circle at the main entrance. The second theme is begun by the largest gable being offset to the right of the entrance, after which the slightly smaller, but much lower gable, echoes this shape on the left, leaving the single dormer on the right to complete this phase, with support from the projecting chimney which is checked as it rises and displaced to the right. Finally the theme is restated for the second time by rectangles of ascending scale, starting with the doorway itself, then by the single-storey bay projecting forwards, and lastly by the two-storey bay projecting sideways and outwards and intimating a further play beyond. And if we move round, *Pl. 184*, an L-shaped mass within a larger L comes into view on the south, the turrets in the corners acting as pivots, and steps like a forestairs, *Pl. 186*, as well as twin gables, *Pl. 187*, to outweigh the end gable around which we have come, the sprightly composition of the extension set against that of the staid older service wing by which it is slightly overtopped.

Pitkerro is a very effective remodelling of an old building and Lorimer felt he had learned a lot from it. 'Been at my Pitkerro job all day', he told Dods. 'I always want to get another job in exactly the *same style* when I've done one. If I got a very large and purely domestically treated Scotch house today, *now* with the experience I've had of that I think I *could* give it beans. There is nothing in the world for teaching one like having to turn out the work.'

First, however, he had to complete the usual alterations he had in hand including Frank Tennant's house, Hyndford, where he was remodelling the basement and adding a drawing room, '41 × 25 × 16 feet high and the centre part of the ceiling domed up. 4 very tall windows' of which one was to be 'carried down to the floor and opened, the lower part casement fashion with an ogee stone balcony outside, this for whispering sweet nothings when she gives a dance, and I've arranged it so that they get circulation when there is a crush. I'm rather keen on this job,' and he drew the plan in his letter to Dods noting also a small wooden oriel 'to get view of the sea and Bass Rock'. Among the other bits and pieces he was called to do were a number of charming Lorimer rooms in other houses – Aldourie in Inverness and Logie House near Dunfermline being among them. He was called in to Balcarres again to build the unpretentious but charming estate office as an L-shaped stone block of one floor with corbie-stepped gables, and he built his second (and last) Tudor house which was in North Berwick for Robert Craig, *Pl. 181*, Bunkershill, as it is called, was perhaps by way of an answer to John Kinross who had just built Carlskempe for Craig's brother, and which Lorimer found 'infinitely finer' than anything Mitchell or Wilson ever did, but he concluded, 'God help the man that has to pay for it.'

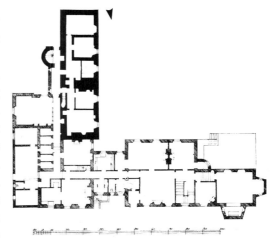

[79] *Pitkerro, Forfar, plan of extended house.* C.L.

The next large remodelling was also in English style and near Buckingham. Barton Hartshorn was a small Cotswold style manor house of 1632 which has been incorporated into Lorimer's scheme as the smoking room and boudoir, *Fig. 80.* A drawing room was added on one side, a dining room and kitchen quarters to the other and additional bedrooms above. He was called back some years later to double the size of the kitchen quarters and to lay out the grounds appropriately for what had become quite a grand establishment.

The manor lay near the end of a cul-de-sac and close to the church, and a general tidying up of the whole area was undertaken, and farm buildings nearby cleared away as well as the Fox public house. A short drive was brought from the north to a large new forecourt beside a huge walnut tree which formerly stood close to the house. Flower gardens were laid out with Gertrude Jekyll's help, around the south of the house on terraces stepping down to the lawns beyond. The vegetable garden was put east of the service wing. On the west, extensive yew hedges provide a compartmented garden with one alley running southwards at an angle across it from the church, apparently to screen those going to church by the footpath it formerly enclosed. Later, new footpaths were established away from the environs of the house, to lead around the east and west sides of the manor's extensive grounds.

[80] *Barton Hartshorn, Buckinghamshire, plan of extended house.* C.L.

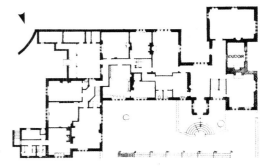

North Oxfordshire was a region Lorimer knew already but it was the first time he had been called to work within its traditions, *Pl. 188.* The random stone walls match the existing with one small difference in the way the new pointing is not flush but recessed a little. Brick was used for the chimney stacks, probably for cheapness, as well as tiles for the roofs from the claybeds of Bedfordshire rather than the straw thatch common in the borders of the Cotswolds or stonesfield slates used within. He also omitted the label moulds on the window lintels and widened the traditional proportions of the windows, as was done with the style by other architects including Lutyens.

Country house work was what Lorimer preferred to any other, perhaps for social reasons as much as for any other. He had found his first years in practice hard going and as one small job came in after another he had put his back into each one with the intention of making each client 'a friend for life'. He had had doubts whether such work would ever lead to anything larger and he told Dods he felt that, 'If you are to rise to the top and not be a mere hack you *must* specialise, just as a man is an occulist or a throat doctor or an accoucheur – you must be a house architect, a hospital architect or whatever it is.' A magnificent start to his practice had been provided by Earlshall but apart from a few small scale jobs little more country house had come in. The elaborate schemes for Mounie and Hallyards had remained only pretty exhibition drawings and he told Dods, 'I sometimes wonder if I'm exciting myself enough, if I shouldn't be putting myself out of joint over competitions for all kinds of infernal buildings, because here I am always over little things', and even went on to ask Dods whether he would advise him to make 'a great effort to get into a big commercial practice.'

Lorimer took every job he could get in his early days but he had few links with commerce. He had worked on the homes of Mackenzie and Burrell but neither had found other work for him. The final scheme for Clousta Hotel cannot have been one with which he was very happy, and his public house at Glencraig in Fife was a once and for all commission in 1902 from which nothing further had come, nor did anything come from the four tenements at Eyre Terrace in Edinburgh which he built at that time, and the later alterations for Mackies shop in Princes Street proved so troublesome that he turned his back on them and left Matthew to complete the job.

If he did not avoid commercial architecture entirely, he was unimpressed by its achievements, telling Dods of his belief that 'The men of the present day who get into a very big way and have all sorts of buildings going on at the same time seem to me *without exception* in the course of a very few years to go to utter seed'. He met William Dunn, whom he knew from Maclaren's office in London, and they went on a tour of Glasgow's new buildings including several by J. J. Burnett. 'You never saw such vulgar stuff', he told Dods, or such 'hurriedly thought out looking stuff as well, of course I slanged them, and says D[unn] "The conditions make it impossible to do anything better, all the floors were the same height, etc. etc.", now if this is so, which I verily believe, seeing the way they have to be rushed up, and that the doing of them in my sort of way so that they don't fall down involves the keeping of an enormous staff, isn't one far better to steer clear of this sort of thing altogether, to try and stick to a line of country that you feel an all seeing providence intended you to work in, and by *setting definite* limitations to yourself to make a reputation for doing fine work.'

180 ABOVE LEFT *Craigmyle, the forecourt.* R.S.L.
181 BELOW *Bunkershill, North Berwick, a Tudor mini-mansion.* S.R.M.
182 ABOVE RIGHT *Craigmyle, Aberdeenshire, the main facade.* R.S.L.

183 ABOVE *Pitkerro*, a photograph with Lorimer's comments on the changes.   R.S.L.

184 BELOW *Pitkerro*, from the garden, with the new extension on the left.   R.S.L.

185 OPPOSITE ABOVE LEFT *Pitkerro*, the approach to the entrance.   C.L.

186 OPPOSITE BELOW *Pitkerro*, the joining of the old with the new.   P.M.

187 OPPOSITE ABOVE RIGHT *Pitkerro*, the external stairs.   P.M.

The increased flow of work which Lorimer began to get after 1900 showed he was achieving a wider recognition. Rowand Anderson was in half retirement by 1903 and Washington Browne was mainly occupied with banks and commercial buildings. The surviving office records, although fragmentary (and Lorimer gives the impression of having begrudged having to spend more than the absolute minimum time required for them) do tell of a multitude of alterations and minor remodellings too numerous to be individually mentioned. The large scale work included a plainly designed wing which he added to the Jacobean styled North Esk House for Loretto School, *Ol. 239*. The Glen, another Bryce house near Innerleithen, was burnt out and he was called in to reinstate it. He wrote, 'Am to breakfast with the young Tennants who have a shooting lodge', telling Dods, 'am enjoying the job but am a bit nervous of it. It will be so tremendously criticised as they have such a huge lot of influential friends. However if one doesn't make a hat of it, it will be all the better.' The Gothic woodwork he designed for it included an oak wheel chair, the central newel and all the balusters with carved spiral flutings, while Beattie did the dining room ceiling entirely by hand work. The Baronial shell remained unaltered except for the rebuilding of the terrace at main floor level which was associated with the remodelling of the garden.

Lorimer took a weekend with the Clydes at Briglands which he had partly remodelled for them already. 'He's a most thrusting young advocate. The man I've just been altering 27 Moray Place [in Edinburgh] for, and I did Briglands for him some time ago. Now he's talking of making sundry additions which were planned some years ago but left over, and I'm glad they were as I think I can do them better now, and it will make a very characteristic thing, there's to be a "gallery" fifty feet by fourteen feet, off one side of it a billiards and recreation room, and at end of gallery a guest suite of rooms. The gallery is to have a mansard roof which will butt up against the new gable. I'm to work all this out.' The billiards room is placed in an L-shaped extension from the end of the long wing which had been added to the early house before Lorimer began to work on it in 1897, *Pl. 26*. The windows in this wing as rearranged by him are too regularly placed to harmonise with the two irregularly arranged blocks at either end, and charming though most of the details are, the L-shaped chimney stack of the billiard's wing seems to express a lack of resolution in the composition seen from the south. A lodge and a large garden pavilion, *Pl. 28*, completed this scheme and for once he expressed no doubts to Dods writing as the second phase began, 'Drove out in a little dog-car with the builder and his man with an old heavy footed mare that looked as if it had a foal "at the drop", rather enjoyed the day.'

Part of Lorimer's work seventy years ago was in improving accommodation which had become too cramped or ill arranged to meet the standards of the day. Minto House, a spacious house designed by William Adam in 1738 and added to by Archibald Elliot (*c.* 1810), required services and additional kitchen stores and offices. The house, now derelict, is a large three storey severely classical L-plan building with a low parapet roof. Internally it had been considerably altered by Maitland Wardrop in 1859. The lower wing added by Lorimer had a steep roof quite out of character with the rest of the building set behind a

188 OPPOSITE *Barton Hartshorn, Buckinghamshire; Gertrude Jekyll collaborated on the garden.* R.S.L.

thick screen of planting which hid it from the forecourt entirely. It was reached by a separate service drive. The experience of this job was found rewarding by Lorimer despite a 'bucketing three months' because 'these sorts of jobs teach one that it is as important to *design*, to provide special places for your pipes, plumber pipes, telephone wiring and all the various and suitable things required, as it is to provide your staircase or your drawing room, that's the sort of thing experience teaches and if an all-providing providence sends me any more jobs, this sort of thing is going to be carefully provided for either near the staircase or in the *corners* formed by an octagonal room or a circle ended room'. Architects were always damning plumbers, he said, when they were themselves to blame for not providing the proper facilities required by all the services and he went on to write that another thing he 'was mad keen on now is getting right away from all this d----d old fashioned construction. I hope soon to have in my spec[ifications] no wood lathing, brandering or strapping to be done to any portion of the works'. Brick was still little used in Scotland and the solid masonry walls were always backed by a light framework of timber to take the plastering, a constant source of trouble in the humid climate. 'What I'm longing for, is a man to come along to me and say "look 'ere young fellah, I'm a new *man* and I want a new house, constructed in the most up to date manner and I want it to be characteristic of all the best that can be done now, I want new furniture, new fixtures, new *everything*, the only condition I make is that there is nothing old about it anywhere". Wouldn't that be a problem to make you spit on your hands and get your coat off.' He was feeling ready 'to do a fine thing if one devoted five or six years to it', and at that point Cameron Corbett introduced him to Sir Andrew Noble who was about to build a mansion saying, 'Here's a promising young architect who you well might consider.'

Sir Andrew Noble soon commissioned Lorimer to build him a mansion at Ardkinglas, the West Highland estate he had bought in 1905. It lay at the landward end of Loch Fyne ringed about by the mountains of Argyll. He was a man of more than seventy years and in something of a hurry, so that the question of spending five to six years in designing the mansion which was to become the best known of all Lorimer's houses did not arise. Speed was the order of the day and he told Dods immediately what he intended to do. 'This big new job I've got on Loch Fyne, I mean to handle, as I've never handled a job before. The ground is to be broken on the first of May, and the dear old gent wants to eat his dinner in it on 1st August, 1907 – if he does it'll be a record', *Pl. 19*. Fifteen months would have been quick going for a mansion of this size, and Ardkinglas was to be built on a site remote from all supplies of material and labour. The stone could be extracted from a nearby quarry on the estate, yet it could only be extracted in small pieces. Accordingly, sandstone for all the window, door and gable dressings had to be brought in from Dumbartonshire by puffer, and a new pier had to be built to offload these small steam boats. The labour had to be brought in also and a hutted camp was built which at one stage held over two hundred men.

Lorimer adjusted his construction to speed up erection wherever he could. 'I'm going to do all the internal walls of brick, so if we have a fine dry summer and autumn, I think it's conceivable we may manage it, but it means straining every muscle', as he and his staff were doing already with the drawings. The working drawings were finished in a little over three months since he first saw the site, leaving him ready to 'dash onto the F[ull] S[ize drawings] and get them all out', and the fact that Scott Morton's contract amounted to about £7,000 suggests that Lorimer used their designers to help do this quickly (because Grieve's share was less than £550).

The site is an old one domestically. A castle of which no trace remains is thought to have stood north of a small loch now called the Caspian, which itself is situated where formerly the burn nearby discharged into Loch Fyne. The earlier house stood well back from the loch in the lea of long established woods and more than half of this house was taken down when the new house was built and four thousand pounds spent on remodelling part of it and also some stables. A still earlier house stood for a few decades in the eighteenth century nearby, when the current practice was to provide a walled garden at a distance from the house and such a garden still exists to the north near the Caspian. Lorimer's original scheme for Rowallan had strung out the public rooms as a south range linked around two courtyards to a north range two hundred and twenty feet long, and even longer, but Ardkinglas, also covering about one hundred and fifteen thousand square feet of ground, is more compactly planned around one courtyard and measures roughly one hundred and forty by one hundred and thirty feet, *Fig. 81*.

Perhaps Lorimer's experience with smaller houses had persuaded him of the need of shelter at the front entrance, so departing from the traditions of the sixteenth century of which he was so fond, he incorporated a large open porch which opens to a low hall dimly lit by one window to the courtyard, *Pl. 192*. The grand staircase to the piano nobile is at right angles to the direction of approach, placed so that a central line of stone piers splits off the staircase to the right, lit by tall mullioned windows at its half landing, from the dim depths ahead leading to Sir Andrew's oval office. The billiards room, which Weaver particularly liked, is reached by raised dais, *Pl. 193*, 'where there are writing tables and steps leading down to the billiards room proper. The players are thus saved from the distraction of having people walking about on the same level near the table and spectators can draw up chairs to the railing that guards the edge of the raised floor and look down at the table', *Pl. 194*.

The piano nobile in the north west range is devoted to the public rooms, all of which have direct views across or down Loch Fyne. The saloon, in plan, is just over two squares in proportion, and is forty two feet long entered slightly off centre and closer to the deep bay at its west corner which immediately directs attention to the long view down Loch Fyne. The fireplace at the other end has a huge granite lintel eighteen inches deep and is flanked by decorative pilasters of delicate proportions following the traditional pattern. A small lobby set unobtrusively in a corner, like a closet, gives access to an open staircase curving down to the pleasance in an S line of steps, no two alike, with complications for the masons which have already been referred to. He had used open stairs roughly similar in form at Hallyburton some years earlier. The corridor leading past the saloon gives onto the upper

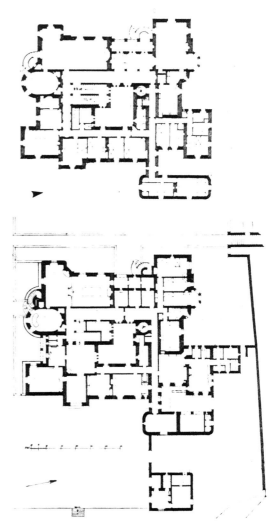

[*81*] *Ardkinglas, Argyllshire,* ABOVE *first floor plan;* BELOW *ground floor plan.* C.L.

hall, not a dark place as at Rowallan, but one filled with light from both sides. The sitting area in it beside the fireplace, *Pl. 195*, looks out into an arcaded loggia from which an even more curving staircase leads down to the terrace, *Pl. 156*. The dining room which opens from the far end of the hall is provided with windows to give views across and also down to the loch, as well as two windows overlooking the tree enshrouded Caspian to the north-east, its surface in summer white with water lilies. The larger window, a bay, is placed to throw easterly morning light diagonally across the room.

The south-west range comprises the principal bedrooms, with subsidiary bedrooms mostly put over the public rooms on the north west. No two bedrooms are alike, each varying in shape, some with bays and some without, the ceilings flat, segmental or combed, all decorated by Thomas Beattie and Sam Wilson with traditionally inspired patterns based on natural forms. The plainly practical servants' bedrooms are grouped over the service quarters on the north-east.

The plan of this house is very simple in principle, around which an infinite variety of inflexions have been worked, as Hussey would have it, in an expressionistic composition evocative of the surrounding mountains, and it is true that the massing does embody many switches of scale in what can only be described as tumbling rhythms. The side of the house facing the loch, for example, has been set down some six feet as well as back a couple of feet almost exactly at its middle with effects which are not fully resolved. The higher half with the tall saloon windows is not strong enough to hold its own with the lower half, with its Baroquely curving stairs, its arcade (possibly influenced by Gordon Castle as it was before the Baxters rebuilt it) and the lively play of window heads. The ambiguities of this arrangement resolve themselves in the oblique view from the west, in which as the lower half recedes, the higher and closer half is strengthened, and as the corner is turned the south-west facade steps down, recalling the stepped courses of earlier Baronial work without resembling them at all closely, *Pl. 198*.

Harling was intended for the house but it was omitted. The local granite which is mostly green in colour appears golden at a distance with the attractive and characteristic glitter of all granites. The dressings around the door and window openings and on the stepped gables are of Dullator[1] which weathers to a pale brown tinged with mauve. It does not weather well but the quarry had been open for too short a time when Lorimer chose it for this to be known.

The whole site offers magnificent views across Loch Fyne to the mountains beyond, and being enclosed on the other three sides by mature trees, has all the feeling of a loch side dell nestling beneath its own mountains. The drive which enters the site crosses the burn by an old bridge some hundred and fifty yards south of the new house and then leads straight across to the former house to the west. The new house has been sited to the right, on the northernmost tip of the platform offered by the site, and above the Caspian, so as to take full advantage of the long view down to the loch. The drive to the new house could have been driven on a straight line from the bridge. Evidently, the ground did not suggest it to

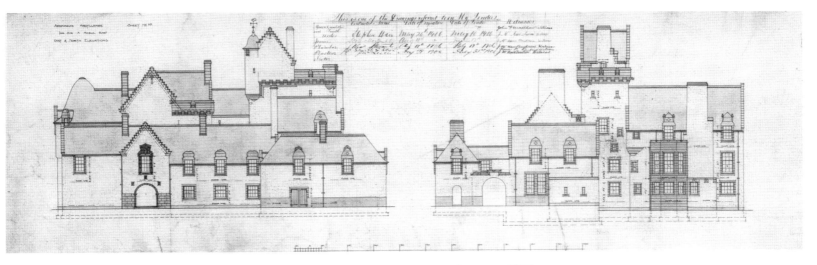

189 ABOVE *Ardkinglas, Argyllshire, elevation showing intended harling (not carried out).* R.C.A.M.

190 BELOW *Ardkinglas, laying the foundation stone; Lorimer on the left, Sir Andrew Noble centre.*

Ian Mackenzie

191 OPPOSITE ABOVE *Ardkinglas, under construction (topping out).* R.S.L.

192 OPPOSITE BELOW *Ardkinglas, from the approach drive.* R.S.L.

193 ABOVE LEFT *Ardkinglas, the upper level of the billiards room.* R.S.L.

194 BELOW LEFT *Ardkinglas, the lower level of the billiards room.* R.S.L.

195 BELOW RIGHT *Ardkinglas, detail of fireplace of upper hall.* R.S.L.

196 ABOVE LEFT *Ardkinglas, the freely-modelled hydro-electric dam.* R.S.L.

197 ABOVE RIGHT *Ardkinglas, hydro-electric generator house.* R.S.L.

198 BELOW *Ardkinglas, from the* W. P.M.

Lorimer or Sir Andrew and the old driveway was retained almost as far as the earlier house, at which point, a new spur was swung away to the right to the new house. If it is not an eye-sweet curve, a description Lorimer would have challenged, it provides a semi-circular line of approach which is highly effective in showing off the house from many aspects.

The entrance facade, *Pl. 189*, provides a lively display of horizontals, and the reiterated eaves and ridges provide a stabilising element in a cacophony of forms. The roof is covered with Caithness slates which weather to a colour and tone close to that of the walls, and give neat regular little shadows to echo the eaves line, over and over again, unlike the ragged blue-grey Ballachulish slates of Rowallan which provide narrower courses to dapple the light falling upon them. Whereas the sombre glitter of the slates of Rowallan associates them with the sky, the slabbing of Ardkinglas does not glitter at all but seems to grow out of the walls, with the chimney stacks set not in the gables as tradition demands in Scotland but mostly in the middle of the various blocks.

The composition overall seems to follow a rule of three. The corbie gable over the entrance is echoed immediately behind but higher, before the shape is repeated even higher upon the watch tower. There are three west facing gables, one at the end of the entrance block, another intermediately over the servants' bedrooms to the east, and the last back on the west and high over the salon. The plat (horizontal step) of the front entrance, too, is re-echoed by the roof parapet over the main stairs and on the outlook tower by the parapet next to the beacon stance. To complete the design there are also three bell cast roof caps.

Brick construction was still not common in Scotland and if the drawings show that some walls have cavities, they do not form a continuous defence against the penetration of damp. Since any Scots architect would expect damp to be pushed through the joints between the impermeable pieces of granite, or 'sucked in' by them as J. J. Stevenson has put it, it seems that after the harling which would have prevented this was omitted that the central heating and numerous coal fires were to be relied upon to keep the building dried out. All the bedrooms have fireplaces and the absence of any insulation whatever in the roof space above suggests that they were intended for almost continual use. There was no local supply of electricity so the water power of the adjoining burn was harnessed. A dam, *Pl. 196*, designed like a natural spill of pebbles and boulders was built and water led through a leat above the burn to the generator house, *Pl. 197*, also built of large pebbles and set near the house on the service road which follows its banks. The services within the main house rise in a large trunk with a built-in vertical inspection ladder and a drain at its foot to take care of any leaks.

A large Baronial house may be set appropriately within a landscape of highland grandeur, either by a deliberate understatement of a building made severe enough in character to rise directly from an unreclaimed site, which is more or less what Lorimer was to do with Dunderave on the other side of the loch a few years later; alternatively, effects can be used in its landscaping broad enough to suit the grandeur in scale of the landscape itself, and this is what he chose to do at Ardkinglas. The north-west front overlooking Loch Fyne is set over a long terrace, *Pl. 198*, whose strong sideways thrust, unlike Rowallan's, has been checked at

[82] *Ardkinglas, the steps from the lochan to the terraces.*   P.S.

regular intervals by wide buttresses, each of which is carried up the parapet wall in a sharp taper. Sir Andrew authorised the execution of this terrace, 'As per model', and two lower terraces were treated merely as grassy steps. A pleasance was laid out on the south-west as a flat hanging garden with a pool and fountain enclosed by flower borders and a yew hedge. The lead figure was by the Bromsgrove Guild. The isolation of these features suggests that more planting was intended or has not survived. The Caspian and the walks around it were in existence before Lorimer began his work and he has linked the end of his long terrace to them by a magnificently simple stone staircase of very subtle curved inflexions, *Fig. 82.*

When the house was finished and Sir Andrew had taken up residence Lorimer went for his final tour of inspection. 'The wife was with me at Ardkinglas over last week end' he wrote, 'and as the weather on the Sunday was *superb* we enjoyed it. Vi motored to church with Miss N[oble] and I wandered around, and I tell you I had a lump in my throat, as if I was saying goodbye to a child. I made a tour – the power house, the dam, the water works, then down the hill again to the home farm, the garage, the kennels, the pier, the gardens. All done and finished up. Never in my life have I *enjoyed* a job like that, it all went with such a swing. I managed to make everyone keen' and I 'had the finest clerk of works man ever had', [James Grieve who had superintended Manderstone for John Kinross] and he concluded, 'I do think ours is an attractive profession, the way one's life, one's thoughts and heart and soul are intimately bound up with one particular spot for a couple of years or so.'

He had been thinking as he worked on Ardkinglas of his own roots in the country and he wrote to Dods of how he had been getting 'a great lesson in tree planting from [Lord] Clyde', who lived in Briglands. 'He's been doing a lot of it. Am quite determined to do a lot at Auchentrail as soon as I can afford it', and he said he wished the family had done it twenty years ago when they bought the property. 'If we get flung out of Kellie, a dozen years hence and I had to build at Auchentrail, my belts [of trees] would be beginning to look quite decent and I feel nothing would satisfy me, but making a little place of my own. Making your own sheds and garden, etc., and what a ripping occupation.' He began designing his never to be realised dream house as a playful composition, the roof sprouting bell caps here and there to his changing moods.

Lorimer was also working on two medium sized houses. Barguillean, *Fig. 83*, set amid an Argyllshire moorland, a long house with harled walls and slated roofs, reflects the waning influence of the cottage movement, *Pl. 207*. The overall composition was still very varied and the roofs still high but the absence of gables, the numerous hips and wide overhanging eaves are part of the general swing back to classical formality at that time. High Barn was the earliest of Lorimer's medium sized houses to have a formal entrance facade combined with an informal garden facade, a theme he repeated several times. Sheildaig, in the Hermitage, Edinburgh, reverses this arrangement, *Fig. 85*. Although it was the first of Lorimer's new houses to have a definitely classical character, its entrance facade is irregular, with the entrance put in an open arched porch set between a projecting hipped bay and a Dutch gable over the stairs, whereas the garden facade is symmetrically flanked by bow fronted wings.

[83] *Auchentrail, Lorimer's design for a Fife dream house for himself.*   R.C.A.M.

The effect overall has something of the sweetness of his second remodelling, St Marnocks. The east wing was added later by James Dunn.

Three other commissions for classical buildings were in the office at that time including a church, a library and a mansion. St Peter's in Morningside, Edinburgh, *Pl. 209*, was a Catholic church which he told Dods was 'to be in the upstanding and primitive manner. All white washed brick inside and there is a little presbytery to be worked with it.' It was all to have, Hussey tells us, 'As much Italian flavour as was compatible with its locality and low costs'. The locality was a corner site which has since been surrounded by the advancing ranks of South Morningside's four storey stone tenements. The exterior had to be of stone, therefore, and for this, Hailes Quarry, some five miles off, was again chosen with dressings of Prudham, whereas the interior, *Pl. 210*, was built wholly in brick, for lower costs, and the Italian effect left, in the main, to low-pitched pantiled roofs and a diminutive campanile. A house for the priest and a school hall had also to be provided and were placed to take account of the angles and directions of the sun, *Fig. 86*. The priest's house is put on the corner to leave it open on three sides and attached only to the church along its north wall. The school hall is placed on the west and across a small court enclosing four trees. The northern part of the site is left for the highest building – the church. Wide eaves keep down the scale of the house and hall, whereas the height of the church is emphasised by the use of parapets, with stepped copings like those of his earlier Tudor buildings. The mullioned windows and chimneys of the priests' house carry Gothic motives, none of which is particularly Italian.

99

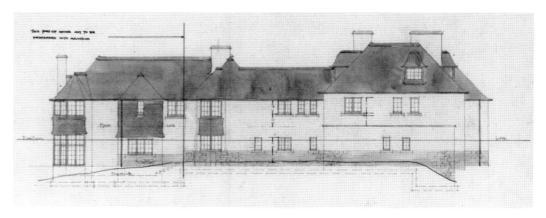

[84] *Barguillean, formerly Achnahanit, Argyllshire, an elevation.*   R.C.A.M.

The cruciform plan of a romanesque church was adopted, lit by tall rounded windows which are echoed internally by the brick arcaded aisles, and by the wooden wagon roof of the nave. Its arched form appealed to Lorimer for structural reasons and he habitually used variations of it. The tie beams closing the trusses against sideways thrust made it possible to use them over the relatively slender brick piers. The arched theme is then repeated over the aisles by narrow brick arches tied by twisting steel rods taken through to black tie plates in the nave, shaped as various emblems, the length of the church was also accentuated by the sanctuary having been put in a recessed apse with a huge painting executed under the direction of Frank Brangwyn on the end wall, and with the ritual choir in front kept as low as possible. The side chapels also had large paintings including a Malcolm Drummond. Eleven of the stations of the cross were by John Duncan, and the stained glass was by Maurice and Alice Meredith Williams. The length of the church, one hundred and forty feet, was placed along the back of the site and across almost its full width, with the subdivisions of the church kept as shallow as possible for economy yet giving a depth of effect to this severe and spacious interior.

Lorimer had been helped by working for a generous private patron and through a priest with very clear ideas of what he wanted. The final effect was an interior of warm but austere spirit, with warm textures of floor and walls to head height and all above white, providing an excellent foil for the many works of art and craft, and for the untreated and natural Oregon pine roof above. In Peter Anson's opinion it provided the 'Finest catholic church in Scotland'. The liturgical changes of recent years have required unfortunate alterations which do nothing to improve St Peter's.

The library extension for the University of St Andrews, which Andrew Carnegie commissioned and Lorimer designed, *Fig. 87*, is largely unchanged although much extended in the same style, *Pl. 208*. Its classical exterior for which masonry walls were used to enclose a tall reading room and access stairs in the central block as well as the book stacks with steel and glass floors in the two wings, forms part of what has become a quadrangle. It has no

[85] *Sheildaig, a neo-classical stone & slated house in Edinburgh.* P.S.

[86] *St Peter's Church, Morningside, Edinburgh, plan.* C.L.

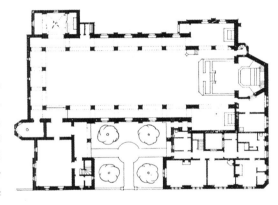

[87] *University of St Andrews Library, plan.* C.L.

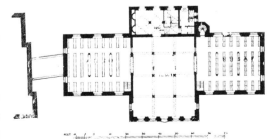

entrance at that side, however, leaving a withdrawn character, an effect in no way helped by the way the basement windows are cut by the ground level when seen from any distance. The reveal of the flat arches over these same windows has been chamfered in a flat curve, possibly to lessen the eye-catching effect of the emphatic convergent lines of their rusticated joints.

If the relationship of the two bottom floors is not altogether satisfactory, the main floor is better composed, but even there, the generous proportions of the windows to the book stacks make the narrow windows of the reading room seem mean in comparison, even though they are placed more closely. This building could have been designed as satisfactorily within a collegiate style if not in the Baronial but the classical style has allowed a flat roof to be used with an open balustraded parapet which keeps it in scale with the other buildings around it. The sharply canted pediment incorporated in the centre of the balustrade recalls early renaissance work in Scotland.

1905 brought another classical commission which gave enough freedom for him to make a really 'fine thing' of it. He was called in to remodel Wemyss Hall,[2] an unassuming harled house by Sir William Bruce, in Fife, and it led to such extensive works as to amount virtually to a new house. The original house had had a large service wing added in Victorian times but it was still too small to house all the owners' possessions, because if Mr Sharp was by no means the biggest man in the Dundee jute trade, he was no inconsiderable collector of antiques.

The house stood a little up a south facing slope with a large walled garden behind stretching out on both sides and surrounded top and sides by plantations of trees. These dispositions made it impossible to replan the house with an approach from the north. The existing entrance to Wemyss Hall, since renamed Hill of Tarvit, and now in the possession

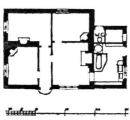

of the National Trust for Scotland, was on the South and served by drives from east and west, so it was decided to leave the old walled garden alone and to approach the remodelled and extended house from its sides. This allowed the Victorian extensions on the north to serve as the service quarters, and a new wing to be wrapped around the front and sides of Bruce's house and on the site of the existing drive, *Fig. 88*. The east and west approaches were then re-linked across the front of the new house but far enough down the slope to provide a generous space for a garden free of traffic routes. The eastern spur was retained to give access to the service wing north of the house and a new spur was brought in from the west to a forecourt in front of the new main entrance put in the west side of the new house. Lorimer had to provide an interior which called for a drawing room to house Sharp's French furniture, a Baronial hall for his Jacobean furniture and tapestries, *Pl. 204*, and a Georgian dining room *Pls. 205, 206*. Scott Morton did much of the detail design and the main woodwork (£6000). Beattie did all the plaster work *in situ* in the drawing and dining rooms, and Wilson that of the stairs and also the library. It may well be that Lorimer's first thoughts were to begin again and drawings exist of a long low scheme with a mansard roof above the ground floor and tall stone dormers rising more than head high from the first floor level in the French manner, *Pl. 199*. The final scheme is much taller and retains a French flavour.

Lorimer's interest in garden design, founded on his experience of the walled garden at Kellie, had so far been directed towards shelter and the example of other early walled gardens like Edzell. Yet terraced gardens seem particularly appropriate to a hilly and mountainous country like Scotland, and of Barncluith Garden,[3] a uniquely terraced garden, begun near Hamilton early in the Seventeenth century, Lorimer remarked in a talk on Scottish gardens he gave in 1897: 'It is the most romantic little garden lying on one side of a great wooded valley, it is a veritable "hanging" garden. Four or five terraces one above another sticking on the side of a cliff the general angle of which is about 55 degrees.'

The gentler but still steeply sloping hillside of Wemyss Hall was to provide him with an occasion for building a garden with extensive terracing. He told Dods as he started on site, that Wemyss Hall 'lies on the loveliest slope to the south and we've got a heap of stuff from our excavations etc., which I'm spreading out in the form of a long terrace so that the chap will *need* to build a great terrace wall fourteen feet high and about one hundred and forty yards long. I think he's on for it, it'll cost him a couple of thousand in the sweet bye and bye', and in this way the house was as carefully fitted to the hillside as the garden was moulded to the house, *Pl. 200*. The west side of the house opens on the forecourt where screening is mostly contrived by the terracing on the steep cross slope. The left side of the forecourt, as it is approached from the west, is closed off by a high retaining wall above which lies the old walled garden, whereas the right side of the forecourt is lined by a balustrade which overlooks a deeply sunk rose garden on its south. The form of the house echoes the terraces but in counterpoint to their descending levels. The main entrance within an arcade of three arches is placed to the left of the main mass and thereby tucked in towards the hill. It is supported on the left by the smoking room, a lower mass but advanced about a foot, and on the other side by the more ornamental large shape of the bay window closing the end of the forecourt to the right, and giving the drawing room a side view along the approach drive and an oblique view of the sunken rose garden.

Steps beside the house lead up from the corner of the forecourt arriving first at a small intermediate garden, dominated by a single circular border raised two feet, within a retaining wall and overlooked by the smoking room which is also at a half level (and reached inside from the first landing of the main stairs). A further flight of steps leads up from this small garden to the extensive old walled garden, where a path extends along the top of the retaining wall which provided views across the valley through gaps in the planting, after which cross walks leading to the vantage points higher in the garden allowed views over this screen of planting.

Since the whole of the west and south facades are open to view from the south-west, Lorimer took great pains to set up a turning movement to harmonise the transition from the assymmetrical arrangement of the entrance facade lying across the slope to the symmetrical arrangement of the south facade lying along its contours, where the bowed ends of the house enclose a balustraded terrace and steps. All the public rooms have french windows to this terrace which overlooks two further imposing terraces below, *Pl. 202*, as well as a large level expanse of lawn extending to the drive. The detailing of the south facade shows the introduction of many switches. Windows surmounted by doors opening on balconies are alternated with doors with windows above, balanced upon the central window with a sundial and recess for a figure above, and providing the rhythmic interplay in which Lorimer so delighted, *Pl. 203*. Ernest Wilmott, writing in 1911, felt it was a house showing influence both of early English Renaissance and the more severe style introduced by Inigo Jones, and based on Italian precedents in that 'the small scale of the rusticated "quoins" and window framings and the absence of horizontal lines between plinth and eaves combining to give a romantic element to a design which has also much of the simple breadth and dignity associated with the late style'.

The setting of Wemyss Hall, as of Ardkinglas, shows the same alternation in attention to distant and near views. The drawing room and study have long views but the dining room also looking across the valley had a near view sideways into a small eastern rose garden surrounded by banks of evergreens which also acted to screen the service area, *Pl. 201*.

It is difficult enough to protect buildings from the ravages of time and man, yet gardens offer an infinitely more difficult problem. Small plants become large, even huge, or a tree essential to the whole effect is uprooted and not replaced (like the walnut tree at Barton Hartshorn), and the clipping of hedges can do no more than maintain the intended shape very roughly. The gardens of Wemyss Hall which were reshaped by Lorimer for this new house have suffered many minor changes which have greatly changed its effect. The hedges have encroached on the architectural stonework in a way that cannot have been intended and where the sunken garden was open to the south a tall hedge completely encloses it. The evergreens around the east rose garden have gone, leaving the clutter of fire escapes behind in full view, and in the walled garden behind, the rectangular plots, formerly busy with fruit, flowers and vegetables, are now empty and grassed over to reduce the costs of maintenance, leaving but a ghost of its former self.

Lawrence Weaver, the architectural editor of *Country Life* began to review Lorimer's work in it from 1905. Clough Williams-Ellis, from whom Lorimer was twenty years later to win the competition for the Stowe Chapel commission, has written how Weaver 'ran' a number of young architects one of whom was Lorimer. He was commenting on how Weaver struck up close friendships with Lutyens and Lorimer and became both their confidant and publicist. Weaver would stay at Kellie when visiting new work by Scots architects and Lorimer is well represented in many of the books he based on his articles. It is probably due to him that Lorimer was to become known as the Scottish Lutyens. Lorimer, like Lutyens, was usually entrusted with the gardens and layout of the grounds, as well as the house, and often the interior and its furnishings as well. He had been influenced in his early work by Norman Shaw, as was Lutyens, but he did not develop a classical and formal manner later in his career as did Lutyens and Shaw before him, and even though he received a number of classical commissions it did not become his chosen style. He was at work in 1905 on another, more characteristic, mansion for Sir Thomas Carmichael. The plan followed the traditional L within which a quite untraditional corridor eight feet nine inches wide ran from one end of the main block to the other, with doors at either end, 'Don't you think that's rather good?' he asked Dods. Usually his corridors were carefully variegated so that this one may well have been intended as an exhibition gallery as well. Sir Thomas's finances had suffered, and Lorimer and Burrell had attended the sale at Christie's in 1902 when he had sold his art collection. He had begun another collection, but Hailes Quarry from which he drew much of his income was nearly exhausted and the project for the mansion at Skirling was abandoned – probably when the estimated costs were known. Perhaps it is as well since it was for a hill top site and would have undoubtedly been draughty.

Lorimer continued to design the occasional simple building in harl and slate, like Muirfield, a small nursing home at Gullane, where the single storey buildings are arranged in a splayed group. Woodhill, a small simple design from this time for Barry, in Forfar, is a gem. The previous house on this bosky site had to be demolished because of too extensive dry rot. The site is flat and the new house is to be seen gleaming through the trees as the driveway loops towards it in a big S, to reach a range of low outbuildings which stretch towards the house from a low round tower left from the earlier house. This pleasant but shadowed approach ends at a porch which juts out hospitably from an otherwise austere northern facade, *Pl. 211*, with the entrance which leads in to the main rectangular block of the house (the lower service wing is hooked round from the far end) *Fig. 90*. The compact circulation within is relieved by a spacious stair well, the rooms are generous and well lit, arranged traditionally as individual compartments, overlooking a walled garden, a private arcadia which renders superfluous any need for complicated spatial effects in planning, *Pls. 212, 213*.

[90] *Woodhill, Forfar, plan.*   C.L.

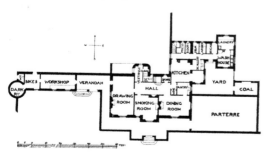

202 LEFT *Hill of Tarvit, the terrace steps.* R.S.L.
203 RIGHT *Hill of Tarvit, the French windows to the*
terrace. R.S.L.

204 LEFT *Hill of Tarvit, the panelled hall.* R.S.L.
205–206 RIGHT *Hill of Tarvit, dining room.* R.S.L.

207 ABOVE LEFT *Barguillean, Argyll.*   R.C.A.M.
208 BELOW LEFT *University of St Andrews Library before extensions.*   R.S.L.
209 ABOVE RIGHT *St Peter's Church, Morningside; priest's house at right.*   R.S.L.
210 BELOW RIGHT *St Peter's Church, Morningside, interior.*   R.S.L.

The exterior is harled and Scotch slates are used, as for all Lorimer's later work. The planes of the main roof are slightly belled, and the low eaves cut by stone dormer heads, and a Dutch gable as well as sash windows, provide an overall vertical emphasis and only the downswept roof over the laundry suggests Arts and Crafts influence by its Voysey-like profile. The garden facade of this disarmingly simple dwelling at first glance provides the effect of symmetry. The Dutch gable is placed centrally but the windows arranged differently on either side suggest rhythms of infinite variety.

Election as Fellow to the Royal Institute of British Architects was a foregone conclusion for someone with so much work to his credit by 1906, but Ernest Willmot's book *English House Design* shows that by 1911 Lorimer was as well known for his English work as for his Scottish. Ardkinglas was included as an example of 'the typically Scottish work which Mr Lorimer knows so well how to handle', as well as Wemyss Hall, and Barton Hartshorn was illustrated to show that 'he is equally at home with work more characteristically English in expression', as well as some cottages at Lympne. Mr Lorimer was moved to begin sending work to the Royal Academy in London. Two years later, 'some recent work of Mr Lorimer' filled most of the February issue of the *Architectural Review* and in 1913 he collaborated closely with Weaver to fill an entire Architectural Supplement of the *Country Life* with 'The Work of Sir Robert Lorimer' in mid career.

Lorimer had too many large commissions to his credit for them all to have been included in the supplement and Lympne Castle, probably begun in 1905, was one which was not. Lorimer told Dods of this 'most attractive job. It stands on the top of a plateau and slopes away very steep to the south looking over Romney Marsh and the sea over to France. A most attractive situation and I think I see my way through it.' Edward Hudson of *Country Life* had been about to let Lutyens loose upon Lympne Castle when Lorimer's client F. J. Tennant stepped in and bought it. Lorimer had already made alterations to a house in North Berwick for him some years before but since his father had left him three million pounds. 'I rather like a job south of London,' Lorimer confided in Dods, 'which takes you up every eight weeks or so in a sleeper at someone else's expense, and one is able to keep in touch a bit with what is going on'.

The castle which stands on a bluff next to the church, *Pl. 214*, had been a grange of the See of Canterbury until fifty years before, according to Weaver, and Hussey says that it was earlier fortified against the possibility of French attack. It had since been used as a farm and a whole clutter of buildings to its north had first to be cleared, after which Lorimer had to link the new extensions to it by a corridor from where they are set back on the only flat part of the site which has views of the sea, *Fig. 91*. The castle had a glorious old hall, far larger than any other he had worked with hitherto, but which had been much altered when an additional floor had been inserted. This was taken out and windows and roof were restored on the model of the one original oak tie beam that remained. Oak linen fold panelling is carried about half way up the walls with plain white plaster above. A large panel of fifteenth century Burgundian tapestry dominated this magnificent chamber.

LYMPNE CASTLE, KENT.

FOR F.J TENNANT. ESQ^{re}

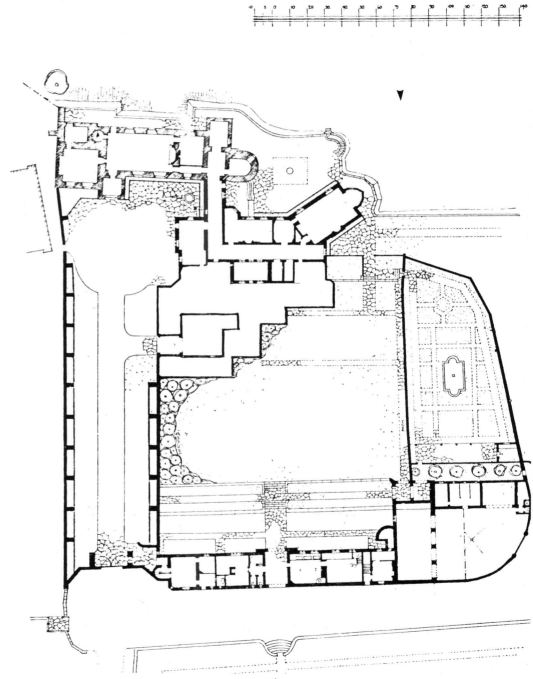

[91] *Lympne Castle and gardens, Kent, plan.*   A.R.

The massing of the new buildings was difficult. The seaward side of the castle had hardly been touched, so a low square turret near its east end was made higher to balance the curved keep at the west, and an old bastion below was linked within a new long curving terrace wall which runs below both the old and the new buildings, *Pl. 215*. The keep, a dominant and most interesting block, projects sideways to the west from the longer and lower, but less interesting, shape of the hall which faces south across the marsh. The new dining room has been made the second mass in interest by being given a high gable to echo the half gable of the hall where it abuts the keep, as well as a six sided bay-window to respond to the shape of the keep. The way the dining room is projected forward gives it three external walls and the oblique angle at which it is set to the hall or keep avoids any clash with them.

The landward side of this group of buildings is planned around several courtyards for shelter on this exposed site, *Pl. 218*. The entrance gate, a great oak portal, set in a recess in the external wall, *Pl. 216*, gives on to a long narrow court which leads past the new wing with its low eaves line, dormers and high upswept gables like a lower version of Barton Hartshorn, to the old castle across its end. There the existing porch at the east end led to the old kitchen quarters which were not only on the edge of the Cliff, but also at the boundary of the site, making impossible any extensions to that end of the building. Accordingly they had to be put on the west, and the second and separate subsidiary entrance that this necessitated emphasises what an intractible planning problem the remodelling set Lorimer.

The general contractor had been a local man, stone was quarried on the site and was so plentiful that the whole approach drive was paved. The subcontractors were all from Edinburgh. The interiors have exposed wood beams, much oak panelling and no ornamental plaster, *Pls. 217, 219*. Most of the heating radiators are concealed in recesses behind wrought iron screens by Hadden. The furniture was mostly antique. *The Architectural Review* told a story that had been put about that Lorimer was building a 'Scotch Baronial' castle in Kent, whereas in truth the additions had been connected by the narrowest of necks to the old castle so as to leave it 'to tell its own story'.

A smaller alteration job of 1907 was Craigroyston, a large symmetrical villa above the foreshore at Pilton in Edinburgh castellated in style. An east wing was added in matching masonry continuing the existing levels of floors and window openings with a stepped Tudoresque parapet above. In 1908 he was called in to reinstate Monzie Castle after it had been gutted by fire. A simple L-shaped tower house had stood on the site since the sixteenth century and John Paterson had added a large castellated block in the Adam style in 1795, with four nearly detached corner turrets, *Fig. 92*. Each floor consisted of three large rooms each running from front to back between cross walls.

This was the rigid framework within which Lorimer had to plan. On the ground floor the entrance hall is set in the central compartment and Lorimer began by introducing two rows of columns as an aisle to lead to the back where a new grand staircase was to be built, *Pl. 220*. All the rooms on the *piano nobile* to which it leads have been reshaped and the floors replaced in reinforced concrete to provide fire checks, all hidden beneath ornamental ceilings for

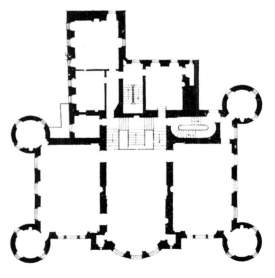

[92] Monzie Castle, Perthshire, plan of piano nobile.
C.L.

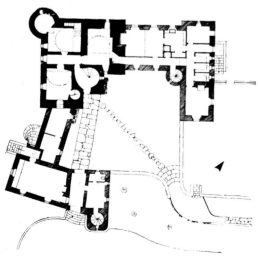

[93] *Dunderave Castle, Argyllshire, plans,* FROM THE TOP *second, first, ground floor.* C.L.

which Beattie did the plaster work in the diningroom and the drawing room, *Pl. 221,* in which Hubert Paton modelled four figures. All the furniture was entrusted to Lorimer, and much of it is to his own design. Another large scale internal remodelling was Galloway House in Wigtonshire – a huge Georgian house built by John Baxter from 1740 onwards and enlarged by William Burn in 1842 – undertaken in 1909 with plaster work by Beattie on the walls and ceiling of the hall and of the staircase. It was so skilfully done that reference to the drawings is required to be sure of what is Baxter and what is Lorimer. At Dawick in Peeblesshire, Lorimer was asked by the Balfours to add a wing to a neo-Jacobean house built by Burn and greatly enlarged by Burnet's ex-partner John A. Campbell as recently as 1898. The estate has become famous for its collection of trees, the house is pleasant in character but not outstanding nor has Lorimer made much effort to blend closely his additions to it. At Ayton House, near Abernethy, another mid-Georgian house enlarged by Burn, he improved the quality of the interior with some fine woodwork; and he has also carried out internal remodellings to a number of Edinburgh houses including 6 Heriot Row, 7 Eton Terrace, 4 Douglas Crescent for Douglas Strachan, as well as to the New Club in Princes Street, which was largely a matter of panelling carried out by Scott Morton (for £1,639) for a fine large dining room (which still exists partly reconstituted within the new building executed by Lorimer's last pupil but one – Alan Reiach).

Dunderave Castle in Argyll was no more than a shell by the end of the nineteenth century, *Pl. 225.* This MacNaughton stronghold had been built in 1596 on the landward side of a small windswept promontory on Loch Fyne, itself the site of an even earlier fort, and in 1911 Lorimer began to remodel the Castle for Miss Noble from Ardkinglas on one of the most dramatic sites he was ever given to work on. The difficulty with such towers of pronounced verticality is how to integrate the additions which for comfort and ease of circulation must be longer, lower and horizontal in accent, *Pl. 226.* His first scheme shows such wings extended flatly both south and east roughly on the lines of the later scheme, but with the access path to the main entrance at the foot of the old tower brought in diagonally from the south-east. Charming though that would have been it does not match the subtleties of the final scheme, *Fig. 93,* in which the view from the south is blocked by further building and the diagonal path leads only from the house to the terraced garden which follows the line of the drive, *Pl. 227.*

The main entrance now has to be gained by way of a pend through the southern range. Apart from the inconvenience of having to walk, sometimes in the teeth of a westerly gale, to this pend and the snug enclosure of the courtyard as one crosses to the front entrance, the view as you leave the house, especially in calm weather, of bright waters dancing in the eye of the sombre pend is as dramatic as any watergate.

Lorimer treated the old tower as he had treated Earlshall. He repaired where necessary and he made changes which were unavoidable. The main entrance was left open to the foot of the turnpike stair, and the vaulted undercroft of the ground floor around it used for stores and a cloak-room. The only large room in the tower, the red banner hall on the first floor,

211 ABOVE LEFT *Woodhill from the approach.* P.M.
212 ABOVE RIGHT *Woodhill from the garden as laid out
by Lorimer.* R.S.L.
213 BELOW *Woodhill today.* P.M.

214 OPPOSITE ABOVE LEFT *Lympne Castle, Kent, from the* S.E.   R.S.L.
215 OPPOSITE ABOVE RIGHT *Lympne Castle entrance gateway.*   R.S.L.
216 OPPOSITE BELOW *Lympne Castle from the* S.W., *with dining room angled to the view.*   R.S.L.
217 ABOVE LEFT *Lympne Castle, corridor.*   R.S.L.
218 BELOW *Lympne Castle, the rose garden.* R.S.L.
219 ABOVE RIGHT *Lympne Castle, stairhead.* R.S.L.

220 LEFT *Monzie Castle, Perthshire, the stair-well and entrance hall beneath.* R.S.L.

221 ABOVE RIGHT *Monzie Castle, the drawing room with furniture by Lorimer.* R.S.L.

222 BELOW RIGHT *Monzie Castle, part of the tiled kitchen.* R.S.L.

was given an open timber floor over it. The heavy beams, close set and carried on wall plates on wood brackets, have been roughly finished with the adze to lose any regularity the saw might have left. Lorimer had used beams at Lympne but he usually chose concrete beams and floors as a fire barrier. Even so his remarks on first visiting Gertrude Jekyll's house showed how much he liked their appearance. 'All the oak in the house is the most beautiful sort of silvery grey colour. I asked her if it was all *old* timber – no, all new but the reason of the colour is it was all coated with hot lime – one man coats it over, his "mate" follows on [a] quarter of an hour later and cleans it off and, *voilà!* you have oak that looks as if it had been there since the beginning.'

The only necessary structural changes were openings for the doorways to give access to the new wings. The new east wing shaped in another L was joined to the tower to form a U in plan, the linking arm being kept to a single storey with attic dormers in its roof to keep it in scale with the diminutive front entrance. The south wing, also an 'L', although taller, was kept empty of windows to the court but still seemed likely to compete for attention with the old tower. Lorimer did not content himself with drawing alternatives or making small scale models, but had full size profiles erected on site. They decided him to swing the south wing to an oblique angle with the tower, and to angle the pend and part of the south wing so that the approach path approaches the front entrance at a slight angle.

The south wing included a west facing open loggia facing down Loch Fyne, *Pl. 223*, the view gained through a screen of ancient windshorn beech trees, most of which have since been uprooted by gales. The library on the upper floor of the south wing, was reached by way of this loggia or by some stairs rising near the pend, and this isolated position gives it clear views down and across the loch, and detaches it from all the household bustle apart from the flower room which abuts it.

Lorimer retained the original drive which follows a rough sea wall of water rounded boulders putting it a little above the level of high tide. Another wall, two metres high and of similar construction, has been built behind the drive leaving some large ash trees to sprout irregularly from within it. The pleasance set above yet another terrace is devoted to a narrow lawn and flower beds which lead from the corner of the courtyard to a garden house perched like a watch house at its far end. All of the divisions of the garden set in the lea of the Castle are small in scale, and the kitchen garden slopes uphill above a third terrace as far as the service drive which approaches the house from the north-east.

Lorimer was designing for a client who could keep coal fires burning whenever needed to keep this building dried out in its highly exposed situation. In recent years the tower, with walls five feet thick or more in places has had to have special treatment against the penetration of damp, in particular from westerly gales. The bedroom walls are panelled and arranged by Lorimer to have bands of wide low panels alternating with tall narrow panels, the different rooms in various woods including bird's eye maple. Beattie and Wilson carried out the decorative plasterwork and Hadden the ironwork. Thus a lonely tower set between the tumultuous waters of the loch and the rugged wooded mountains behind has had new

[94] *St Andrew's Church, Aberdeen, Rood Screen.*
O.D.

[95] *Duncraggie, Brora, sketch.*   P.S.

buildings and gardens knit to it in a scale and character entirely appropriate, and the garden pavilion with its steep hipped roof is the only domestic touch amid a general spareness of effect with no hint of prettifying. As Lorimer learned at Earlshall a highly exposed approach road but makes the house court the snugger by contrast.

Pittencrieff House, a run down sixteenth century building of three floors near the Palace in Dunfermline, was a straightforward job since the only ceiling of any interest over the dining room could be taken down and re-erected. The ground floor became a club, the first floor three rooms, and the top floor a museum gallery sixty nine feet long with a ceiling arched up into the roof space. Beattie did much of the plasterwork and the Dunfermline Carnegie Trust, for whom the work was carried out, received a very fine building. Lennoxlove in East Lothian, which had been extensively remodelled by Sydney Mitchell just a few years earlier, was a minor job which was beautifully done. The new fireplace in the fifteenth century vaulted hall shows Lorimer in 1912 working with the lightest of touches. Beattie carved the coat of arms over the main entrance.

The Thistle Chapel had established Lorimer as Scotland's leading exponent of the Gothic but it was three years before he received another Gothic job of any importance. Dunblane Cathedral, a thirteenth century fabric replacing a Norman building, was added to and altered a number of times before suffering the vicissitudes of the Reformation, and the timber roof of the nave had fallen in through the subsequent neglect. The choir continued to be maintained as a parish church until 1890 when Rowand Anderson restored the whole fabric, and in 1912 Lorimer was called in to finish the job by refurnishing the interior, *Pls. 228, 229*. It was the first lofty church interior he had had to work with, the effect of upwards of sixty feet was greatly accentuated by the tall windows without transoms to interrupt their great height.

The reredos had long been swept away and he proceeded to make good its deficiency by a range of panels hung on the wall below the severely plain windows of the east end. The muntins between each bay of the woodwork were treated as columns attached to the wall before being swept up and forward to form a cantilevered and vaulted canopy. The arch shape over each bay repeats that over the central window above, and the narrow ribs at the edge of the boards forming the backing of each bay take up the rhythm and number of the mullions of it. Each archivolt carries a carved panel of the seven acts of mercy.

Although some of the original medieval stalls remained, Lorimer preferred to design anew. New choir stalls were provided in two rows, those in front with narrow panels, ones behind with wider, their divisions repeated by the slightly projecting canopy over them which was richly carved to contrast strongly with the plain masonry above. Haffits, at the end of each range, are carved as poppy heads. The organ case is also richly carved and is set on the north side of the choir where windows are lower than elsewhere, and its stepped form rises above them and even a little above the triforium's sill. Its decorative open front projects a little more than the stalls canopy and the organist is placed out of sight at a console facing the choir. Stone paving was laid to replace the glazed tiled floor and Louis Davis

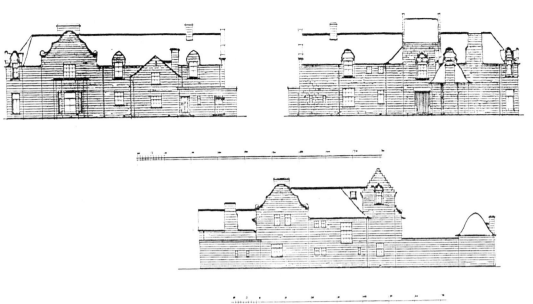

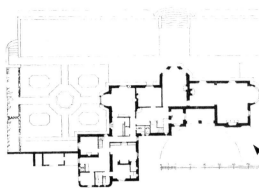

[96]–[97] *Rhu-na-haven, on Deeside, Aberdeenshire,* LEFT *elevations,* R.C.A.M.; ABOVE RIGHT *plan,* C.L.

designed the stained glass in the windows on the south side of the choir.

Loretto School, which had given him a number of minor alterations, commissioned science laboratories for which Lorimer produced an uninteresting building, *Pl. 231*, a gym – 'a lovely hall with dark planked walls' under a gambrel roof, *Pls. 232, 233*. The cricket pavilion is a charming harled building with delicate wood posts, the roof hipped, tall and slated, *Pl. 234*.

Restoration work often put the emphasis on the interior and its decoration and the number of purely internal remodellings he continued to get like Glenmayne, Gattonside, and Hunterston suggest that he had attracted a regular following to his Lorimer style of interior decor. Stables at Kinellan, gates for Balcaskie, a complete remodelling of Westerlea in Murrayfield, inside and out (an early work of J. J. Stevenson's), and of the garden, furnishing at St John's, Alloa, and St Andrew's Episcopal Cathedral at Aberdeen, *Fig. 94*, at which he also added a porch, were among the commissions which kept his office busy in the years leading up to the First World War. His new work during this period showed a considerable variety in house design. Duncraggie in Brora, *Fig. 95*, was a 1911 design for a smaller house in the manner of Barguillean, and he turned to Woodhill for the details of a much larger house in its manner at Aboyne.

Rhu-na-haven is situated on the outskirts of Aboyne in Aberdeenshire in the depths of the Dee Valley on a low bank past which the river flows. The house was built of regularly coursed blocks of granite with a roughly axed finish, and of a warm grey which shimmers with dappled light against the dark beech woods which approach it on three sides. The plan was based on the one main in line double aspect block from which the service quarters are

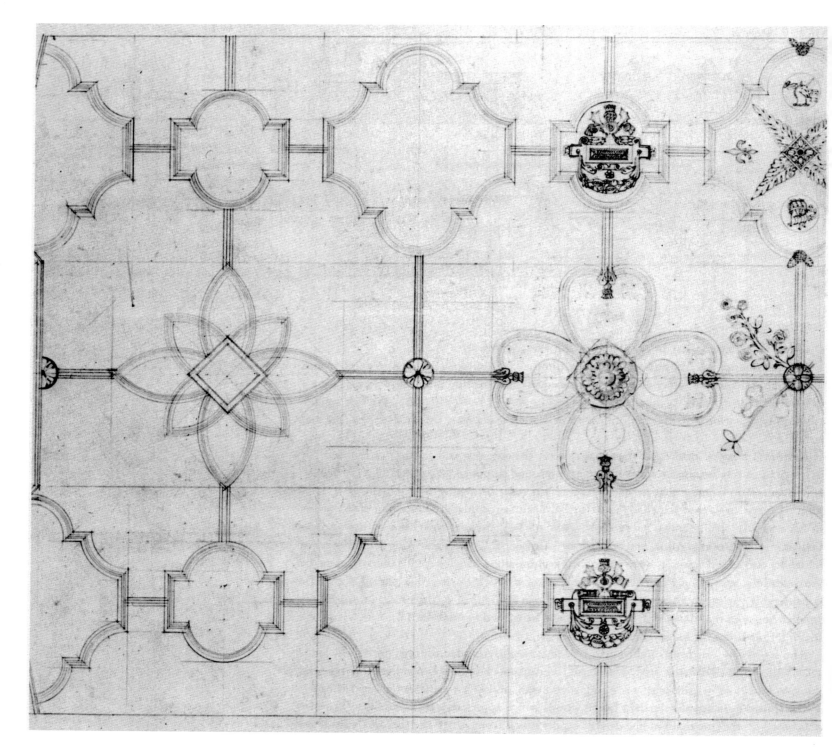

223 LEFT *Dunderave, a Baronial fastness on Loch Fyne.* P.M.
224 *Dunderave*, RIGHT *a stained glass window by John Sutherland*, R.S.L.; OPPOSITE *ceiling design*, R.C.A.M.

225 ABOVE LEFT *Dunderave, re-roofing, the first stage of rehabilitation, and before demolition of the old cottage.* R.S.L.

226 BELOW LEFT *Dunderave, from the* W. P.M.

227 RIGHT *Dunderave, entrance court under construction.* R.S.L.

231 ABOVE LEFT *Loretto School, Musselburgh, science laboratories.* R.S.L.

232 MIDDLE LEFT *Loretto, the gymnasium.* R.S.L.

233 BELOW LEFT *Loretto, an interior.* R.S.L.

234 RIGHT *Loretto, the cricket pavilion.* P.M.

hooked to the north from the east end, *Fig. 97*. The emphasis is then shifted within this simple massing by a constant variety in subsidiary elements. The drawing room appears to be set in the middle of the riverside facade between symmetrical wings but the library wing to the west, and under a hipped roof, is slightly longer and set a little farther forward than the east wing, *Pl. 235*. The smoking room, *Pl. 237*, and dining room are in the east wing whose roof ends below a tall Dutch gable facing downstream. The eaves line has been kept to one level throughout the house, except for a dip over the service quarters, and its long line contrasts with the many richly curved Dutch gabled dormers by which the combing ceiling bedrooms are lit, *Fig. 96*.

The approach from the north is by a simple gateway flanked by low granite walls capped by a deep coping made up of river cobbles. The lodge to the right is a low granite square with a low pyramidal slate roof, and farther off and to the left, and also among trees, are separate staff quarters past which the drive leads to the northern side of the main house. Its withdrawn character is emphasised in Woodhill fashion by the tall narrow, and in this case, corbie gabled miniature entrance tower, *Pl. 236*, old examples of which can be seen in Fife burghs like Culross or Pittenweem. If Woodhill is a gem then this very special house is like a circlet of gems, a diadem or a tiara.

The Corner House at Gullane, *Fig. 98*, designed immediately afterwards, for Robert Pitman, is another low house of complete horizontal emphasis built in a warm sandstone with tall hipped roofs of Caithness slates. Hussey found its anglicised understatement easier to assess than the Scottish vitality of Lorimer's major works, yet 'far from being commonplace,' he admitted, it 'bears the impress of the master mind. Its rough walls, slightly battered, and over the entrance and at the returned end slightly overhung; in its clear roof and perfectly proportioned chimneys we see [an] assured distinction.' The same may be said of Lorimer's last house in Colinton, now called Stone House, *Pls. 238, 239*. Both have beautifully proportioned rooms, a few Scottish features and are built from Scottish quarries, and yet the overall character is closer to some of Guy Dawber's Gloucester inspired houses (like Ashley Chase) than anything else.

[98] *Corner House, Gullane, sketch.*   P.S.

The variety in these designs must reflect clients' preferences as well as Lorimer's and if stockbrokers then preferred Tudor in England, Scots financiers usually preferred the Baronial. Laverockdale for J. A. Ivory on the then southern edge of Colinton below the Pentland Hills was one such house. Built of sandstone, the roof 'thekked' – to use the old Scots term, according to Weaver – with Forfarshire slates. It is no larger a house than the largest of the earlier Colinton Cottages, and has a main block on three floors, the top floor, largely combed, is devoted entirely to the nursery and children's quarters, *Pl. 241*. Ivory had a lot of eighteenth century furniture and the stair balustrading, as described by Weaver, is in 'Mahogany neither stained nor polished but rubbed down with rotten-stone and oil, a treatment which not only gives a rich colour, but leaves a surface soft as silk.' A particularly fine herbaceous garden was laid out, but it has been long since simplified out of all recognition.

[99] *King Edward VII Memorial at Holyrood Palace,*
competition drawing. A.N.

Lorimer, for all his wide experience in laying out the grounds of buildings in the country, was rarely asked to do so in towns. He did prepare a scheme for a national memorial to King Edward VII to be erected at Holyrood, which was illustrated in *The Builder* with the comment that the scheme had 'been approved by the committee of which the Lord Provost of Edinburgh is Chairman', *Fig. 99*. The design was not one of Lorimer's best and it comprised a gateway across Abbey Strand at the foot of the Canongate with the buildings on either side cleared away. Photos exist of a model of another scheme of a more pleasant design, *Pl. 240*. It may be that Lord Rosebery, who owned some of the property which would have been swept away, objected. The scheme was not proceeded with and some months later a competition was held which was won with a design by Washington Browne for a Bernini colonnade on the lines of St Peter's. It also necessitated demolishing the buildings on either side but, when it was found there was insufficient money to build it, wrought iron gates were substituted, which the new sovereign preferred anyway. At almost the same time a watermill in the centre of Galashiels was taken down and Lorimer was asked to lay out the free area. There had been thoughts of a garden, but Lorimer was loath to cover in the stream and his design provides a deep pool with a tall sculptured column rising from its centre, surrounded by stone balustrades and paving. The conception, says Hussey, is 'typical of Lorimer at his happiest. It comes as a charming surprise, this submerged fountain in the middle of the busy lowland town.' It is called Cornmill Square.

Lorimer's next mansion, Formakin in Renfrewshire, was also for a stockbroker who had been known to him for many years as a collector of art, Lorimer telling Dods 'It ought to be an interesting job, want to make it the purest Scotch I've ever done'. He had told Dods nearly ten years earlier that 'his wife constantly said he overdid things.' Then after two years, while staying at Briglands he reached the conclusion that he had become 'simpler and broader now. I am more able to leave things alone in detail, but I feel I am not continent enough with myself yet.'

Formakin, the last of the trio of completely new Scottish mansions he was ever to be given, shows how much he had learnt from the first two. He had been impressed by the way Miss Jekyll had first bought the site for her house in Surrey, 'and laid out a complete place there, paths, gardens, bought a barn that was being demolished, then erected it and some other buildings above the garden, and left a hole in the centre of the ground for the house'. In similar fashion John A. Holms, who had been Lorimer's best man, acquired Millbank, a large farm near Bishopton south of the Clyde, and first altered the farmhouse to live in while the gardens matured on lines planned by Lorimer. The walled garden of the farm which was above it to its north on a gentle south facing slope, was replanted as a pleasance, *Pl. 243*. A second walled garden almost as large as the first was extended to its east, *Pl. 245*. A large vegetable garden was put across their northern edge above another impressive terrace, and a garden pavilion and tool store with a bell-cast roof provided.

The materials for the new house were sandstone, as at Rowallan, and Easdale slates for the roof, as at Ardkinglas, thereby providing its warmth of effect without its glitter in Lorimer's most resolved and calmly composed mansion, and one which befits the wide plains south of the Clyde. The details are equally restrained. There are no curved flourishes in ornament, only a few archways and the merest suggestion of bell-casting to the turret roof caps. Even the plan is much simplified, *Fig. 100*. There are no internal courtyards and their absence allows all the public rooms to have two aspects. They are all set in one group of three-storey blocks loosely linked as a U, and with their high gabled roofs and big stacks they dominate the longer and lower service wings on their east.

Lorimer told Dods enthusiastically of the plans adding, 'I think its rattling good for Holms' special requirements', by which he meant his collection of tapestries, and when he submitted the drawings of the house to the R.S.A., the *Glasgow Herald* commented that 'Mr. John A. Holms must be singularly strong minded if he can withstand the fascination of Mr. Lorimer's drawings for his projected residence' because it felt that Formakin 'extends an invitation to the art treasures of Mr. Holms'. It suggests that Holms' erratic behaviour was already known, though he was not by any means the only collector to be taken over by his collection.

Years passed as the garden matured and adjustments of all kinds were made to the designs for the house until building was begun probably in 1910, since the fabric was finished, photographed and in the *Country Life* by September, 1913. Labour had been hired directly by Holms through James Grieve, the master of works who had supervised the work on the Thistle Chapel, Ardkinglas and Dunderave. Lorimer spent many long days on the site with

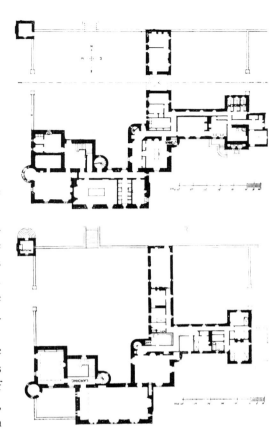

[*100*] *Formakin, Renfrewshire, plans.*   C.L.

him probably because Holms was something of an umbrella architect, given to changing his mind as he sketched things out in the sand with his umbrella, a habit he well may have caught from Lorimer. The site visits regularly extended overnight in the beginning, with Lorimer spending the night at the farm, as the two friends discussed and argued the details. The office diary for 1911 notes that models of the scheme were being considered and regular meetings are noted until 1915.

Weaver tells of the room to the west being 'built round' a Persian rug of great interest, and of the great chamber on the south being made twenty feet high to display a group of French tapestries on the conquest of India, and of working out in great detail the positions of all the larger pieces of furniture. This might have produced Lorimer's perfect work, built and matured over a period of about ten years, but activity was halted by the war with the interior still unfinished. Holms' financial affairs had fluctuated since he had been worth a 'quarter of a million', and only a little more work was done in the early 1920s. Even if the garden is his finest, and the layout of the grounds meets all Lorimer's preferences – the house open to the landscape on one side, *Pl. 244*, to the garden on the other – nevertheless the house was destined to be yet another of his unfinished masterpieces, although it remains his most harmoniously proportioned.

In this middle period of Lorimer's career, his work – like that of Lutyens – had been championed by Lawrence Weaver, and Lorimer's many restorations, his mansions and smaller country houses, had become known to all readers of *Country Life*, many of whom had never been to Scotland and had given him the reputation of being Scotland's leading country-house architect. The war of 1914 closed this era of large country houses and apart from a few further restorations and remodellings he had to turn to other work. 🍎

Antique tile.

235–237 *Rhu-na-haven, Aberdeenshire,* ABOVE *from* S.; BELOW *entrance forecourt & study.*   R.S.L.

238 ABOVE *Stonehouse, Colinton, from the forecourt.*
                                                    P.M.

239 BELOW *Stonehouse from the* S.   P.M.

240 ABOVE *King Edward VII Memorial competition, model by Lorimer.*   R.S.L.

241 BELOW *Laverockdale, Colinton, the nursery attic floor.*   C.L.

242 ABOVE LEFT *Formakin, Renfrewshire, the lodges and gate.* C.L.

243 BELOW LEFT *Formakin, the garden.* C.L.

244 RIGHT *Formakin, from the* S.W. C.L.

245 *Formakin, from an archway in the garden.* C.L.

246 *Balmanno Castle, Perthshire, the lodge seen from the castle.* P.M.

7

The War Years

The fact that Lorimer's buildings were so varied in style puts him with the common run of architects of his time but the quality of his response sets him above them. Scotland had offered him opportunities of only a tenth of the scale of England's, yet he had stayed in Edinburgh where he had specialised as far as his circumstances would allow. The excellent work he had executed in Fife and the Lowlands had led to other work on spectacular sites beside sea lochs and in Highland glens, but with the outbreak of war the country house work, which was the mainstay of his practice, had dropped off. James Morton, a longstanding friend of his in the textiles business, was having a medium-sized house designed for a site at Brampton near the Roman wall in Cumberland, and even though it had been staked out it was abandoned. Other projects which were too far advanced to be abandoned without considerable loss included two country houses in Scotland.

Midfield was a small eighteenth century classical house at Lasswade near the coalfields south of Edinburgh. It had been burnt out shortly before war began and Lorimer was asked to rehabilitate and extend it for Mr Hood, a coal owner, *Fig. 101*. The opportunity was taken to remove various oriel windows and other features which had been added in the nineteenth century, and apart from a general tidying up, a new wing with a dining room was added, its windows one pane wider but otherwise matching those reinstated in the existing building, *Pl. 248*. The interior was refitted with plaster panelling and woodwork in Lorimer's Georgian manner, *Pl. 249*, with occasional Arts and Crafts devices like baskets of fruit introduced into the ornamental plasterwork. A flower garden with great textural effects was laid out with stone edged borders and stone paved paths within which a circular stone pool with a column and figure provide the focus, all set between the two arms of this simple Georgian house. Lawns extend from the edge of the garden to an ancient and massive hedge of yew in the middle distance, *Pl. 247*.

Marchmont, the second classical remodelling undertaken at this time, was an imposing country house built to Thomas Gibson's design. In 1913 Robert McEwan, a close friend of Lorimer's and also a music devotee, had bought it and he had then decided to remodel it completely. Lorimer had extended Bardrochat in Ayrshire for him eight years before. Marchmont had three storeys and was rectangular in plan but for narrow wings only slightly advanced at either end, *Fig. 102*. Single storey pavilions were advanced at right angles to the main block on each side and were linked by curved screen walls surmounted by balustrades at the level of the *piano nobile*. The design was pleasing, despite the small (almost square) windows of the top floor which gave the whole building an underlit and withdrawn look,

[101] *Midfield, Lasswade, plan of rehabilitated house & new wing.*

C.L.

yet the massing was both clearly articulated and satisfactory in balance.

Mr McEwan found that there were practical problems with its plan. Meals had to be sent from the kitchen to the dining room by a trolley-way over fifty feet long, the bedrooms were underlit, and the attic floor rooms were lit only by skylights. The house was said to be very cold, and the succession of doors from one side of the building to the other through both the drawing room and salon could only have produced draughts. The main entrance was moved down from the *piano nobile* to the ground floor which may have helped. As for the rest: the bedrooms were given larger windows, the attic ceiling was raised within a new mansard roof and Lorimer provided dormer windows which crowd the six urns which had been silhouetted formerly against the pale, sky reflecting, roof of Gibson's design, *Pl. 250*.

The clear formality of Palladian planning is rarely matched by the most convenient arrangement of rooms and if the changes made by Lorimer provide some improvements in their disposition, many of them came about as a result of providing considerable increased accommodation. The library and the dining room have been transposed, and also the kitchen with the scullery quarters, and yet kitchen and dining room remain almost as far apart as before. Services and plumbing, however, have been concentrated in two vertical ducts serving the bath rooms and lavatories which have been provided on all floors, and more servant quarters have been squeezed in.

The interior now offers an intriguing mixture of old and new work: the trophied plasterwork in the salon executed in William Adam's manner was repainted pale grey with the enrichments picked out in white; the original plaster ceiling of the library – now the dining room – was combined with new plaster work on the walls treated in Georgian manner; plaster work on the new staircase was enriched by trophies modelled by Thomas Beattie in the manner of William Adam, and elsewhere at the main stairs, first floor lobby and music room, a profusion of flowers and fruit appears quite alien to William Adam's manner, yet common in Lorimer's work, *P. 251*.

Much of the furniture is massively Georgian in its proportions and was designed by Lorimer and made by Whytock and Reid, and the music room also shows Lorimer's fine feeling for wood. He and McEwan, as ardent music lovers, agreed upon a relatively plain room, and it has been put on the first floor of the north pavilion. The walls of this room which measures sixty five feet long by thirty three, were wainscotted in oak arranged in very large panels divided by Ionic pilasters, and are surmounted by a large plain coved ceiling with a small panel of ribbed plaster decoration at its middle and thirty feet above the floor. The full sized organ which covers one end wall has been treated in an altogether more lively fashion as befits the focus of the room. The pierced casing of the pipes above the keyboard have been treated with flowing rhythmic curves, and are flanked by pairs of panels pierced with arabesques, over which the parapet carries six little fauns modelled by Louis Deuchars and Joseph Hayes and carved by the brothers Clow, as well as four celestial musicians sculpted by Pilkington Jackson.

If Lorimer has knit old and new together with his usual skill inside the house, the altered massing of the exterior has many additions which have the effect of double vision. Originally the three blocks appeared to be linked by the curved screen walls. However, the need to provide much more accommodation has led Lorimer to add an extra floor to each wing but they have been set back to rise above their original east fronts which have been retained as screen walls. The need for linking corridors on the first floor means that in similar fashion they rise above the curved screen walls. Gibson's scheme may have had added – since the drawings have been lost – a backstair in a projection rising as far as the *piano nobile* in the middle of the south facade. Lorimer has extended it upwards to the level of the cornice, putting a projection on the north facade to almost match it, and has extended the mansard roof over both these bays. Hussey considered that these 'excrescencies' were 'of great value in buttressing the increased height of the facades and thus connecting them with the wings'. Yet, since the bays also weaken the effect of the corners of the front facade, as do the new front walls of pavilions weaken the effect of the old by standing up indeterminately behind them, Lorimer's architectural stuttering shows more that he was asked to cram too much accommodation than would fit properly within the old walls.

Other parts of the building show the influence of similar difficulties. If the chimneys have been grouped to a more satisfactory arrangement of stacks, then the existing floor levels have not permitted him to give the three arches of the new entrance porch sufficient height to give this feature the prominence it requires even after the support of the other decorative features on the floors above is taken into consideration. Even the darkness of the porch might have been acceptable for a Baronial building like Ardkinglas but it does not suit the classical. Hussey was forced to admit that the eye 'finds no central point on which to rest', and he goes on to suggest that the unresolved duality between the two halves of the facade, or between the upper and the lower parts, derives from Lorimer's Gothic propensities and that it would have helped had he followed his earlier intention of taking the mansard up to a ridge instead of a flat roof. Be this as it may Lorimer seems to have been beaten so far as the east front was concerned. The brief admitted no satisfactory solution without destroying even more of the old building than he did, and even the west front suffers from a massing in which the individual elements, part cramped by the old work, have not been brought entirely into balance. The layout of the surroundings did not require treatment other than a simplification of the Victorian garden on the west. Grotesquely shaped borders and urns have been swept away in favour of a broad lawn with a fountain at its centre.

Eight sizeable jobs were in the office in 1914, after which the following year brought in a country house remodelling at Foss in Perthshire which was abandoned at the design stage, and three fire restorations. Lorimer had strong feelings on the hazards of fire and had become something of a specialist in them. His office diaries contained many newspaper clippings describing country houses which had been burnt out and he often wrote to their owners to tell them of his experience in such rehabilitation work.

Whitekirk Church, in East Lothian, had been burned down by suffragettes. A new roof had to be provided and some Gothic furnishings, which he carried out sensitively but

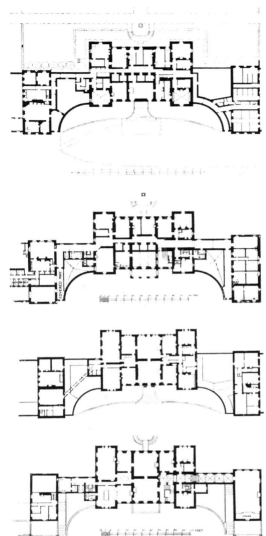

[102] *Marchmont, Berwickshire, plans,* FROM THE TOP *ground floor before & after remodelling, second floor before & after remodelling.* C.L.

without enough regard, in James Richardson's hyper-critical view, for the random fragments of early carving which had been displaced in the fire. Since he and Lorimer seem never to have reached full agreement on how old building fabrics should be treated, another work – the rehabilitation of large parts of Dunrobin Castle in Sutherland – offered Lorimer not only a welcome opportunity for the interior design for which he had become celebrated, but also one without archaeologists breathing down his neck.

Dunrobin was being used as an auxiliary naval hospital in 1915 when the part added by Sir Charles Barry between 1835 and 1850 was burnt out, *Pl. 272*. The castle is claimed to be the oldest inhabited house in Scotland. The original keep which was built in 1275 had been enlarged until it was surrounded by newer buildings, mostly in the style of the French Renaissance. Walls were repaired, concrete floors put in and a new roof installed to make the building weather-tight but it was not until 1919 that the interior finishings could be carried out.

One of Morton Sundour's factory buildings in Carlisle had also been burned down and Lorimer's old friend James Morton called him in to design a replacement building. Although Lorimer had had long standing links with the textile trade through R. W. Mackenzie and, to a lesser degree, through Scott Morton, his friendship with James Morton was probably of later growth and he must have been chosen for the project of the Brampton house because of his pre-eminence by 1913 in country house design and, although it proved abortive, it brought Lorimer and Morton close together. Morton's son Jocelyn tells how his mother found it necessary to tell their English governess that she must not show her surprise that the great Sir Robert Lorimer should stand by the fire to eat his porridge which he referred to as 'them' – since it was customary in Scotland in those days.

James Morton was to influence Lorimer strongly on his views on industry. His firm had been started by his father Alexander in Darvel in Ayrshire. Both father and son were highly resourceful men whose initiative took their firms into many different fields. Alexander, who began as a hand-weaver, went on to adapt the processes of Nottingham's lace machines to such effect that he was employing over five hundred workers by 1897. James became interested in the 1880's in the fabric designs of William Morris and especially in the quality of the dyes upon which he insisted. The firm had branched out into tapestry weaving and carpet making to keep the former hand-weavers in work and, when there was no more labour available around Darvel, a branch was started in Carlisle at which the fire was to happen in 1914. Lorimer produced the design and, with some goading, all the working drawings in two months for a modern weaving shed. The design was for a simple utilitarian brick affair with pleasant proportions and interesting brickwork decoration. Another job on the west was Conheath, to the north in Dumfriesshire, which involved a simple farm house with a Queen Anne character, as well as some remodelling of a small chapel nearby for which Lorimer designed an interior with severely simple lines.

The long family ties with Kellie Castle seemed broken when his mother died n 1916. As his plans for a new house at Auchentrail had not been realised, *Fig. 83*, he bought Gibliston

247 ABOVE *Midfield, Lasswade, the garden.*   R.S.L.
248 BELOW LEFT *Midfield, from the* S.W.   R.S.L.
249 BELOW RIGHT *Midfield, the drawing room.*

R.S.L.

250–251 *Marchmont, Berwickshire, interior &*
approach facade. R.S.L.

252 ABOVE *The Morton Sundour factory, Carlisle, entrance.* P.M.

253 BELOW *Gibliston, Fife.* C. Lorimer

254 *Balmanno, from the lodge archway.*   P.M.

from a distant cousin, Sir Archibald Campbell, *Pl. 253*. He let the farmland which went with this Georgian house, and in the event his brother Jack (James had died of fever in South Africa) was able to take over Kellie on a new lease, from whom it was to pass to Hew, Robert Lorimer's second son, the sculptor, from whom, with most of its contents, it has finally passed into the hands of the National Trust for Scotland.

Shipping was in high demand in the First World War and the next two jobs of any importance came from Glaswegians in this business. William Burrell sold off most of his fleet for sixteen million pounds and then bought Hutton Castle, an entirely undistinguished house which was a mixture of Baronial work from various periods. However, it sat commandingly on the top of a low hill in Berwickshire around which the River Whiteadder looped, very close to the border, and it set Lorimer dreaming of fine things, *Fig. 103*. He was instructed firmly that building prices were too high to allow more than putting the place in order to receive Burrell's collection, which had already reached fabulous proportions. Any large extensions were to be deferred until after the War and Lorimer was asked only to improve the service quarters and provide a few extra bedrooms. Perhaps Burrell warmed enough to encourage Lorimer to produce a full scheme and for him to attempt to persuade Burrell to accept a scheme for entirely building the castle on the lines of Formakin. This would have been appropriate for Burrell's tapestries, since Formakin had been largely modelled around those of Holm's, but it was acidly rejected.

The alterations were commenced and soon the Clerk of Works had written to complain that Burrell's habit of issuing streams of instructions whenever he inspected the works was leaving men idle while the drawings were adjusted. Extra costs began to be claimed by the contractors and Lorimer replied to Burrell's complaints about them saying, on one occasion, that he had warned him that reducing existing walls by four and a half inches was not only very costly but left precious little to show for the expense. This was how the job went for which Lorimer had been hoping over a period of fifteen years in the belief that it would allow him to do an appropriately grand building for Burrell's magnificent collection. Instead he was abruptly dismissed and when further work was commissioned, it was Reginald Fairlie, one of Lorimer's pupils, who got it. The results were so poor as to suggest that he could not cope with Burrell either.

W. A. Miller was the other Glaswegian in shipping who decided to invest some of his profits in a sixteenth century tower house in Perthshire and then asked Lorimer not only to remodel it but also to lay out the grounds and to furnish the house from top to bottom. Balmanno was a domestic tower protected by a moat, the eastern side of which had already been filled in to provide easier access to the castle. Lorimer proceeded to fill in the rest of the moat to provide space for a series of walled gardens which now surround three sides of the house.

Despite the war the job went ahead quickly. 'Perth 10.10 with Mr. Miller and Lucas inspected castle and water supply and arranged for survey also to make and submit sketch plans for restoration and additions of house and gardens', so reads the entry in Lorimer's

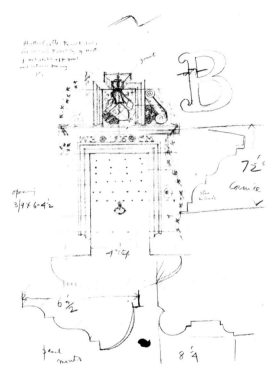

[103] *Hutton Castle, Berwickshire, detail sketch of doorway.* R.C.A.M.

[*104*]–[*105*] *Balmanno*, THIS PAGE W. *elevation,*
OPPOSITE N. *elevation.*   R.C.A.M.

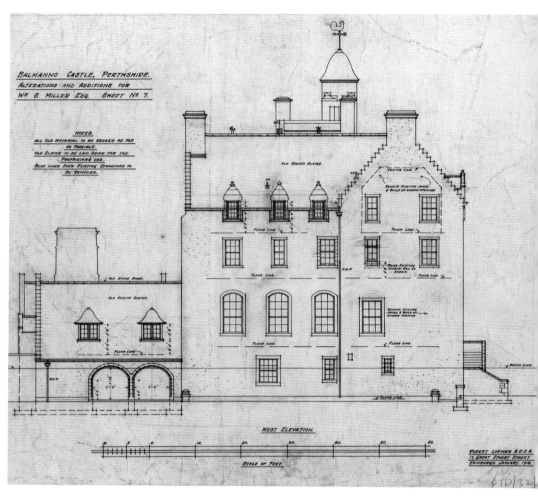

diary for 26 May, 1916. A little over a fortnight later he went over again 'to inspect and go over the sketches on the spot'. General approval of his scheme followed in October and a visit to Earlshall with Miller was arranged. Yet Balmanno was not so romantic as a sixteenth century moated house would suggest and it left Lorimer much to do.

Moats are not so common in Scotland as to be automatically considered a liability. Balmanno, however, sat on the slightest of rises circled by the moat which was fed by a burn coming off the hills to the south. In terms of the wider landscape, the moat can only have sat awkwardly in it, like the artificial canal it was, poised above the long gentle slope down the fields to the north. Furthermore, the filling in of part of the moat may well have rendered much of the remaining water brackish.

The site near Glenfarg is too far inland to incur the direct force of the gales sweeping off the sea yet the flat carse on the edge of which it sits is scoured by every wind that sweeps inland along the Tay, *Pl. 257*, and which makes desirable, even necessary, the high shelter

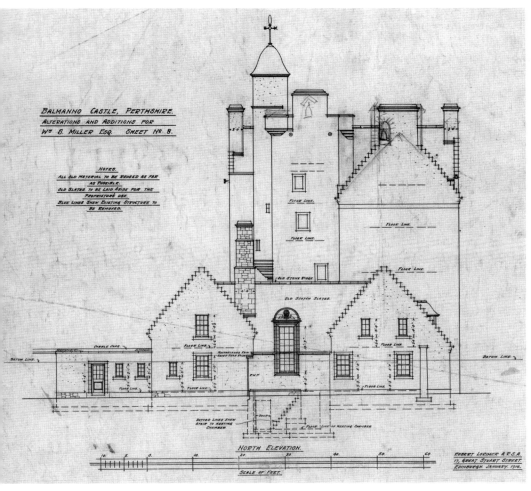

walls which have been used for the group of interlocking courtyard gardens. The house itself was reasonably convenient yet like all tower houses too tall to provide properly serviced groups of rooms on any one floor, and so new service quarters were provided in a low two storey L-shaped wing attached to the castle to form a U in plan lying across the end of the entrance court, *Fig. 104*. This allowed the vaulted undercroft to be used for the dining room, *Pl. 268*, and cloak rooms, *Pl. 269*, and for the other public rooms to be concentrated around the turnpike stair on the first floor.

Beattie and Wilson modelled the ceilings with their customary skill; Hadden the wrought iron work; Scott Morton with a little help from John Watherston and Nathaniel Grieve undertook the woodwork (contracts for £9,149, £1,036 and £1,120 respectively) for which a wide variety of woods – mostly homegrown – were used because supplies were short: walnut in the billiards room, oak wainscotting in the drawing room (formed from the former entrance hall), mahogany in the parlour next to it, and much home oak. The

123

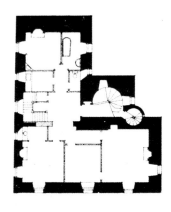

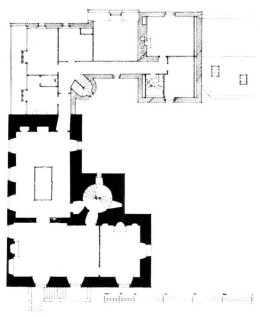

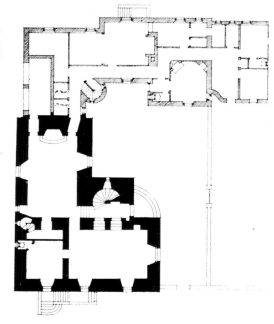

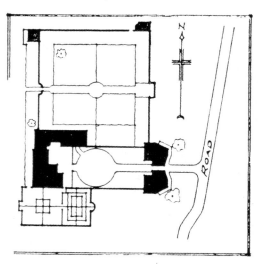

[106] *Balmanno*, FROM THE TOP *second, first &*
ground floor plans, layout of gardens.   C.L.
255 OPPOSITE *Balmanno from the forecourt.*   P.M.

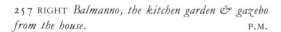

256 LEFT *Balmanno, the gazebo in the walled kitchen garden.* C.L.

257 RIGHT *Balmanno, the kitchen garden & gazebo from the house.* P.M.

258–259 LEFT & RIGHT *Balmanno, from the kitchen garden.* P.M.

260 ABOVE LEFT *Balmanno, the gazebo from the house, looking* N. *from the tower.* P.M.

261 BELOW *Balmanno, the sundial garden on the* S. *from the rose garden.* P.M.

262 ABOVE RIGHT *Balmanno, roof detail.* P.M.

263 OPPOSITE ABOVE LEFT *Balmanno, the kitchen garden from the tower.* P.M.

264 OPPOSITE BELOW *Balmanno, the sundial garden looking towards the rose garden.* P.M.

265 OPPOSITE BELOW *Balmanno, the forecourt from the tower, water-spout bottom right.* P.M.

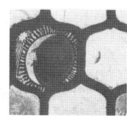

266–271 *Balmanno, details from interior,* ABOVE
LEFT *wash-hand basin recess,* P.M.; BELOW LEFT
antique tiles, P.M.; ABOVE RIGHT *dining room with
Lorimer furniture,* C.L.; BELOW MIDDLE *'through the
looking-glass' on the stairs,* P.M.; BELOW RIGHT *stained
glass in tower by the Camms,* P.M.

bedrooms are finished in elm, ash, pine and larch, the washbasins set in tiled recesses, *Pl. 266*, and the heating radiators also in recesses behind fretted oak covers.

Whytock and Reid supplied all the furniture in this top and bottom job, most of it to designs evolved by Lorimer over the years: long modern lounging chairs, escritoires based on French and Dutch examples, and Sheraton type chairs mingled with curved chairs derived from French examples, to provide a range which might have been amassed in the old castle over the centuries. Antique paintings are worked in as panels over the fireplace in the panelled bedrooms, and for once there were no tapestries to take into consideration.

Balmanno has Lorimer's last and most elaborate compartmented garden, and it has the particular interest that it was Lorimer's favourite commission. Like Earlshall, the drive approaches the side of the house. He straightened out one kink and placed the arched lodge across the drive as it turns towards the castle. Through the dark archway is a long walled forecourt mostly stone-paved but with some grass, with the castle rising sheer from its far end. The colours are stunning, an ivory tower, pewter coloured walls and grass like jade, *Pl. 255*. Across the court, and near the house, is a low balustrade to keep the area adjacent to the house free from vehicles and a small gate gives access to the plain oak front door which is dwarfed by the towering walls above.

A doorway in the flanking wall in the corner to the left leads through to a rose garden sheltered by high walls except on its west: to the left we find roses set snugly in stone-edged borders between paved paths; to our right across the waist-high wall is a sundial garden with low walls on all sides, *Pl. 264*, to give wide views across the fields to the south and west, *Pl. 261*, and an open staircase leads up to the door of the drawing room. Thus the sundial garden is like a lobby set between the house, the rose garden and the spreading lawns along the whole west side of the house; a lobby sparsely planted yet exquisitely proportioned in itself and wholly delightful to linger in before moving on to the richer delights of the rose garden or the stretches on the west which Lorimer has left as open as possible to contrast with the sheltered enclosure of the three other sides.

If we return to the forecourt, we find another door which gives on to the large kitchen garden on the north. It is a large square enclosure with high walls linking the buildings set at each of its corners: south-west the house, south-east the lodge, north-west a gazebo beneath a bell cast roof, *Pl. 256, Fig. 107*, and north-east a large potting house. Across the middle of the garden, and lying east and west, is a wide grass alley between oak trellises (in the French fashion) for espaliered fruit trees. These trellises, as in most other Lorimer gardens, are long since gone but his sketch-books show how much he loved to sketch examples he found in France, at the Luxembourg Gardens and elsewhere at the châteaux.

Balmanno was yet another example of Lorimer taking a Baronial building muddled by the various additions of the seventeenth and eighteenth centuries and tidying it up to something close to its original sixteenth century character, *Figs. 105, 106*. Each feature has been studied closely to assess its effect upon the whole composition and minor adjustments made too numerous to mention other than a few: he put fifteen feet on the staircase tower, he shifted

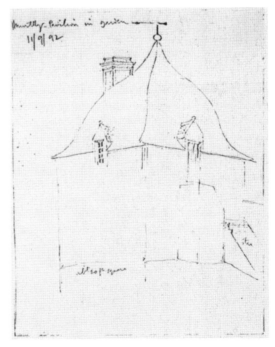

[*107*] *Lorimer's sketch of the pavilion at Murthly, Perthshire.*   R.S.L.

the chimney stack to the centre of the gable, and he lowered the eaves of the south range to push the top windows up into dormers. He then designed a garden of forms which find little place within the Baronial tradition itself, and yet which harmonise perfectly with the building, a harmony achieved primarily by the firmest restraint in proportion, and secondarily through using methods and forms of construction closely following those of the original building.

Balmanno is said to be the only commission Lorimer received in which he would have liked to live himself but then it was like home from home to him, and Kellie is not far off, in Fife. Mrs Miller was not impressed, however, and he was bitter when she refused to move from Pollockshields in Glasgow telling Dods that 'she prefers living in her apartment with red petticoats round all the lights'. Perhaps, though, the middle of the war was not the most comfortable time to be moving to the depths of Perthshire.

Lorimer had been fifty when the war started and Matthew thirty nine. Both had growing families, since Lorimer had married late, and each had four children. The office had been situated on the top floor of a Queen Street house before Lorimer uprooted it to move to much larger and more imposing offices in Great Stuart Street only a short walk from Lorimer's home in Melville Street and one occupied earlier by the leading architect, William Henry Playfair. The office kept going at a much reduced level after Matthew had rejoined the army as a Major in the Royal Engineers' Signals but by 1917 no work whatever was coming in and Lorimer closed the office for nearly a year. When he met Richardson, on leave from the Royal Scots, in Princes Street he declared things were so bad he might have to get rid of Matthew, who was on half pay presumably, 'I strongly advised him against doing such a thing,' Richardson declared roundly.

Lorimer had retained close links with Weaver even though *Country Life* did not publish any of his work during the war itself. When Weaver and Gertrude Jekyll had collaborated on a book *Gardens for Small Country Houses* which was published in 1912, Lorimer had been asked by the R.I.B.A. to review it for the *Journal*. As a friend of both the authors he had been happy to do so because he believed that if any architect may have 'a few stray glimmerings regarding the arrangement of terrace steps', and indeed the long stone staircase which descends the bank from the house at Ardkinglas to the loch had been illustrated by them, yet, as he said, 'When it comes to planting – like the old Scots gardener "he gets fair wandered among a' the names"', and because of this, he found the planting plans by Miss Jekyll of 'extraordinary value'. He had submitted a short article on the Fairy Fountain in Berlin which he had visited in 1913 and Weaver had published it early in 1914.

There was also all too much spare time for other things for Lorimer. Like so many other members of the Art Workers' Guild to which he belonged, Lorimer had become very concerned about design and its role in industry. The 1912 exhibition in London had sold very little and members were increasingly concerned by the success of the *Werkbund* in Germany in promoting an improvement in design and growth of its industry. He had visited Germany in 1913 to see the *Werkbund* exhibition but it was only after the war had begun that a group of manufacturers and designers in Britain got together to present a memorandum to the Board of Trade on the state of design in industry, and among those who signed this memorandum was James Morton. The Design and Industries Association, better known as the D.I.A., was set up a few months later in April 1915, and the first manifesto of aims of this association was to include an article by the principal of the Edinburgh College of Art, Morley Fletcher, as well as one by Lorimer himself. Two other friends of his were also on the Council, F. W. Troup and Weir Schultz (who had changed his name to Schultz Weir at the start of the war), and Lorimer joined them on the Council soon afterwards. An Edinburgh branch of the Association was formed the following year and he chaired its inaugural meeting at which Fletcher spoke on 'Simplicity in design for lettering and colour work'. Lorimer's diaries show that he attended regular meetings. In 1918 he went down to London to give one of the addresses to a meeting held to consider the textile trades, and he remained on the Council until 1926.

Supreme individualist though he was, Lorimer could no more than any other architect set aside the technical problems which arise in the day-to-day contact with building. He had seen at first-hand the Germanic thoroughness with which Muthesius had approached his study of British architecture some fifteen years earlier and he told the Association of it. It was clear to him from his visits that 'In Germany the possibilities and limitations of the machine have been welcomed instead of being regarded as a hindrance.' Neither he (nor Gropius and le Corbusier later) foresaw the paralysis in variety to which the economics of flow production would lead, despite Morris's prophecies. Lorimer cheerfully cited Wertheim's store in Berlin as an example of good modern design and as Morton's factory showed, he could turn out a functional yet pleasing design when required. If other additions to the Esk Mill in Musselburgh in 1917 included a Baronial turret and wrought iron gates with a highly ornamental overthrow, he was not altogether out of character in an organisation like the D.I.A. which could proclaim in 1918 that 'the last thing we should father is this idea of standardisation.'

One standard design which he did make was for a W.C. suite carried out in collaboration with members of the British Medical Association. It was put into production by Messrs Shanks of Barrhead, and was called the Remirol, which is Lorimer backwards, *Fig. 108*. It was slightly lower than others made at the time and he got Shanks also to develop a porcelain cleaner as those already on the market were too abrasive. Years later he entered a competition for a new telephone box for the G.P.O. and was disgusted that Gilbert Scott won it, *Fig. 109*.

Affairs were still very slack in 1916 when he helped organise a loan exhibition of antiques at the New Gallery in Edinburgh in aid of the Edenhall Hostel for limbless soldiers and sailors. Burrell and Holms contributed. He filled in time also by writing an article on stained glass, and also one on the home production of timber, and he occupied himself with plans for remodelling Gibliston after the war. He wrote to Dods as the war entered its closing stage to tell him how he had been 'asked rather suddenly to take up the job of principal

[*108*] *'Remirol' W.C. suite.* *shanks.*

Shanks' "Remirol" Washdown Closet

Section

Plan

architect to the Imperial War Graves Commission' for Italy and Egypt.[1] Had a letter about it fr[om] Sir F. Kenyon of the British Museum and then was summoned to London by wire to a meeting and it was fixed up.' This was probably on the recommendation of Lutyens, a friend of his for more than twenty years, and so a chapter of Lorimer's life began which was to take him as an official architect on eleven tours of duty across Europe and around the Middle East, in which he travelled tens of thousands of miles as he worked on the design and layout of more than thirty three British war cemeteries.

Kenyon's letter had stressed the need for an immediate start to the work. Seven hundred people were already engaged on the huge task of locating the graves and registering the names of a million men who had mostly been buried where they fell, and Kenyon and his committee were in the process of compiling a report setting out a design policy. When Lorimer was asked how soon he could begin, he replied 'a week' and he left for Italy seven days later and was already at work there when his post was officially confirmed. He was making a whirlwind tour of inspection as he told Dods, 'I don't believe anyone has seen so much of Italy in fourteen days as I have.' He was escorted everywhere by various technical advisors and they visited 'a number of pathetic little cemeteries with their rows of wooden crosses. This was right up close to the front-line and shell fire even going over our heads at one place. They made us wear tin hats.' Thus in thirteen days constantly on the move he had spent seven days working, four and a half days sightseeing in Genoa, Brescia and Rome, and a day and a half on long journeys.

The next three days were spent in clearing up his notes and working out sketch designs for the cemeteries he had been to, which he left 'to these boys on the spot to work out', and he returned through London where he reported to Kenyon at the close of a tour of about five thousand miles, and noted that in 'two to three weeks probably start for Egypt on the same errand'.

A few weeks later he found himself in Egypt after 'a most pleasant voyage, never rough enough to be disagreeable and we were at a table with old Lord Kitchener, brother of the great man, and a friend of his, Napier, and we found we had many mutual friends.' They landed at Port Said and Lorimer went on to Alexandria, from where he wrote to his wife telling her how he talked at dinner to a nice looking youth at the next table, who was dining alone, and we had a delightful talk, [he was] 'Australian but had done six years [of the] medical course in Edinburgh and loved it and had been captured doing medical work in Turkey and been $2\frac{1}{2}$ years a prisoner of war and [was] now on his way home – I was so glad I talked to him, I'm getting over my horrible shyness that's been such a bug-bear to me all my life', a shyness so many people had misread as aloofness or even arrogance. He went on to Cairo where he was put up at Shepherd's Hotel and taken under the wing of Major, the Honourable Percy Thesiger. Life was much more comfortable for him in Egypt which was a base area, than in Italy which had been a theatre of war. At Christmas he motored to Bethlehem where he stayed in a monastery for several days before he returned to Egypt for another ten days' work interspersed with visits to galleries, museums and shops. He

[109] *Design for a telephone box.*   S.R.M.

completed designs for ten cemeteries which were much larger than those in Italy. They were mostly near towns which had raised all sorts of extra administrative problems, and before leaving he was required to submit his report in person since Egypt had its own War Graves Committee.

He took ship for Macedonia where he spent a further seventeen days touring cemeteries and making designs. At this time not all the cemeteries to be developed had been decided and some he worked on were subsequently closed and their graves transferred. He wrote to his wife that he would be 'content with doing samples of the cemeteries here if that will save some time', but he was able to delegate the working up of his sketch designs to a 'lance corporal ARIBA who I've appointed my deputy . . . he's to be promoted captain for this job which means a rise fr[om] 1/3d a day to £300 a year', and Lorimer arrived back in London after nine and a half weeks away.

Twenty months were to pass before his next overseas tour which took place late in 1920. Meanwhile, he had been asked if he would advise on the cemeteries in Britain where 'there would be some 100 to 150 cases where your advice either in the details or in an advisory manner may be required.' The work involved siting the War Cross, providing inscriptions where needed and generally advising on landscaping and layout, and he accepted this appointment. Further tours of duty in Italy and France took place in 1921, in Egypt and Greece in 1922 when he noted '15 nights in a steamer only 5/- per day allowed in expenses'. He began his return by train after spending five hectic weeks away. He was asked on his return if he would advise also on the cemeteries in Germany, and late in 1922 he began yet another tour of inspection there. Still further tours followed and the work continued for nearly a decade, during which time a steady stream of drawings arrived at the office in Edinburgh, to be opened up, pored over, approved or corrected, and parcelled for their return.

The interior refurbishing of Dunrobin Castle began in 1919. Lorimer expected the work to finish by June next year and he told Dods that the cost would be 'about 50 thou, and I'm getting 10 per c[ent] on this contract and Tulloch Castle restoration for Vickers will cost 25 if it goes on, and another job for one of the Nobles 15000'. This was internal woodwork for Glendoe, a house which overlooks Loch Ness. The work at Tulloch was also mainly internal. He spoke also of two jobs in England at 'twenty thou[sand] a piece. Again if, in fact its the if, all the time, but I think I see bread and butter for another year ahead.' The jobs in England took several years to complete and were probably Hurworth Hall near Darlington and Balls Park, Hertfordshire, a brick house in the Inigo Jones style to which he added a wing in matching style. The dining room had dark blue painted walls and a white coffered ceiling with simple low relief plaques of animals planted at intervals in which Hussey saw Swedish influence.

The interior work at Dunrobin was typical of Lorimer. He fitted up the library in his Georgian manner, finished in home grown sycamore with a plain coved plaster ceiling and fitted bookshelves. Cedar and larch were used for the Duke of Sutherland's private suite.

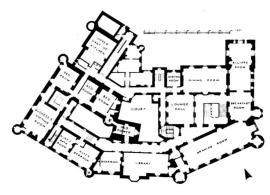

[110] *Dunrobin Castle, Sutherland, plan.*   C.L.

The dining room was panelled in Scotch oak, with a plaster ceiling modelled by Sam Wilson, divided into deep coffers by heavy beams covered with freely worked patterns of vines. No cornice or plaster frieze was incorporated and, instead, a line of Italian paintings was worked in above the panelling and below the ceiling, on all the walls but the window wall. The paintings of mythical figures grouped against almost black backgrounds draw the eye inexorably, before they drop to the portraits hung on the wall below, to produce a slight clash of scale. Hussey saw this as another of Lorimer's failures to deal properly with the subtleties of classical design but it is just as likely that having been asked to incorporate them he could find no better way.

The drawing room showed no such disunity, *Pls. 273, 274.* This magnificent white painted apartment is seventy-two feet long by twenty five feet wide and is like a long gallery lit by six large windows looking down upon the formal gardens set south and at the foot of the steep bluff on which this house sits. The long walls of this room end in a taper where it meets the dining room at an angle and is yet another example of Lorimer's skilful weaving of formal elements within an irregular grouping.

The decor was also worked around an imposing array of art objects. Two similar classical fireplaces, triangular in plan for burning logs, with surrounds of Hopton wood stone with green marble inlays are surmounted by Venetian paintings. The fireplace near the centre of the back wall was flanked by two large Brussels tapestries in a group which created a centre of balance between the differently treated ends of the room. The other fireplace, on the west, was flanked by arched openings, one a door and the other with shelves for china, whereas the east end of the room beyond the splayed walls is reduced to a deep square bay with a window looking over the sea. This lack of symmetry may have prevented a ceiling treatment divided into regular bays, and Lorimer has adopted waving lines of curved ribs laced together to Jacobean effect. The mouldings are shallower than in the dining room, more delicate in effect, and sit above a delicately moulded plaster frieze.

The success of the drawing room more than counter-balances the imperfections of the dining room and it corresponds closely enough to Lorimer's own prescription made eighteen years earlier in a letter to Dods, to suggest that it closely follows his own preferences. He had told Dods that 'a drawing room should be above all things a place where you can have a pleasant time, and should have a *number* of large comfortable sofas, and a stuffed armchair or two, *all* those things should be covered with strong washable material preferably striped. The things should be of the simplest form, and should have stretched across the back of them tight fitting muslin covers either plain or powdered, or better still plain with a monogram in white. The chair coverings should be *warm* in colour and the curtains the same and the walls and cornice entirely white painted. A simple chimney piece with a *large* picture, in a very small gilt frame being in a panel prepared for it, and from the shelf to the bottom picture about eighteen inches plain as background. For some garnish of china some good big things, and simple. There should be no china, and very few nick knacks lying about, just one or two of the real joy for ever sort. Then if there's to be china, let it be a mass of it in a recess in the wall with shaped shelves. Still life or decorative pictures hanging in the panels above the doors into the room and some needle pictures and other choice things, but not much on the walls; lots of books but not lying on tables, if a show table is required let it be the cabriole big bellied frieze Queen Anne type with glass in top only. In this the Gothic libraries will be safe from the well meaning but sometimes fatal flick of the domestic duster. The chairs, other than those described above, should be low in the seat and *quite light* so that you can lift them about with one finger, and people forming themselves into *groups* at the various sofas.'

Behind this list lie reasons of choice based on scale as well as on comfort, nor has the manipulation of light been forgotten: 'The flood of light into the room should be softened by white muslin curtains hanging quite straight and these and the before mentioned curtains should both come out of a curtain box so that the rods are not visible to the nude eye.' Finally he takes up the floor and its requirements: it should be made of 'random oak boards and either a thick thing with no pattern on top or simply some Eastern rugs. The hearth should be of marble *very large* and flush with the floor. The fender a little hinged steel thing set on the marble', and he summed up finally by saying 'the room should really look as if it was used, and everything in it should look just right, but there should be no feeling of the curiosity shop, in fact perfect fitness.'

Lorimer had been presented with an inscribed silver cigar box by the Duke at the completion of the works, during which time he had shown a sure and subtle touch as he dealt with all the complications of a conglomerate building and its numerous works of art. The first spate of alterations to country houses which followed the end of the war ended and here was a pause until 1925, after which in the last four years of his practice he was called on to renovate Craigiehall near Cramond (by James Morton), *Pl. 276*, as well as to Touch near Stirling for the Buchanans, for which Ian Mackenzie remembers he insisted upon oil-fired central heating saying 'We must move with the times.' Place next to the Abbey in Paisley, *Fig. 121*, and to build extensions to Glencruitten near Oban and Braidwood near Lanark.

Antique tile.

The war had left much distress and unemployment and the inequalities implicit in the scale of the houses on which Lorimer had mostly worked were increasingly questioned. Almost no new country houses were to be built after the war and none were designed by Lorimer. In Europe a modern style consciously emulating the sleek appearance of machines was arising. It was international in its character and in the hands of the second and subsequent generation of architects anonymous in appearance. Britain was slow to adopt it. The Empire Exhibition staged at Wembley in 1926, for which Weaver was director of the U.K. Exhibition, included photographs contributed by Percy Nobbs from Canada, as well as others on behalf of the late R. S. Dods from Australia, and of Lorimer's Thistle Chapel and furniture.

By this time Lorimer's architecture, orientated as it was to the country and the individual, seemed anachronistic by the standards of the emerging new style which was directed towards towns and the masses. No matter that it was to fail in most of its high hopes for

rebuilding cities on Utopian lines, it came to colour the views of almost every critic. By 196
T. W. West put the widely held view that, 'The work of architects like Lorimer represent th
end of a defunct tradition that few would wish to revive now that a more genuin
understanding of architecture has made it clear that each age in the past has built mainly i
the style appropriate to its time.' Such simplistic views have since lost favour for a numbe
of reasons without any clear alternative views emerging.

The technical assumptions of the international style have proved equally misplaced. Th
design of the smaller houses remained entirely a matter of appearance and yet all traditiona
building methods were declared obsolete and have been discarded in favour of the method
which – it was believed – would provide houses in millions, would be disposable and almos
as cheap as nappies. The widespread legacy of crumbling or even tumbling buildings which
has resulted have sent maintenance costs sky-high, while traditionally built houses like
Tuethur in Carlisle 1923 – so named at Lorimer's suggestion because it provided mid-week
accommodation for James Morton between long weekends elsewhere – has entered its
second half century as sound as ever and with reasonable care good for another couple o
centuries. Indeed it seems that most of the crafts of building were killed off just as
diminishing resources had come to make nonsense of the wasteful methods on which large
scale industry so much relies.

Antique tile.

272 ABOVE LEFT *Dunrobin, exterior.*   C.L.
273 BELOW *Dunrobin, the drawing room.*   C.L.
274 ABOVE RIGHT *Dunrobin, cast plasterwork for recess.*   R.S.L.

275 ABOVE LEFT *R. S. Dods, Lorimer's closest confidant.* E.F.

276 BELOW LEFT *Craigiehall, Barnton, Edinburgh, new bay window at left.* J. MORTON

277 ABOVE RIGHT *Niederzwherhen War Cemetery, Germany.* C.W.G.C.

278 BELOW MIDDLE *Cavaletto War Cemetery, the Asiago plateau, Italy.* C.W.G.C.

279 BELOW RIGHT *Boscon War Cemetery, the Asiago plateau, Italy.* C.W.G.C.

280 ABOVE *Doiran War Cemetery, Macedonia, Greece.* C.W.G.C.
281 BELOW LEFT *Sarigol War Cemetery, Macedonia, Greece.* C.W.G.C.
282 BELOW RIGHT *Lahana War Cemetery, Macedonia, Greece.* C.W.G.C.

283 *Niederzwherhen War Cemetery, Germany.*

C.W.G.C.

8

A Decade of Memorials

The war years had been very thin for Lorimer and when Dods, *Pl. 275*, wrote to commiserate with him, after hostilities had ended, he wrote back to say, 'You've been looking over the *C[ountry] L[ife* magazine] and the enormous number of places for sale, and said to yourself "What will poor Robin do then poor thing." Well, its a rummy time, we seem to live from day to day, from hand to mouth, but I and Matthew and three draughtsmen and five apprentices and a typist seem to be busy all the time. How much of it will really come off I don't know.'

The office was at work on improvements to a number of houses, an extra attic floor was being hurriedly added to a University building at 10 George Square in Edinburgh made up of 'a lot of standards and felt and muck', and he spoke of the 'endless flood of memorials of all shapes, sizes and costs' which was dominating his practice. Indeed he was to exhibit almost nothing else at the R.S.A. from 1920 to 1926. One single account book includes one hundred and sixty seven commissions for them, and it was prophetic of the way Lorimer's practice would be carried that Weaver should have included far more designs by Lorimer in his book on memorials published in 1916 than by any other architect.

The dead from every village and town had been buried in more than fifteen thousand cemeteries. Loretto was among the schools which commissioned Lorimer to design a memorial to its former pupils struck down in their youth and he designed twenty individual memorials to them as well, *Pl. 287*. Schools in England included Westminster, Eton, Stonyhurst and Rossall, *Figs, 111, 112, Pl. 296, 297*, (for which Lutyens recommended him) and he unsuccessfully entered the competition for one at Harrow. The University of Edinburgh installed its memorial to his design in Playfair's Quadrangle, and he was asked to design memorials for many of the mansions he had worked on including Ardkinglas, Balcarres, Dunrobin, Minto and Wemyss Castle. He designed memorials for the Border Regiment and for the Sixteenth Royal Scots, as well as simple crosses for villages scattered across Scotland. Paisley erected an equestrian statue as its memorial which he, with Mrs Meredith Williams, won in competition from over two hundred other entrants. Some memorials took the form of stained glass windows or wrought iron gates, the Burgh of Galashiels built offices as a memorial, *Pl. 290*, and in Perth the ancient Church of St John's was restored by him as the county's memorial, *Pls. 286, 288, Fig. 122*.

As Lorimer and his staff struggled with the vast task, the work of the overseas war cemeteries continued, including a number which were only abandoned at the design stage. Large stone monuments to his design were erected at Queenstown in South Africa, *Pl. 300*,

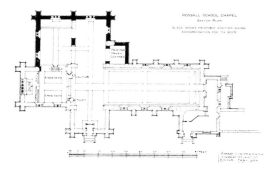

[*111*]–[*112*] *Rossall School Memorial Chapel (extension)*, ABOVE *plan;* BELOW *interior.*   O.D.

Doiran in Northern Greece, and Chatham, Portsmouth and Plymouth for naval memorials to those who had lost their lives around Britain's coasts. Grave plots for the war dead in no less than one hundred and eighty seven cemeteries throughout the United Kingdom were laid out to his directions. Even the last major work for which he is mostly remembered was to be the memorial in Edinburgh Castle.

Dods, like Lorimer, had written an article laying out his views on how the dead should be commemorated but his health had become so poor that he was little involved in such design and was soon to die. Voices were not lacking in England or Scotland to decry the money and effort being put into memorials and to urge that it be directed rather to housing and hospitals for those who had survived. Some such building was done, and maybe not enough, but Lorimer was not being asked how to spend the money for Scotland's National War Memorial but what architectural form the Memorial should take. It has become no easier to judge this issue with the passing of time, yet the partisan and unfair attacks on Lorimer continue as when Christopher Harvie, writing on *Scotland and Nationalism* in 1977, contemptuously dismissed Lorimer for having merely 'built meticulous reconstructions of seventeenth century castles for millionaires', apparently without realising how much other work Lorimer has done. If Socialism was one of the few things on which Lorimer did not agree upon with William Morris, it was because he found that, despite all its local vagaries, its egalitarian creed is international in its inspiration whereas he himself was not only deeply individualist, he was also a nationalist culturally.

Robin Dods was failing in health and Lorimer, in one of his last letters to him, was able to write that he was doing 'a power of work these days in the house and what a mercy the phone is on these occasions, and the fact that one's house is near the office, as we're really very busy and understaffed at present. I've been approached – re the Scottish Nat[ional] War Memorial Scheme on the Castle and have been making a report and sketch plans'. Six architects had been invited to submit work from which Lorimer had been chosen to act for the nation. The project had begun as a Scottish reaction against Lord Mond's proposal for an all-British memorial in Hyde Park, and the Duke of Atholl had protested that 'He' [Lord Mond] 'had not the right to speak for the Scottish nation . . . if the Scottish nation wanted a memorial they would put it up with their own hands in their own country, and with their own money'. The General Officer Commanding in Scotland sent out a memorandum on the matter to all Scottish forces which urged, 'No nation in the wide world has in its capital a finer and more natural monument of war than Edinburgh's Castle', and made the plea for a memorial chapel to be set within it.

A year later the Secretary of State appointed a committee of twenty eight to consider the whole matter, quite a few of whom were very well known to Lorimer. He wrote to Dods, 'The *castle scheme*, you'll twig from my report what I'm after. The last few days have roughed it all out $\frac{1}{2}''$ – and have now a man putting it down to $\frac{1}{8}''$ – Atholl – chairman of the show – had pot luck with me here one night and stayed till 12 going over my report and discussing procedure and both the sec'r'y and the Under Secretary for Scotland have had it all explained o them by me – and seem to like it, oh! it will be fine if it comes off.'

The committee's deliberations were published in 1919 as command paper 279, and Lorimer's own report was attached as an appendix. He proposed that Crown Square, which was already enclosed on three sides by the old palace and banqueting hall, should have the barrack block to its north replaced by a low but sturdy range of cloisters, on the back wall of which individual memorials might be set to 'specially distinguished' soldiers and sailors. A short corridor from the middle would connect a shrine to be set father north on the highest point of Castle Rock, like an octagonal chapter house with tall buttresses and its roof hidden by the parapet, *Fig. 125*. J. J. Burnett, who was on the committee, favoured the accentuation of the mass at the top of the rock because too many lofty erections had been reared on the lower ledges of the rock and it would offer 'a return to historical correctness', *Pl. 284*. However, dissent on this had appeared and Lorimer commented in his report how 'an erroneous idea appears to have got abroad that the proposal of your committee was to erect on the apex of the rock a commanding structure in the form of a church or chapel which would . . . be a conspicuous feature' whereas it seemed 'what is wanted is a building which will not materially alter the familiar silhouette'. The design was submitted to the building committee whose main task had become the raising of funds, and Lorimer thought 'it seemed to meet with entire approval'. No less than five advisory panels were concerned between whom affairs were to move very slowly.

Lorimer retained his links with London even if his practice still remained firmly rooted in Scotland. The Design Industries Association and his war cemetery work took him to London regularly, he had been exhibiting at the Arts and Crafts Exhibitions there for a quarter of a century and at the R.A. for more than ten years when, in the middle of 1920, he wrote to Dods telling him that 'for some reason that *I* can't account for they're electing me A.R.A., you c[oul]d have knocked me down with a feather – easy. Got home late to dinner one night about the 23rd April and the servant handed me a wire that had been 'phoned through, "Warmest congratulations on your election as A.R.A. this afternoon. *D. Y. Cameron*". I happened to be going to London that night, so saw Cameron next day, and he told me Burnett [J. J.] was runner up with "Dawber", and one or two other following on with a few votes each. It's the first time a *non-resident* Scotchman has ever been elected.'

As Lorimer had a busy week ahead of him he rang Weaver before he left London and asked him if he thought it would matter if he did not attend the banquet and found' he took the view that as they'd screwed themselves up to do this very unusual thing, of electing a non-resident Scotsman, that it would be discourteous not to go, so I bundled myself into the train again on Friday night, put on my best bib and tucker and went to the banquet and was received by your old friend Webb' (Dods had worked for Aston Webb before returning to Australia). Lorimer found Webb no orator but a very good chairman. 'I ought to have gone up 10 days ago', he continued, 'to get my diploma and sign the roll – but wired at the last I couldn't and have now been summoned for 10 June.' He reminded Dods of the day when a weekend in London cost 32/8d and complained that with sleepers etc costing £10 a weekend

[113] *Sketch for bronze panel by Maurice Meredith Williams.*   R.C.A.M.

cost 'over £20 *every* time', and this 'wretched romp will have cost me about £50. I suppos[e]
subconsciously it does one good professionally, but "a hae me doots".'

He was working, he told Dods, on a memorial in Carlisle that was to have been [a]
competition but that the meeting of 'all the Carlisle architects' called to advise on i[t]
'unanimously agreed to recommend that I s[houl]d be employed. Wasn't that pretty good fo[r]
a body of architects. So I'm struggling over the design for a 40 [feet] high cenotaph in a park[.]
Price £5000; little W.M.s seem still to come in at about the rate of two a week – they ar[e]
always difficult to design, and this cenotaph business is a teaser. . . . How I wish you were a[t]
my elbow to give me some tips with your ready wit.'

A number of opponents of the Scottish National War Memorial scheme had emerged. Si[r]
Herbert Maxwell a longstanding friend of Lorimer's resigned from the committee because
he had come to feel that it was inappropriate to put so much money into a 'masonr[y]
memorial', and when Lord Rosebery wrote a letter to the press likening Lorimer's design t[o]
a 'jelly mould' he provided a slogan around which opposition to the scheme rallied.

The main committee was not convened between 1919 and 1923 but late in 1920 th[e]
building sub-committee substituted an enclosed gallery for the open cloister as a place t[o]
house the regimental memorials. One of the panels with a say on the design was the Ancient
Monuments Board of which Lorimer was himself a member. However, James Richardson,
Inspector of Ancient Monuments, was also a member and he was Lorimer's greatest foe. It
had begun from a clash of two fiery temperaments. Richardson was still incensed sixty five
years later as he told me how, after joining Lorimer in the early years of this century as an
improver, he had been set to draw a perspective of a house which he set up precisely and
correctly. Then Lorimer came along and told him it would put the clients off because it
looked too high and that he was to lower the ridge line of the roof. Richardson also had the
archaeologist's strict regard for historical fact and he found Lorimer too prone to
'improving' old buildings. When he and Lorimer came to face each other at the Ancient
Monuments Board he challenged, and proved, that Lorimer's perspectives of the Scottish
National Memorial diminished the true height of the shrine and its effect on the skyline, and
finally in November 1922 he succeeded in getting the Office of Works to erect a full size
model of the memorial made of wood and canvas. A storm of protest followed, and
although the model was torn to shreds within days by a westerly gale, the trickle of
protesting letters became a flood. Lorimer wrote back claiming that this 'nightmare
erection' had given no 'adequate idea of the silhouette . . . or of its light shade and colour'.

The damage had been done and the opposition had become so strong and vociferous as to
make likely the abandonment of the scheme. Early in 1923 the Duke of Atholl met the
Cockburn Association[1] which seemed set to condemn the scheme out of hand but he met
their criticisms by saying how unfortunate it was to be criticising a scheme that was not only
obsolete but which had never been put to the committee. He disclosed that Lorimer was at
work on a third scheme to convert the existing barrack building across the north side of
Crown Square to which a Gothic apse would be added on its north side. The motion of

ensure which had been prepared was withdrawn as it was seen to have become 'perfectly meaningless.'

Throughout the long controversy Lorimer was still at work on innumerable domestic alterations, and also at work on the war cemeteries which had to be conducted within complex and different administrative arrangements of each of the four overseas countries for which he was responsible. He visited the Egyptian cemeteries again in 1922. He had spent much of this time on his first visit in the company of Arthur Hill, the horticultural adviser from Kew, with whom he had got on very well finding him a 'delightful enthusiast'. They had visited the Botanical Gardens together and Lorimer had been shown 'the forbidden fruit that notty Eve gave to Adam, and I can't blame the poor blighter for accepting it'. The Kenyon Report had suggested that the 'main features of each cemetery will be given by the trees or shrubs planted in it', and Lorimer, with Hill, drew up long lists of suitable plants for his purpose, although where the cemeteries were part of an existing civil cemetery, or an extension to one, existing planting might also have to be incorporated.

The Kenyon Report of 1918 for the Imperial War Graves Commission had laid down guidelines for laying out the cemeteries for all the principal architects entrusted with their design, with an overall intention of creating a sense of unity of expression in all of them. Two central monuments were to be incorporated in each cemetery wherever possible. Sir Edwin Lutyens had suggested a large War Stone twelve feet long and it was accepted as a kind of altar to be put on the east of each cemetery with the graves before it facing east 'as the army faces now'. However a cross, as a symbol of self-sacrifice, was felt to be indispensable also, but that the size, pattern, and position be left to the designer for each cemetery. After Sir Reginald Blomfield had designed a particularly fine cross for this purpose, it was adopted as a standard design and made in four sizes to suit the different scale to be found in cemeteries of varying sizes, and regulations were drawn up to govern the use of them as well as the War Stone.

The very number of headstones in each cemetery, all repeating a standard design (there were eight and a half thousand in the ten Egyptian cemeteries) made a regular arrangement essential, and it followed that such symbolic features as the Cross of Sacrifice and the War Stone had then to be placed in a clear formal arrangement with them. Lorimer had placed these features on a central axis at Suez and Cairo, terminated by the Registry House built of stone on simple classical lines. Cypresses and a great profusion of shrubs were planted and at Port Said the Registry House, which is also the gate house, was flanked by tall palm trees planted long before Lorimer settled on the layout.

Lorimer's letters and notes reveal his great interest in the arts of Egypt and his enjoyment of the social scene, but he said little on the landscape. He went on to Macedonia and although travelling was arduous in its wild uplands he was more at home there. Many of the seventeen sites were far from human habitation and this allowed him an extra freedom in design. The sites were larger than required for the grave plots alone and this provided the opportunity to shape the perimeter walls freely by setting them back from the boundaries of

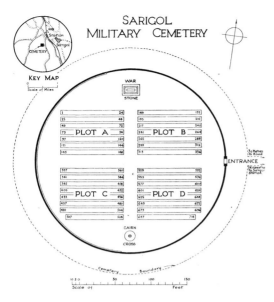

SARIGOL
MILITARY CEMETERY

[114] *Sarigol War Cemetery, Greece, plan.* C.W.G.C.

[115] *Struma War Cemetery, Greece, plan.*

C.W.G.C.

STRUMA
MILITARY
CEMETERY

KEY MAP

the site where it seemed to suit the surroundings. There were few craftsmen, and those not very skilled, and this set other limits on the designs. For these reasons, as well as because many of the cemeteries were in Muslim areas, the cross was omitted and conical stone cairn built in its place with a small cross on top. Eight sites were abandoned.

The cemetery at Sarigol sat amid flatly rolling uplands; they were deserted, extending as far as the eye could see, and were virtually treeless, *P. 281.* The six hundred and eighty eight graves were arranged four square with cross paths and were loosely surrounded by a waist high wall circular in plan, *Fig. 114.* The entrance gate is to the side nearest to the road and leads to the middle of the main path, the cairn is at one end of it and to the west, the altar stone on the right (and at the other end) to the east. A generous belt of cypress trees which follows the perimeter grew up into a tall screen within which the graves lie beneath more delicate flowering trees.

At Karasouli where the plot slopes up the hill from the road the fourteen hundred graves are enclosed by a rectangular wall. The gateway is at the lower end and a central path leads up to the cairn at the top. There is no altar stone. Kirechkoi in a similar situation and with about half the number of graves, is rectangular but placed along the slope, and the central path is extended up the hill into a large bay in the east wall and past the War Stone up to the great Cross of Sacrifice. The bay looks as though it were a late addition after more graves had been transferred from other sites.

Struma, with nine hundred graves, follows the dispositions of Karasouli except that a small bay has been projected from a side wall to house the War Stone, *Fig. 115,* whereas at Mikra the entrance is on the side and the central axis is terminated by the War Stone and Cross of Sacrifice at either end, each set out in bays in the boundary wall. The desolation of these graves, left on sites so lonely and so far from home, is felt less at Lahana, another rectangular cemetery, set within sight of the village, *Pl. 282.* The only approach is by a footpath which diagonally climbs the low rise, on which it sits like a small acropolis, to arrive at the gateway near the middle of one of its long sides, *Fig. 116.* The visitor is thus brought in behind the cairn which is slightly raised up in an apse projecting towards the path but a little farther along the wall to the right, whereas the War Stone on the other side of the cemetery and lower down remains out of sight until the gateway is reached. In this way the features of the cemetery come into view one after the other, and even the very long rows of graves are not over emphatic since they are marked only by the low rectangular blocks.

The elements of these simple cemeteries were few but a great variety of effect from the formal and military, to the informal and human, has been introduced both by their differing positions of access, and by the direction of slopes and the arrangement of the graves themselves, which in some cemeteries had been decided before the design was begun. An idea which had been voiced, that the lines of headstones would carry on 'the military idea', had the drawback that large groups of graves also produced diagonal lines of headstones with a restless effect. The reduction of this diagonality by using Hopton wood panels inset in concrete blocks as grave markers can be seen at Doiran, *Pl. 280.* Hussey said that they vere used to avoid headstones being 'broken off and used by the peasants for walls of their pigstyes', and the concrete blocks were keyed to continuous beam foundations of concrete.

All the cemeteries were richly planted and many grew up to look like thick and secret coppices from outside. The Doiran site comprised a whole hill top of forty acres of which Lorimer reported that it overlooked 'the blue expanse of Lake Doiran facing La Couronne and the Belashitza range of mountains standing purple against the sky'. A large stone pylon was erected outside the cemetery on this picturesque site, built of dressed, but roughly finished stone, with a lion sculpted in white pentelicon marble. Lorimer had visited the 'historic mountains whence the great blocks used in the construction of the temple of Zeus and the Acropolis buildings were obtained', and had found that the concessionaire for the quarrying was an Aberdonian.

He paid his third visit to the Italian cemeteries in 1923. The number of graves for each cemetery had been mainly an administrative matter and the seven hundred and fifty graves on the Alpino plateau of the Asiago could have been concentrated at one site. Five sites had been chosen, however, each to contain between one hundred and one hundred and eighty graves, and all were set amid wooded mountainous surroundings reached by such primitive tracks that Blomfield's cross was found to be too fragile to be transported across them and the War Stone too heavy. The original procedure was reverted to, therefore, and Lorimer was allowed instead, to build up crosses in rough masonry blocks with something of the ruggedness of Celtic granite crosses, which he has set in apses in the boundary walls, and the War Stone has been omitted altogether. The result is a group of woodland cemeteries freely shaped like those in Macedonia, and small enough in scale to be like village graveyards, though not quite so informal in their effect.

The gateway at Boscon, *Pl. 279*, a rectangular enclosure with the corners rounded, was placed in the middle of one of the long walls and opposite the Cross of Sacrifice which sets up an axis between them which is obstructed by the lines of headstones which face the cross but are carried right across the entrance. Barenthal, similarly, is in a narrow valley bottom on a wider, shallower plot but it has been given a broad grass walk which follows the axis between gate and cross. The cemetery at Granezza, which is set back from the road on a grassy slope, is square in plan with an apse in all four sides, and it follows Barenthal in having a central walk between gate and cross. Magnaboschi, however, which is almost square in plan has no central walk, *Fig. 117*, yet the entrance by being brought forward into an apse allows space for the sideways displacement of the paths without the feeling of being crowded by the graves. The last of the Asiago cemeteries is Cavaletto, another cemetery which is square in plan with apses in all four wall, *Fig. 118*, and set on a flat site in a much broader valley. The gateway, unlike those of the other four cemeteries, is set at the side which leads in at right angles to the lines of headstones which stand facing right to the cross in an apse on that side. The mass of headstones does not dominate the entrance and the effect is more like entering the south door of a church with a congregation facing the altar, *Pl. 278*.

The Director of the Commission later called this group of cemeteries 'as impressive and

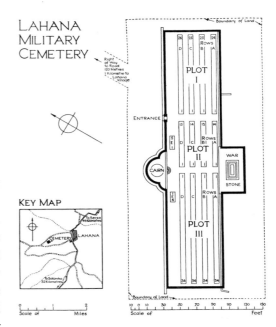

[*116*] *Lahana War Cemetery, Greece, plan.* C.W.G.C.
[*117*] *Magnaboschi War Cemetery, Italy, plan.* C.W.G.C.

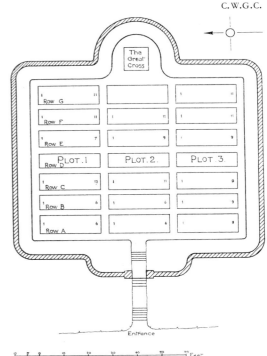

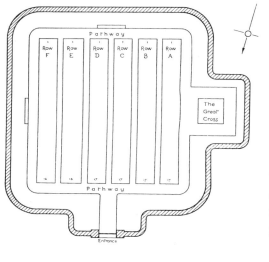

[118] *Cavaletto War Cemetery, Italy, plan.*
C.W.G.C.

[119] *Montecchio War Cemetery, Italy, sketch of site.*
R.S.L.

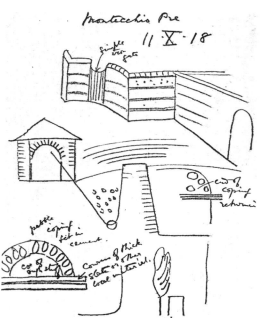

artistically perfect as anything in the world', and King George and Queen Mary arranged to come to open them officially. Lorimer went out to Italy with his wife, a little beforehand, to see that all was ready. He started at Montechio, a line of communication cemetery in the plain of Lombardy. His earlier survey note showed him disposing the features of this cemetery within the site limitations and scenic possibilities, *Fig. 119*. 'A charming site on slope in orchard, view over Venezia and winding river Astico, opportunity for central walk and stone at end, cross at top of hill', and he had laid out the simple gateway and path to lead through the graves arranged in tiers up the slope to a high terrace wall over which the cross rose against a background of vineyards and the distant blue Alps. He left Montechio and when he reached the Asiago, perfectionist that he was, Lorimer expressed himself dissatisfied when he found that the cemeteries were not yet sown or 'semée with wild flowers, which was what we hoped for, and the interior of the walls have not yet been planted close with small leafed ivy'.

The appointed day arrived and Lorimer and 'the whole population of villages turned out to see the Royal programme', which he found moving. After a while 'a fleet of seven Lancia cars was seen approaching and the whole ceremony was gone through in dead silence, the word having been passed round that that was what was correct: the K[ing] saluted the cross and then made a general inspection of the cemeteries. The arrangement was that the children were not to be allowed in till the K and Q were gone, but he said let them all come in now. So all these hundreds of tinies, came in among the K and Q and their suite and placed their bouquets some on the cross others at the headstones.' The tour ended afterwards at Dueville where Lorimer had 'a few final words with their majesties' before he and his wife returned home.

Gothic work was increasingly hard to find after the war and Lorimer's first commission was from Pierpoint Morgan who had visited the Thistle Chapel and had then commissioned Lorimer to refurnish a chapel on Long Island. There was no long history associated with the building to tie Lorimer down and the organ case, which is one of the smallest he designed, is also the most decorative, and apart from a label mould running around like a picture frame, the rest is entirely a matter of low carved plastersque ornament without any suggestion of structural stiffness. William Laing remembers how woodwork which had been meticulously carved by the Clow brothers, was set up in Grieve's workshop in Washington Lane and numbered before being taken down for transport. Two joiners were sent to the United States to re-assemble it also working for six weeks to put the finishing touches to the font, *Pl. 280*. Oak entrance doors which have an almost domestic character outside, and a highly decorative treatment on their inside were installed with ironwork by Thomas Hadden including four clenched hinges carrying thistle motifs inside as well as out (Grieve £10,525 and Scott Morton £6,912).

On the death of Dr Macgregor Chalmers, Lorimer took over the restoration of Paisley Abbey. A virtual rebuilding had been begun in 1785 since only the nave of this great cruciform church had remained intact after the tower had fallen and destroyed the choir in

284 ABOVE *Montage of the first scheme for the Scottish National War Memorial.* S.R.M.

285 BELOW *Lerwick War Memorial.* Ramsay

286 ABOVE LEFT *St John's Church, Perth, Lorimer with site agent.* R.S.L.

287 BELOW LEFT *Loretto School, Memorial panel.* R.S.L.

288 ABOVE RIGHT *St John's Church, Perth, from the N.W.* R.S.L.

289 BELOW MIDDLE *Font for St John's, Lattingtown, U.S.A.* R.C.A.M.

290 BELOW RIGHT *Galashiels Burgh Buildings, Selkirkshire.* R.S.L.

291–292 LEFT *Stowe School Chapel, exterior &*
interior. R.S.L.
293 ABOVE RIGHT *Margaret Swan, neé Brown,*
Lorimer's secretary. MRS. FERGUS HARRIS
294 MIDDLE RIGHT *J. F. Matthew & family, Robert*
furthest left. S.R.M.
295 BELOW RIGHT *Department of Zoology of the*
University of Edinburgh. C.L.

296–297 LEFT *Rossall School Memorial Chapel, exterior & interior.* R.S.L.
298–299 RIGHT *St Andrew's Church, Aldershot, interior & exterior.* R.C.A.M.

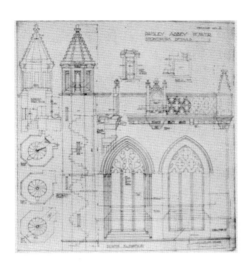

498. Rowand Anderson had been called in 1897, and in 1911 had been succeeded by Chalmers, who had carried up the choir walls and the base of the tower before he died. (He was a cousin of Lorimer's and some fruitless negotiations ensued between the widow and Lorimer about taking over his practice.)

The inflection of the Abbey's Gothic walls is strongly linear with tall windows ending in slightly more pronounced curved tracery at their tops than at Dunblane, *Fig. 121*. The ribs of the vault which radiate above them provide long plain panels of infill. A. G. Lochhead, Lorimer's assistant, found the springers as built had been incorrectly set out and took much trouble to redesign them, Mrs Chalmers having refused to hand over the drawings for him to see how they should have been. Lorimer had the size of the bosses increased, and richly carved and gilded. The effect of the plain stone infill panels was then adjusted to them by applied gently coloured patterns, although some of the bosses suggest applied medallions rather than carved structural members.

The woodwork follows the lines of Dunblane. The reredos panelling, however, is not taken the full width of the choir but conforms to the window above it. The waist high linen fold panelling is continued round in two projecting wings which culminate in carved angels rising up with lighted torches in their hands. The whole arrangement is spatially more complicated than Dunblane's, perhaps to reflect the complicated rhythms of the vaulted roof but without in any way echoing its shapes. The details are consequently treated with less structural emphasis than Dunblane's but, so as to provide a suitable immediate setting for the carved stone altar table, it is set upon a number of shallow steps, the bottom one of which is broad enough to give space for the throne and kneeler set on either side.

Louis Davis executed a number of the windows. Douglas Strachan the east window and Lorimer drew up a plan for the rest to be executed as donors came forward. In those ways Lorimer completed the work more decoratively than Chalmers would have done yet in almost perfect harmony with the earlier work. The only effect Lorimer had on the exterior was to substitute a parapet for the spire which Chalmers had designed, and even that was partly a

[*122*] *St John's Church, Perth, perspective.* R.C.A.M.

measure of economy and partly a continuing unease about the foundations, despite Anderso having spent a great deal of money on them.

The restoration of the Church of St John was begun as a memorial to the men c Perthshire who had fallen in the war, on money raised by 'The People's Million Penn Fund', by private subscriptions and by Lord Forteviot among others. This twelfth centur church has the squat simplicity of a Celtic Cathedral like Iona, *Fig. 122*, but had been muc altered at the Reformation and the interior had been partitioned to form three separat assemblies. The interior was stripped, various piers and windows restored, and the roof c the nave renewed as an oak barrel vault with painted panels and plaques.

The wood furnishings provided by Lorimer reflect the pronounced horizontal emphasi of the church. The stalls are less vertical in emphasis than the Thistle's and the organ case i kept within the general confines of one arch although it is strongly projected. The pulpit said to have been a reproduction of John Knox's, is to Lorimer's own design. The wa memorial shrine was set up in a bay added to the church in 1828. The stone carving was b Donaldson and Burn of Edinburgh and the bronze statue of St John the Baptist was b Finandra Bose, an Indian sculptor working in Edinburgh. The stained glass window o Michael the Warrior angel is flanked by angels representing Courage, Faith, Fortitude Hope and Magnanimity and was designed by Mrs Meredith Williams. The windows carrie out in thick white glass in varying tones are by H. Hendrie, and a lancet window in the nort aisle by Douglas Strachan. The exterior was left alone except for the raising of the aisles which MacGibbon and Ross had urged earlier should be left low – and the restoration to it original height of the Halkerstone tower over the north porch. As rebuilt by Lorimer, it wa closer to the south porch of Linlithgow than its original form prior to demolition a centur earlier.

St John's was Lorimer's last important Gothic work after which he was only to design th Shrine of Youth for St Giles Cathedral in Edinburgh, some carved doors for St Baldred' North Berwick and minor additions to J. J. Stevenson's Crieff South Church. St Andrew' Church at Aldershot built in 1926, however, shows him taking a new direction. It is one o the very few brick buildings to his credit. The exterior is a simple arrangement of roof stepping up from the entrance porch, which is echoed by the various other arched opening and flanked by a small Celtic round tower, *Pl. 299*. St Peter's, Morningside, with which thi church shares so many features, had an altar with candles piercing the shadow in which i was set. St Andrew's has its altar in a similar recess but, as befits a Presbyterian church, on brightly lit by a tall east window, *Pl. 298*. The arches along the aisles are wider, the roof o the nave is lower, its wood is lighter in tone and receives more light; and although S Margaret's, Knightswood, Lorimer's very last church, executed posthumously by Matthew, had little in common with St Andrew's, its tower with stepped gables and saddle backed roof, and the plain surfaces of the whole building, all hark back to earlier influences

By 1924 Britain, in Clough William-Ellis's opinion, was in 'a definite period of classical character', but even he had to admit that some 'regular Gothic building still goes on bu

with few exceptions, Sir Robert Lorimer, Gilbert Scott and Sir Charles Nicholson for instance, it would be difficult to find an architect who was able and willing to build a 'straight' Gothic building of any considerable scale.' Next year he and Lorimer were among those invited to enter a limited competition for a chapel for a school newly set up at Stowe, an eighteenth century classical mansion whose gardens had been laid out by such as William Kent and Capability Brown. The school needed a chapel grand enough to hold its own with those exhalted surroundings, yet one which could be built for the relatively modest sum which was available. Lorimer submitted a design for a basilica plan with arcaded aisles for which the arches were set on sixteen columns taken from Kent's Temple of Victory and Concorde situated in the grounds, *Pl. 291*. Such an act of vandalism would be unthinkable today and Hussey has accused Lorimer of using 'the classic tongue barbarously, as a good goth no doubt ought to do'. The governors were impressed and awarded Lorimer the commission. Clough, who had regarded himself as the school architect on the strength of work already done there by him, was very disgruntled, particularly as Lorimer had flown in his drawings by light plane at the eleventh hour after everyone thought he would fail to submit them on time.

The interior of the chapel is entirely satisfactory, *Pl. 292*. The arches spring from the columns without any entablature with medallions set in each intrados, and the wagon roof sits well upon them. The seating is arranged conventionally to face the east end with a continuous range of stalls placed in each aisle facing across the Chapel. The entrance is through a pedimented portico which extends to within a metre of the corners of the facade from which it is projected. As though this were not enough, large projecting bays have been added at either end of each side facade and it was perhaps the Goth in Lorimer who felt the need for such discords.

The Zoology building for the University of Edinburgh was begun in the last year of Lorimer's life. The long promised partnership with Matthew had finally been arranged in 1927 and if Lorimer's influence can be felt in this design it was not the kind of building which interested him and the bulk of the work fell on Matthew. Lorimer, who could respond so deeply to the sense of place of his numerous domestic buildings was forced to site this building, the first on an new campus, on the corner of the site to allow further buildings to be added along the boundary roads by ribbon development, *Fig. 123*. He had made proposals for something more ambitious with faculty houses set out on a larger site but finances were restricted and those proposals were turned down. The building, of steel and concrete cage construction to allow large windows of non-traditional proportions, has vestigial classical features applied to it decoratively to humanise the otherwise entirely utilitarian exterior, and the small traditional entrance door has been set in a high recessed porch, a diminished version of that on the National Memorial, *Pl. 295*.

As business had picked up after the war, Lorimer had told Dods how 'Matthew thinks we'll need a huge staff – costing thousands a year to overtake the work – but we'll see'. He was able to work his staff very hard because they believed it was worth while working for

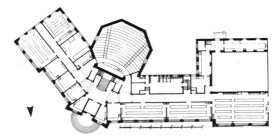

[*123*] *Department of Zoology of the University of Edinburgh, plan.*   C.L.

143

Scotland's premier office. They worked late into the evenings to keep up, but no overtime was paid, indeed Lorimer would make no allowance for it and would complain bitterly if anyone turned up late the following morning. To be fair, Lorimer worked himself as hard but he would have liked to have followed James Morton's example by working three days in Edinburgh and taking some work home for long four day weekends at Gibliston. But there was too much demanding his attention in Edinburgh. He would arrive at Haymarket by train and hurry on foot to the office, where the staff worked like slaves by today's standards – as did the other offices of those days.

There were no tea breaks but Lorimer had his own cup of tea and a piece of cake sent up by the caretaker who lived in the basement. According to his secretary, Miss Brown, he was always preoccupied in his work and was rather thoughtless about the comfort of others. He had a fire in his own office but much of the rest of the building was unheated. Miss Brown used to type wearing tall fur-lined boots which her father, a mercantile captain, had brought back from Russia, and even then she was never warm!

He telephoned his secretary, *Pl. 293*, one Christmas day to tell her, 'I have a lot on my chest and I want to get it down'. She went to Melville Street where he dictated notes on all the symbols to be used for the shrine of the National Memorial, after which he told her to 'go round to the office [in Great Stuart Street] and get it typed'. Miss Brown remonstrated that her mother was alone at home preparing Christmas dinner but he replied, 'Allright, but come back afterwards and do it.' Needless to say she did not return to the office late on Christmas Day and when he found out afterwards he accepted it. It seemed, from the way he pushed everyone, that he felt he had to make up for the thin years of the war. Romantic though he was in all things pertaining to design, he remained very hard-headed about money and he acted always as though he was short of it.

Matthew was still the great talker, *Pl. 294*. Margaret Brown recalled, 'He'd talk all day to the apprentices, anyone. You had to shut him up at times. Then he'd go home to his house in Minto Street [towards the purchase of which Lorimer had given him £650 in 1920] and retire to his basement room to do the work he hadn't done during the day. He also got on very well with the craftsmen.' He was always immaculate and spotlessly turned out. He looked like the city gent whereas Lorimer preferred plain, coarse, tweedy suits and looked like a country squire as he rolled his own cigarettes. The office in Great Stuart Street had distant views to the north, across the Firth of Forth to Fife and the distant Ochil Hills to the south of the Cairngorms, and the garden below was perched on a cliff above the Water of Leith. The Lord Provost, Sir Thomas Whitson, who brought the Loretto work to the office, exclaimed when he first saw Lorimer's room on the first floor, 'How can anyone work in this room? The view is too superb, from my own office I can see only chimney pots and just as well.' Lorimer liked to burn wood in his fire and he so liked its smell that he'd take a glowing log and swing it round and round to scent the air.

The front room was the general office where three apprentices were put and it fell to the junior apprentice to answer the office phone as well as to see all the travellers visiting the office. 'Boy,' Lorimer would roar, as he burst in to send one of them on an errand, and they hastened to do as he bid them because all new apprentices were warned to do *exactly* as he said or 'he would go up in a puff of smoke'. They started each day at the College of Art at eight and came on to the office at nine-thirty to gain experience for which they received no pay. The office closed at five-thirty after which they went to the Heriot Watt College for evening classes. They often got to bed after eleven o'clock so that the only time left for their homework was at weekends. One apprentice whose religion forbade work of any kind on the Sabbath had great difficulty in passing his exams as he couldn't do enough work in his remaining spare time. If there is a hint of exaggeration in Margaret Brown's memories of the office, one can be sure that everyone worked very hard indeed and that Lorimer brooked no passengers.

When Lorimer was about to go off on his annual holiday to Europe the apprentice who was nearest his ear was required to warn the others so that a beanfeast could be held in Lorimer's own office, with food provided by the caretaker. It also had to be a day when Matthew was away for the whole day, and Morton Cowie recalled how one year, when the party was in full swing and just as the 'shagreen box of Lorimer's own special Egyptian cigarettes was being passed around', Matthew returned unexpectedly. 'He appeared at the door and a hush fell, then as poised as ever, he came in and helped himself to a cup of tea and some food, going from dish to dish saying "I'll have one of these and two of these." Then he went in to his office to eat them and never mentioned the affair to anyone again.' Cowie also remembered how Matthew still referred to nine by four inch envelopes as 'first size long' from his earlier stationery shop experience. 'JF', he said, 'had a great sense of humour. He would point out to us apprentices, how to design a W.C. You had to assume the chap using it wanted to read *The Scotsman*, so when he held it out in front of him, the width of his outstretched arms was the "minimum" width of the W.C.'

The influence of surveyors was growing in the office, as elsewhere, although Matthew was in control of all estimating. By the twenties Reid had a room of his own on the second floor of the office, and Gibson, his partner, was jammed in another room with seven assistants. At first they had worked entirely for Lorimer but had expanded to take in work from other offices as well. The specialists housed on the top floor were of a kind no longer to be found in any architect's office. John Sutherland, who had worked in the office of the Lord Lyon King of Arms and who had done much work on the Thistle Chapel, had joined Lorimer, and as a heraldic artist he drew all the full size cartouches needed. He was a striking figure from Shetland, six foot tall, with long grey hair which he bobbed and he had a yellow complexion from working too much indoors. He worked part-time for Lorimer and for the rest he taught at the College of Art. Jack Arthur, who also had a small room on this floor, was a draughtsman who only worked on the inscriptions for memorials and buildings. The drawings were stored in the sub-basement, although abandoned might be the better word. They were piled on the floor and stacked up until they reached knee height. Margaret Brown remembered once finding a young apprentice down on his knees praying. Lorimer had sent him to look for a particular drawing and he told her, 'It's my only chance of finding it.'

In 1926 Lorimer had set out for his second tour of the four war cemeteries in Germany. They were the most formally impressive of his designs, with the exception of Ohlsdorf where the plot was a subdivision of a huge civil cemetery near Hamburg and where the works were mainly to do with planting. The other three cemeteries were all given highly formal wrought iron gates, executed by Hadden in Edinburgh, which were flanked by screen walls and lodges with stone beehive roofs. Niederzwhehren was a long narrow cemetery with graves of former inmates of a nearby prison camp, *Pl. 277*. The gateway gives on to a central walk leading up a gentle slope to the War Stone and then to the Cross of Sacrifice near the top. The effect of this cemetery nestling in the lea of a long coppice amid open fields not far from Cassel is simple but austere, *Pl. 283*.

The British graves at Cologne are set in part of a large civil cemetery as at Ohlsdorf. An existing poplar avenue has been used effectively as the background to the main axis and war stone, and the approach is by iron gates flanked by beehive lodges. The cemetery at Berlin is a woodland cemetery and it was set among fir trees at the confluence of three rides. The graves are arranged in concentric semi-circles about the gate with lodges. The War Stone and Cross of Sacrifice are on the main axis, the War Stone half way back and the Cross near the back. Lorimer considered using whin (gorse) around the edge of this cemetery but was told that the heavy winter snow would flatten it. He had suggested gilding the lettering at Cologne but the Director-General told him he was already under attack for the extravagance of some cemeteries (not Lorimer's) and that he couldn't sanction it lest a precedent be set for other cemeteries.

Lorimer achieved an extraordinary variety in the great number of memorials he designed in Britain, where he borrowed architectural motives with a freedom which conferred sculptural vitality yet brought criticism. The oak screen for Westminster School was of finely carved classical columns and pilasters carrying brackets crossed only by a thin moulding, the entablature having been omitted to give space for large carved flat reliefs of trophies which he introduced beneath some existing windows. Yet the effect was magnificent. The memorial for Eton involved reshaping an old Chantry, and Lorimer proposed to introduce a large new opening into the medieval masonry. When the committee refused to sanction it Lorimer withdrew and his letter conveyed 'so much scorn and contempt for the committee and such a heavy bill that a compromise was out of the question'. However, Lerwick's memorial, the design for which had incorporated the prow of a viking ship, was adjusted without difficulty to the more conventional cross, *Pl. 285*. Lorimer habitually used lettering for inscriptions which was raised by sinking the background – the letters slightly coarsely formed to evoke the vigour of medieval Scots inscriptions. Sir Herbert Baker, on a visit, tapped one such inscription with a cane he was carrying and turning to his son remarked, 'I think we could do a little better, don't you?'

The smaller memorials are mostly within the Gothic tradition. Davenham is a small richly carved bay carried out with the Clow brothers and set with a kneeler between two

[124] *Lorimer's sketch for a typical village memorial (Skirling).* O.D.

146

ines of stalls, *Pl. 301*. The private memorials were usually simple carved oak or stone tablets with a Gothic frame, with an insignia at its head, and the raised inscription below. Some incorporated bronze panels, but all produce the liveliest play of light.

The war cemeteries had involved a public form of design achieved by endless compromises with site conditions, transport and building costs and the numerous officials and advisors, but if ever a building was designed in committee, it was the Scottish National War Memorial in Edinburgh Castle. The cloister of the 1919 scheme had been changed in committee to an enclosed gallery to house the regimental memorials in 1920, but then such a tumult of public protest had arisen that all chance of building that scheme had been destroyed and the third scheme, which was saved from its wreckage in 1923, retains only half the shrine in the form of an apse. David Erskine of Linlathen had already put to Lorimer that: 'Any building on Edinburgh Castle should not be in a definite style either Gothic or Classic but that it should be rugged, rigorous and depending for its effect not on fine details but on mass, light, shade'. Richardson, backed up by a wide range of opinion, was making impossible the consideration of all but the slightest changes to the Castle's 'historic' outline. Atholl pursuing Lorimer's wishes, was battling as chairman of the committee for a building at least partly Gothic, and Sir John Stirling Maxwell became the midwife for the final design when he suggested that it ought 'to be possible, in order to placate public opinion, to retain the exterior of the old barrack building . . . and to build the shrine up against it' instead of making the shrine detached. Lorimer saw that this was the key to the problem, and went home to shut himself up for the weekend – by the end of which he had produced a new scheme, *Fig. 126*.

The final scheme shows its mixed parentage. The gable in which the tall steep roof of the shrine rises above the flatter parapeted roof of the gallery of honour in the old barrack, suggests that had he been allowed he might have put a high roof on both, *Pl. 306*. The gable did allow a south facing window to the shrine to provide shafts of bright sunlight into its interior and he suggested that a lantern should crown the apex of this gable from which a light might shine in perpetuity. Protests were immediately raised that electricity was too vulgar for such a symbolic light, and when a full sized mock up of the lantern was put in place a fresh outcry of the desecration of the skyline arose and idea had to be abandoned, much to Lorimer's regret.

The attacks on the scheme and upon Lorimer had been both prolonged and bitter. He had told Dods in 1919 that were the memorial built it would be 'a smack in the eye to the "enemy" – who have been trying hard to wreck it, incidentally with the hope of wrecking *me*'.[2] He spoke, too, of a 'wild talking irresponsible devil of a secretary' who was making difficulties. It was probably Richardson who was Lorimer's most resolute opponent on the Ancient Monuments Board – on which Lorimer continued to sit even while it was considering his scheme. Many of the attacks were unfair and Rosebery was not alone in using ridicule. The niches and the apse had been borrowed from Stirling which led Richardson's cousin, the painter F. C. Cadell, to quip, 'If Stirling was the outcome of a

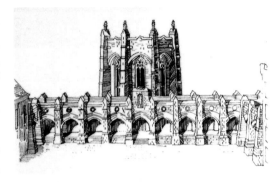

[125]–[126] *The Scottish National War Memorial,* ABOVE *perspective of first scheme,* P.S.; BELOW *plan of final scheme,* C.L.

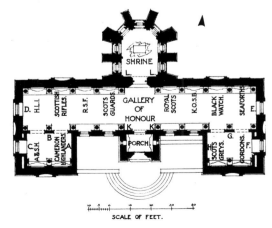

147

good blowout of a medieval banquet, Lorimer's memorial was the outcome of a tea fight and he said rather coarsely, when he heard that Lorimer had told Burrell his name would go down to posterity if he made a large subscription to the memorial, that 'Lorimer's own name would go down to posterity through the Remirol'.

The subscriptions had been coming in despite all the rancorous publicity and work finally began on site in the late autumn of 1923, *Pl. 305*. The masonry of the barrack was patched and the porch and niches built in Doddington stone from Northumberland, which of the available stones most closely matched the original, *Pl. 313*. The interior masonry is in Berwickshire stone from Swinton, and Ailsa Craig provided the polished green granite for the floor. The memorial stands on the crest of the Castle rock which is allowed to protrude naturally and untreated, through the middle of the floor of the shrine. The long narrow track which leads up the rock takes the path of an S from the portcullis gate to pass the six gun battery and through Foog's Gate, past St Margaret's Chapel (the oldest building on the rock) up past the north side of the memorial to Crown Square on its south. Frank Deas, one of Lorimer's closest architect friends, has quoted him as saying that 'proportion, light and shade, dignity and appropriateness to the purpose, were the qualities aimed at in the design', and despite the 'bold and rather heavy type of detail, characteristic of 16th century Scottish architecture' adopted to suit the rugged walls of the old barrack building, its proportions convey an inner harmony of measure whch is worldless communication like a tune.

A lofty arched porch houses the entrance above which a tall mysterious figure of Byzantine proportions – The Spirit of Survival – rises from a corbel decorated with a phoenix as the symbol of resurrection. Above the entrance door, on the inside, is another figure – Reveille – which is gilded radiantly to represent the figure of man purified by the flames of sacrifice, a broken sword in his hand to symbolise the end of the war and set against a circular panel of blue, gold and green for the sun, earth, sea and sky. Immediately opposite, and across the gallery of honour, inside, is the Gothic archway leading to the shrine, *Pl. 308*, in which the large pendant figure of the Archangel Michael carved by the Clow brothers, *Pl. 304*, hangs from its vaulted ceiling and seven plaques, the Planets, designed by George Salvesen, *Pl. 309*, whereas the walls of the gallery carry memorials so numerous that the task represented in merely positioning them must have been considerable.

Despite the variety of the memorials 'Scotland is small enough to know all her sons by heart', and as Ian Hay had noted, although 'you may live in Berwickshire, and the man who has died may have come from Skye' his name nevertheless will be 'quite familiar to you'. Consequently Scotland's mourning is national where England's is more often local which is why 'Scotland alone among the nations has erected a war memorial commemorating in detail the service of every unit of her arms'.

Each regiment has its own memorial in the gallery; the Royal Scots Greys, the Scots Guards, the Royal Scots, the Royal Scots Fusiliers, the King's Own Scottish Borderers, the Cameronians, the Black Watch, the Highland Light Infantry, the Seaforth Highlanders, the Gordon Highlanders, the Queen's Own Cameron Highlanders, and the Argyll and

300 ABOVE LEFT *Queenstown War Memorial, South Africa.* R.S.L.

301 BELOW LEFT *Davenham Memorial in carver's workshop.* R.S.L.

302–303 RIGHT *The Morton Memorial, Darvel, Ayrshire & detail.* R.S.L.

304–311 *The Scottish National War Memorial,* THIS PAGE LEFT *Maquette for St Michael;* ABOVE RIGHT *work in progress;* BELOW MIDDLE & RIGHT *models of exterior & of Naval Memorial within;* OPPOSITE ABOVE LEFT *doorway detail;* ABOVE MIDDLE *Venus, G. Salvesen;* BELOW LEFT *Lorimer & visitors;* RIGHT *stained glass, D. Strachan,* R.S.L.

312 LEFT *The National Memorial, placed centrally in the Edinburgh Castle skyline.* P.M.
313–314 RIGHT *The National Memorial, exterior & interior views.* R.S.L.

Sutherland Highlanders. Each is set in a bay flanked by classical columns above which runs a continuous frieze of all their battle honours.

The great wealth of military detail to the memorials was largely undertaken by Pilkington Jackson who had been introduced to Lorimer by J. J. Cowan when Westerlea was being remodelled. Jackson found Lorimer to be 'diffident in some ways and aggressive in others but craftsmen collaborated well with him. He would give you ideas but he would also take ideas. He had difficulties with sculptors who were difficult but if you were trying hard and kept to your estimate, he was very easy to work with.'

The walls were to be blazoned with the colour of the rich insignia and gilded inscriptions – no penny pinching here – and the regimental colours. The work was given to his decorators Moxon and Carfrae. Sutherland was in charge since so much of the colouring was heraldic but Lorimer came to the conclusion that he would 'never get it right until we get an artist and his palette on the job'. Jackson introduced Miles Johnson who was brought in to harmonise all the colours being used, and as it became too big a job for one man he brought in to help him, Donald Moodie and a young student of painting called William Gillies. The decorators put on the undercoats to Johnson's instructions, and then he and his assistants applied the finishing treatments.

The first thing Lorimer wanted to be coloured was a tree. 'What colour is it to be?' asked Johnson, 'Brown' replied Lorimer, and though brown could mean almost anything, when he found Johnson was doing the work satisfactorily, he let him get on with it with the least supervision. There was barely enough light to illuminate all the carving properly so the green and red had to be kept very light in tone after which they took Van Dyck brown and black water colour and stippled the whole thing to get an equal penetration. Then they went over it with a chamois leather so that the high parts were wiped clear and the dark colour went into the hollows.

Lorimer had asked two things of Johnson as he began work, that 'People should be overwhelmed by the effect of entering, and that it should look as though it was a hundred years old'. When he finished Alex Carrick, the sculptor, came across to say to him, 'Bill, this is not the last job you'll do for Sir Robert', nor was it to be.

The eight stained glass windows in the gallery fill in other parts of the war's story. They are all pale in colour with circular panels inset to let in plenty of light. Four of them follow the colours of the seasons: to the left is the Autumn, and inset a leave train, and munition workers below; Winter shows the last post sounded in the snow, the watch on the coast and a camouflaged convoy nearing Britain's shores; Spring time is to the right, with its flowers as well as an air raid, anti-aircraft guns and an ambulance, and finally Summer is shown by poppies, roses and thistles and a departing troopship and minesweeper.

At the west end of the gallery is the Air Services window showing aeroplanes, airships and observation balloons, and also the women's window with land girls, a munitions worker, a Red Cross motor-cyclist and Red Cross nurses. On the keystones of the arches above is carved a pelican to symbolise sacrifice and the lamp for nursing. The windows at the east end at the naval memorial, *Pl. 307*, are dedicated to those who 'have no other grave than the sea' represented by a destroyer, a troopship, the Forth Bridge in the distance, Rosyth and a submarine, and to the mechanisms of war. Heavy artillery, the machine gun, the tank, bridge building, the bomb thrower, the flame thrower, the armoured car and a trench digger are all shown.

There are several stories that Strachan wanted strong colour in the windows of the gallery but that Lorimer did not, and that Lorimer insisted on duller colours for the windows of the shrine, *Pl. 311*. The balancing of effects fell to Lorimer who had to communicate some unwelcome decisions to the individual artists, but 'what struck me most was the exceptional range of his moods', Strachan has said of Lorimer, it gave him a 'certain portentousness' which made him a bit 'Napoleonic'. The two men were very close friends and Strachan knew him as a deeply emotional man who could surrender himself 'completely to the spell of great music, and I have seen tears in his eyes as he related some child incident that touched him in its tender beauty'.

Other memorials large and small had to be fitted in wherever space permitted. The memorial to the honour of all Scotswomen is at the end of the gallery beneath a window. It is surrounded by the carved and painted insignia of their units. The Women's Legion, the Women's Land Army, the Women's Royal Naval Service, the Voluntary Aid Detachment, the Queen Mary's A.A.C., the Women's Royal Air Force, and the Women's Forage Corps. At the other end of the gallery is the memorial to the nursing services, and the insignia of the British Red Cross Society, the Territorial Nursing Services, the Scottish Women's Hospitals, the General Voluntary Aid Detachment Service, the First Aid Nursing Yeomanry and the Queen Alexandra's Military Nursing Service.

The lengthening list brings out the apalling scale of modern war as well as the complexity of arranging for so many memorials within a single building. Elsewhere upon the walls and piers are memorials to the Royal Naval Reserve, the Royal Naval Volunteer Reserve, the mine sweepers, the 'Q ships', the auxiliary patrols, the Mercantile Marine, the Royal Marines and the Royal Naval School of Music. The two hundred and seven chaplains who were killed are commemorated, and also the Royal Army Medical Corps, the Royal Engineers and the Royal Army Service Corps. Those who served with the South African Scottish, the Tyneside Scottish, the Liverpool Scottish, the London Scottish, The Royal Artillery, and the Household Cavalry are not forgotten nor those Scotsmen who died in English, Irish and Welsh regiments or with the units of the Dominions or Colonies.

Even the beasts of burden were remembered; the elephant, the ox, horse, reindeer, dog, camel and mule, have been carved by Donaldson and Burn from Phyllis Bone's models. There was also a basket of carrier pigeons, a cage of mice and canaries, 'the tunnellers' friends', modelled by Hazel Armour. Lorimer was using well-established sculptors like Carrick, Salvesen, Portsmouth and Kennedy but he had discovered Bone. She was young and had very little experience apart from a few months modelling animals with Carrick. Her first job was a little unicorn for the memorial at North Berwick which had been

esigned by her second cousin James Richardson. She had trained in Paris from where she
ad brought back a small bronze of a mountain goat. Cadell the painter had suggested she
ubmit it to the Society of Eight³ where Lorimer saw it and, having discovered that it was by
 student, he went to see her and asked her to model the beasts of burden for the National
Memorial. She made four models and 'he came across and seemed to like them. He always
eemed to have an eye for putting a piece of sculpture outside a building or inside it. When I
sked him "do these people know they're getting this thing?" he'd say ' "No, but when they
o, they'll get to like it". He had a great sense of humour and I was young enough to take his
dvice, not that he pushed his advice down my throat, but he was so helpful in so many,
nany ways.'

Lorimer, his craftsmen and artists had produced a work that was seen to be, 'Built by
cottish brains, Scottish hands and Scottish money'. If it had taxed Lorimer to the limit it
ad been equally hard on Matthew who had long suffered from migraine and as the
nemorial neared completion he broke down and had to rest. On its completion a dinner for
ll the seventy artists and craftsmen was held by Lorimer and Matthew, who were now
artners, and in 1928 when the University of Edinburgh conferred the honorary degree of
Doctor of Laws upon him, it cited Lorimer's influence upon 'the revival of the best
raditions of Scottish building at its prime, and the stimulus he has given to the fine
raftsmanship of the Edinburgh School of Woodcarving, stained glass and the other
ecorative arts'.

The memorial was opened by the Prince of Wales, at a dedication service in the presence
of the Lord Lyon King of Arms, his Heralds and Pursuivants, Earl Haig, the Secretary of
State, the Lord Lieutenants and dignitaries of the law and church. As the service ended the
asket within the shrine, given by their majesties the King and Queen, stood open, the
Prince waiting beside it to receive the rolls commemorating the dead from the Colonels
Commandant. Sir Ian Hamilton, who bore that of the Gordons, found himself thinking as
he crossed the gallery of honour that 'life is very precious and could surely never have been
created to be flung so recklessly away', and he entered the shrine which surprised him for
being a 'tiny chamber' dedicated to 'a generation of young soldiers – boy soldiers who were
ut down in rows by machine guns at Beaumont Hamel, Festubert, Loos and buried there in
heir kilts as they fell – disappeared in one dreadful moment. And there, hemmed in by so
nany insignias of sorrow – there lies the book – and in that book one hundred thousand
names – Scotland for ever!'

This solemn service had closed when shortly afterwards the first official visitors to be
admitted were the King, the Queen and Princess Mary. The clamour of dissent had stilled
and people from all over Scotland flocked to see their memorial, *Pl. 310*, standing patiently
n long queues to enter. 'Whatever the final verdict may be', wrote Ian Hay, 'that vanished
generation have left behind them something which neither time can efface nor posterity
belittle', *Pl. 312*.

Lorimer was exhausted and he and Pilkington Jackson took a holiday in Sweden. He took

Jackson to look at buildings, Jackson took him to see Carl Milles, and they returned full of enthusiasm for all the things they had seen. Lorimer was created Knight Commander of the British Empire for his part in the design of the National Memorial, after which he was nominated unanimously by the council of the Royal Incorporation of Architects in Scotland as their President for the following year. As he relaxed from the rigorous pressure to which the responsibilities of the Memorial had subjected him, he spent more time at Gibliston where he added a music room, and he found time to write regularly to the London *Times* letters filled with the poetry of life; on the dawn chorus of birds at Gibliston; on the charm of wood fires, and with sadness he wrote sensitive appreciations of his friends who had died.

He still met James Morton regularly, and, indeed, had designed a Morton memorial for Darvel in Ayrshire, *Pls. 302, 303*, and as they talked over Lorimer's Scandinavian holiday Morton was stimulated to go there to see things for himself. He was there when Lorimer was taken ill with appendicitis, and operated upon. Morton arrived back at Leith bubbling over with things he wanted to discuss with his old friend. When he got off the boat he saw on the newspaper placards announcing 'Famous Scots Architect Dies'. Robert Lorimer was dead. There had passed away, Percy Nobbs wrote later from Canada, 'The last of the great romantics, with a name to be put beside that of Philip Webb and Norman Shaw. Like these, a revivalist; like these, a modernist; it was given to him, as to them, to leave the land he loved so well more beautiful in a thousand places than he found it.'

Antique tile.

315 *Sir Robert Lorimer, R.S.A., A.R.A., LL.D.,*
P.R.I.A.S.   Drummond Young

316 *St Margaret's Church, Knightswood, finished by*
J. F. Matthew.   R.S.L.

Postscript: 1929–1979

Lorimer's death was followed within weeks by the stock-market crash on Wall Street and the economic recession in Scotland deepened. J. F. Matthew, who had taken over the practice, received almost no work, so that when his son Robert qualified as an architect in 1931 he had to enter the government service in which he was to rise so high. If times were bad in 1931 *Country Life* was able at last to bring out a book on the work of Sir Robert Lorimer. Lawrence Weaver, Lorimer's close friend, who had been contributing articles on Lorimer's work since 1905, had been given details by Lorimer of all his buildings but he had hardly begun work on the book when he died and the project was passed on to his young colleague Christopher Hussey who had begun some years earlier also to write upon Lorimer's work. Lorimer's first large commission, Earlshall, had established his reputation for fine restoration work, and even if, like so many other country-house architects of his day, he was given far more castles and mansions to alter, extend or remodel than new ones to build, Hussey, by devoting two-thirds of his book to Lorimer's restorations, was doing no more than reflect the interest of his audience of readers of *Country Life* magazine for this kind of work (which embraced all Lorimer's large scale works in England), and his book was to lead to the later opinion, which held that Lorimer had been only interested in historical building.

Lorimer had been asked to build only four completely new mansions but they had been enough for Weaver, earlier, to promote Lorimer as the Scottish Lutyens. Brackenburgh in England was Tudor in style but the Baronial style had been stipulated for Rowallan which was started soon after, and Ardkinglas, begun after a lapse of several years, was also composed within the tumbled rhythms of the Baronial. The last of the four, Formakin, begun soon after Ardkinglas, was intended, by Lorimer's own definition, to be as 'Scotch' as he could make it, and herein lies the all important distinction betweeen the Baronial and the Scotch styles (which being both part of the Scottish tradition are closely linked). The variety of building which is apt to be called Baronial is very wide and extends to those from the fourteenth to the seventeenth centuries. A little of it is truly Baronial, but much more was built for bonnet lairds and lesser folk who had no claim to be considered Baronial even if their buildings lay more or less within the same traditions. Their Neo-Baronial transitional buildings, however, were less defensive in character or sturdy in construction and were usually longer and lower in shape than those of the Baronial, so they shared the unpretentious simplicity of the more unassuming of English manor houses. Simple rectangular blocks were casually grouped together without the diagonal shifts of emphasis brought about in the Baronial by corbelling, stepped string courses, or by the irregular addition of turrets, nor were the quoins much interrupted. A great deal of revival Baronial work, by Burn and Bryce, though by no means all, reflects the transitional Baronial often well garnished with Jacobean enrichment, and Lorimer in his maturity increasingly reached back to the transitional in his search for a pure 'Scotch style', moving away thereby from the restlessness of the Baronial which had so well reflected the turbulence of its times.

A new direction in British architecture had appeared by the time Lorimer had completed his apprenticeship, and one of the most lively Scottish exponents of what has been called the free style was none other than James Maclaren for whom Lorimer had worked briefly (as well as afterwards with Dunn and Watson, Maclaren's successors). Among other things, the free style involved the use of geometrical flourishes as patterns in the abstract and divorced from all associated considerations of construction.

Lorimer was to be more deeply influenced by the Arts and Crafts than Mackintosh or Maclaren but he swayed neither towards pure geometry nor towards the Art Nouveau. Yet the irony of Lorimer's work is that his Baronial work which has been found so often to be too revivalist and historical in character is the very work in which the inherent volumetric geometry provides the basis of the restless rhythms of composition, whereas his smaller and more calmly restrained houses, no less original in their own way than those of Voysey or even Mackintosh, by adopting quieter, less varied rhythms may only seem to reflect the early Renaissance. Consider the example of Woodhill in Forfarshire, its plain withdrawn-looking entrance facade of white harled walls to be seen gleaming through the trees until the S-shaped drive fetches up alongside it, watched over by a tall, narrow, completely Scotch tower which juts forth to receive the visitor, whereas on the south, the facade which opens to the garden is arranged as an elaborately irregular play of form within an appearance of symmetry, *Pl. 320*. Or consider Rhu-na-haven which is very similar in the dispositions of its approach. It has a long south facade of glistening grey granite with tall regular openings sheltering, and below a slated roof hipped at one end, gabled at the other, but brought low so that all the windows of the upper floor push through the eaves and are capped by small beautifully shaped dutch gables. The whole facade is dominated by one large, nearly central, canted bay window focussed up, down and across the River Dee which tumbles past, freshly descended from the Grampian mountains.

These large, but not enormous, country houses are of a type which neither Mackintosh nor Voysey was much asked to undertake. However, Lorimer's smaller – if still generous by today's standards – Colinton cottages (and his Rustic houses developed with them) do bear comparison with theirs, and such buildings which formed a considerable part of Lorimer's practice in its first fifteen years and which are to modern eyes the most appealing, were ignored by Hussey, *Pl. 317*. Hussey became, however, the only general reference to Lorimer's work so, as the years passed by, Lorimer was left out of all architectural dictionaries, and when in 1964 an exhibition was mooted in Edinburgh to mark the centenary of his birth, the committee which was set up to arrange it, working from Hussey, concluded that Lorimer was too revivalist to be of general interest since restorations seemed o form the bulk of his work, and the colony of cottages in Colinton, which Hussey mentioned but failed to describe (or locate), was suggested as a more suitable theme. An observer was despatched to Colinton to see if he could locate them but returned to say that no one knew any longer which they were and the centenary passed without any exhibition being held (and only later did the account books of the office reveal the whereabouts of these cottages).

At a rough count Lorimer had designed upwards of thirty five such cottage styled houses to Mackintosh's handful, and he worked them in to a practice of which they were, not the major part as for Voysey, but one among many other things. The Colinton cottages were begun by Lorimer in 1893 (by which time Maclaren had been dead for three years, Voysey had built almost nothing and Mackintosh was several years away from starting either of his most celebrated houses) when he began to use a mixture of traditional Scots and English features in them. Yet already other early houses outside Edinburgh by him, like the Grange at North Berwick (1893) or Stronachullin Lodge near Ardrishaig (1894) show Lorimer designing in a manner which is as purely Scottish as it is his own. Such houses are less mannered than Voysey's and closer to tradition but their detailing is as varied as his, as is the interplay of their interior spaces. This is not to say that they are better or worse but that they are very different. Voysey so often planned his rooms as subdivisions of a long rectangular block within which the wall faces produce a regularity which is one natural outcome of using brick. Equally the smoothly rendered external walls he favoured, convey not only a sense of regularity but of graceful lightness. Lorimer's cottages, on the other hand, though as graceful in their own way, have stone walls over two feet thick which are solid in fact as well as appearance, and are built of harled random rubble which allowed an easy freedom in modelling, by rounded corners, recessions, corbelled upper floors, all without recourse to the buttresses which Voysey's houses so often employed. Indeed Gimson's Cotswold cottages which are modelled with a similar freedom to Lorimer's provide their nearest English equivalent.

In Scotland comparisons between the harled houses of Mackintosh and Lorimer are inevitable, since they share a freedom of modelling and solidity of effect which derives from their common roots in the architecture of Scotland. However, Mackintosh combines this with themes which are free style and new art interiors which are closer in spirit to Voysey's than Lorimer's. A plainly flat linear use of timber also characterises them since neither Voysey nor Mackintosh was reluctant to use machine finished planks of wood worked into abstract patterns without mouldings, with results which thus foreshadow the weightless disembodied effects of so much design of thirty years later. However, this was but one theme in their richly varied work. Lorimer, as a craftsman interested in the handicrafts, was not only interested in composition but also in assembly and in the way materials are jointed and brought together. Voysey and Mackintosh who were also deeply interested in craftsman-ship were rather more interested in effects and less in means. There are arguments to be advanced for and against the hiding of joints and the elimination of mouldings which so often provided ledges for dust, but overlapping joints also allowed for movement which is inevitable in mixed construction and provided places both to allow such movement and conceal the cracks which may be opened by it (and hence Perret's famous riposte in favour of modern architecture that ornament always conceals some fault in construction). Finally, it may be said that if Voysey's and Mackintosh's designs emphasise the element of space and Lorimer's emphasise the more human sense of enclosure, yet a strong love of nature united all three architects despite their differences.

Voysey, who was seven years older than Lorimer, had lived in and around London since the age of fourteen, and did little work after 1922. He died in 1941 the year after the R.I.B.A. had conferred the Gold Medal upon him. Mackintosh, four years younger than Lorimer, was in virtual retirement from 1911 and died in obscurity in 1928. Lorimer, who died the year following, was at the height of his reputation but was soon forgotten, except in Scotland, a result due at least in part to the geographical isolation of so much of his work. Tom Howarth, in his book of 1952 on Mackintosh (which did so much to revive interest in Mackintosh's work) only credits Lorimer with adopting the native forms of Scottish architecture in 'an attempt to produce a modernised traditional style', as if this were not enough! Fifteen years later interest in Lorimer had revived strongly – particularly in Scotland – and Alastair Service in 1977 remarked in his *Edwardian Architecture* of Lorimer's early houses and in particular on their Arts and Crafts influences and describes Lorimer as 'one of the most notable Scottish architects of the century'. Too many Scottish architects, who were Lorimer's near contemporaries, were lured away to the south – Maclaren, Brydon, the three J.Js (Stevenson, Joass and Burnett) to name but a few. Lorimer chose to stay in Scotland because his heart was in Scottish architecture and he did not build much in the city as they had all done, but his designs for gardens, Rustic cottages, furniture and church woodwork are among the best of their kind and his 'Scotch' country houses have not been surpassed.

From a letter to Dods.   R.S.L.

317 *Pentland Cottage, Colinton.* P.M.

Antique tile at Monzie. P.M.

Antique tile at Monzie.   P.M.

318 *Woodhill, Barry.*   P.M.

Chapter Notes

I

1. The upsurge in national feeling in the latter part of the nineteenth century bore fruit in *The Castellated and Domestic Architecture* by David MacGibbon and Thomas Ross, the first thorough survey published in five volumes between 1887 and 1892. They then capped it with *Ecclesiastical Architecture of Scotland* in three volumes published in 1896 and 1897.

2. Royal Scottish Academy, founded in 1826 to encourage fine arts in Scotland and to arrange exhibitions organised by the artists themselves. It grew out of the earlier schools and institutes of the preceding century.

3. Kellie Castle. Fourteenth century Keep. Another tower was raised to its east with a barmican between, of which all trace has been lost as further additions in the fifteenth to seventeenth centuries linked these two towers together. Large walled garden to the north and east of Castle.

4. Sir Walter Scott's part in the revival of interest in Scotland's indigenous architecture shows not so much in the house Abbotsford which he had built for himself in the Borders (with a number of architects including E. Blore), which was more Gothic than Baronial, but in his interest in Scottish history and in rescuing such bits of its heritage as he was able, some of which were built in to Abbotsford. He wrote also against the despoliation of Scottish gardens by the Victorian improvers.

5. Edinburgh Architectural Association was founded in 1858 and is the next oldest association of the profession in the U.K. to the R.I.B.A. and, in effect, took over from the Architectural Institute of Scotland founded in 1850. F. D. G. Stanley, a pupil of Brown and Wardrop, read a paper on iron in 1859. 'Mr. Brown being familiarly known as the Farm Architect, Mr. Wardrop had a good private connection with the mansion building class.' J. M. Brydon appears on record in 1860. 1862 R. R. Anderson gave the first of two papers on work seen on his Continental tour. J. C. Hay, the 9th President 1867. (From the *History and Reminiscences of the E.A.A.* Two bound volumes typescript by G. S. Aitken, 1913, in E.A.A. Library, Case J, Shelf 4).

6. School of Applied Art 1892–99. Run by Committee of Board of Manufacturers and Rowand Anderson until the Scottish Education Department took over functions of Department of Science and Art in Scotland.

7. Two bound volumes of photos and a typed description of 'the tables and porcelain presented to Holyrood Palace by Sir R. Rowand Anderson LL.D etc.' 1917 are lodged in the E.A.A. Library, Case N, Shelf 1.

8. Earlshall. Hall of the Earls of Fife whose thirteenth century castle formerly stood a mile away in Leuchars (was probably called Earlshall). MacGibbon and Ross, *Castellated Architecture*, Vol. 2, pp. 282–90). The present house was begun in 1546.

2

1. Falkland Palace is set at the foot of the Lomond Hills (1,500 feet) in Central Fife. It has been Crown property from about 1150, although formerly a castle of the Earl of Fife. The thirteenth century castle was to the north of the palace which is fifteenth century and partly in ruins. The Chapel Royal in the south range contains the oak entrance screen, its slender hand-turned pillars, no two of which are exactly alike, which Lorimer used to model that of Earlshall.

2. Wemyss Ware, pottery produced by Robert Herron and Co., Kirkcaldy, from c. 1883–1930, but similar to that developed by older potteries in the area using bold decorations of flowers, fruits and cocks. Mackenzie contributed a number of designs some based on the rookeries at Earlshall. 'They range from the naive to the sophisticated, the latter no doubt due to "improvement" by Wemyss decorators' (P. H. Davis, *Wemyss Ware Catalogue*, Scottish Arts Council, Edinburgh 1971).

3. Edzell Castle, on the edge of the Forfar plain where it reaches the foothills of the Grampians. The fifteenth century keep was enlarged around a court in the sixteenth century when a large pleasance (173 by 144 feet) was added with a high, very decorative, enclosing wall as well as a garden house (now destroyed) and a bath house.

4. Wemyss Castle is in East Fife on a thirty-five foot cliff above the shore. The fourteenth-century keep was greatly extended around a court in the sixteenth century, and again in the seventeenth century.

5. Craigleith Quarry has provided the stone with which Edinburgh is most associated, but Ravelstone was quarried nearby also within the Burgh, and Hailes Quarry, near Slateford (and now

within the district) produced three varieties of stone – 'Blue', 'Pink' and 'White' sandstone. Although they weather almost indistinguishably the white is the strongest and the blue the weakest of these stones.

3

1. *Shrines and Homes of Scotland*, Sir John Stirling Maxwell, London 1937, p. 205. He also instances other unhappy uses of red materials by Anderson.

2. Sparrow's books mentioning Lorimer are listed in the introduction.

4

1. Lyon Playfair 1st Baron (cr. 1892) Sir Lyon Playfair P.C., G.C.B., b. Meerut 1818, Educated Universities of St Andrews and Geissen (Germany). Ph.D, LL.D, F.R.S. Professor of Chemistry, Manchester, Member of Commission for Great Exhibition of 1851. Famine Commissioner to Ireland 1845 etc. Widely active in matters of Public Health. Friend of the family.

2. Whittinghame House, a large classical house designed by Sir Robert Smirke for James Balfour 1817. Additions by William Burn *c.* 1827. Balustraded terraces were added still later to this imposing Victorian mansion. Beil House at which Lorimer attended weekend parties is within a few miles of it and is a conglomerate of tower house, vast Gothic additions of 1814 and a large conservatory rebuilt in 1883 by Rowand Anderson. A large, terraced garden steps down to the Beil Water. 'The Tapestry Room was refitted by Robert Lorimer early in the 20th century' (page 102, *Lothian*, the Buildings of Scotland. Colin McWilliam, London, 1978, p. 102).

3. The rectangular sash window is 'the kind you usually build in Edinburgh [and it] has a certain dignity in its utter refusal of ornament but 'I cannot say it is entertaining . . . I have not

counted them all through the [New] Town [but in] this very Queen Street (with York Place and Picardy Place) there are six hundred and seventy-eight' (John Ruskin, lectures on Architecture and Planning delivered in Edinburgh in November 1853, published London 1891).

4. Rowallan Castle. U-shaped in plan. It is a mansion defensively planned without most of the military trimmings usual for the sixteenth century. There are no turrets or corbelling, merely towers on either side of the main entrance. The rooms are *en suite* without corridors.

5. Mullioned windows were used for monasteries as part of the Gothic tradition in Scotland. Baronial windows were small, often only their upper half glazed with opening wood shutters below. Lorimer echoed such divisions in his efforts to provide larger windows demanded by his clients without losing the withdrawn character of the sixteenth century Scots architecture.

6. Balcaskie. Seat of the Anstruthers since 1694. Bought by Sir William Bruce in 1665 and extensively remodelled on palladian lines after extensive trips on the Continent. Fretwork ceilings by George Dunsterfield. The slope to the east is terraced in 'Italian' fashion.

5

1. Art Workers Guild, founded by a group of architects in 1884 to promote good craftsmenship.

2. What Lorimer referred to as a mother's bowl is called in Holland *Brandewynkom*. It was used as a brandy bowl and anybody who called at the home of the bride during the wedding period would be invited to toast the young couple in three spoonfuls of brandy with raisins. Everyone used the same spoon which was the 'birth spoon' of the bride. The bowl and spoon were kept for these special occasions (note by Sybylle Cole).

3. Royal Scottish Society of Arts, instituted 1821,

incorporated 1841. It grew out of the Select Society founded in Edinburgh in 1754 by Allan Ramsay, modelled on the Academies for debate found in France, as a way of encouraging the Arts, Sciences, Manufactures and Agriculture.

4. Lawrence Turner, author of *Decorative Plaster work in Great Britain*, London 1927, include examples from Kellie Castle, Balcaskie. An Arts and Crafts man well known to Lorimer.

5. The Earl of Leven left £40,000 in 1906 for a Chapel for the Knights of the Thistle if it could be fashioned from Holyrood Abbey by Thomas Ross. Professor Lethaby was appointed to report on the existing building and advised that to rebuild it as a Thistle Chapel 'would be disastrous to it as a great historical monument'. There was some public outcry against this opinion and since Lethaby became master of the A.W.G. James Richardson was inclined to see Lorimer's influence in this. The E.A.A. set up a committee which included Deas which said the building was strong enough to carry a new roof to replace the one which had fallen in, but made no comment on the aesthetics of so doing 'as such does not fall under the remit'. The executors declined to act, and the bequest was allowed to lapse. (E.A.A. Transactions, Vol. V, Edinburgh 1910, pp. 181–92). When the offer was renewed by his sons the site was shifted to St Giles, and Lorimer became the architect.

6

1. Dullatur, a quarry in Dunbartonshire opened shortly before 1907, providing a stone with weathering qualities which have since proved poor.

2. Wemyss Hall. Designed by William Bruce *c.* 1695. A simple, symmetrical three-storey classical house with a hipped, slated roof entered from a southern forecourt reached from east and west drives. Lorimer's remodelling of 1907 by which it is enclosed on three sides carries a faint echo of the French nuances of Bruce's work.

3. Barncluith. A sixteenth-century garden near Hamilton in Lanarkshire. Lorimer found it 'quite unlike anything else' and quoted Walter Scott's essay on 'Forest Trees' in his own paper on Scottish Gardens. 'It is the most romantic little garden in Scotland, lying on one side of a great wooded valley, it is a veritable "hanging" garden. Four or five terraces one above the other sticking on to the side of a cliff, the general angle of which is about 55 degrees. Two little summer houses, great trees of scented box, and the flowers gathered here you feel sure would be not a "bouquet" but a "posy" – such an atmosphere about the place. In the twilight or the moonlight destinies might be determined in this garden.'

7

1. The Imperial War Graves Commission. It began during 1914 as a Graves Registration Unit. The Commission was set up in 1917 to consider what permanent form the cemeteries might take. An advisory committee under Sir F. Kenyon (of the British Museum) drew up a report in 1918, and six principal architects were appointed, of which Lorimer was one, he being charged with the design of cemeteries in Italy, Greece, Egypt, Germany and the U.K. (*The Unending Vigil*, P. Longworth, London 1967).

8

1. The Cockburn Association, founded 1875 'for the improvement of Edinburgh and the neighbourhood', named after Lord Cockburn who had done so much to promote these ends. It has always argued for conservation.

2. It may be that Lorimer was referring to James Richardson as the enemy, however in the hard times for all artists and craftsmen following the 1914–18 war, the Scottish National War Memorial raised wide animosity for various reasons, and Esme Gordon has related at length the tedious affair when three sculptors, Pittendrigh Macgillivray, Birnie Rhind, and G. S. Gamley, not only opposed Lorimer's election as full academician to the R.S.A. in 1918 but accused him of 'practices outside the recognised etiquette of his profession' (*The R.S.A.*, Esme Gordon, Edinburgh 1976, pp. 185–92). Subsequently, no evidence was found to substantiate the charge and this trio may have been only objecting to the way he offered a package deal for war memorials for all services, including his own and a sculptor's when needed, as well as those of the contractor.

3. The Society of Eight. A group of painters founded 1912 who all used light-toned colour. F. C. B. Cadell was one of them (Sir J. L. Caw *Scottish Painting, 1620–1906*).

From a letter.

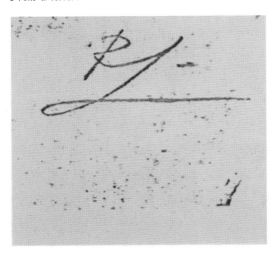

Biographical Notes

Notes on the Architects, Craftsmen, Family Members and Friends mentioned in the text, alphabetically arranged.

ADAM, William, 1689–48, of Kirkcaldy, Fife, and father of John, Robert, James and William the younger, most of whom were educated at the High School, Edinburgh and all at The University of Edinburgh. His works included the Royal Infirmary, Infirmary Street which is now part of the university, and the east side of Hopetoun House (the west is by William Bruce).

ANDERSON, Sir Robert Rowand, 1834–1921, born Forres. Son of a lawyer. Trained for four years as lawyer, then worked in Edinburgh drawing office of Royal Engineers with Col. Moody and R. W. Billings. 1855 trained as architect with John Lessels of Edinburgh. Worked for Sir Gilbert Scott, London. Toured continent, worked briefly for Cuypers, published 'Examples of the Municipal, Commercial and Street Architecture of France and Italy' (undated), started practice in Edinburgh, 1862, with houses and Episcopalian Churches. Married Mary Ross, 1863. Won School Board competition for three schools, 1873. Won limited competition for New Medical School for University of Edinburgh, 1875. P.E.A.A., 1874. A.R.S.A., 1876. Resigned on being passed over for election to full Academician, 1883. Took G. W. Browne as partner, 1881. Amalgamated in 1884 with Hew Wardrop to form, Wardrop, Anderson and Browne, a partnership Anderson carried on alone after Wardrop's early death in 1887 and Browne leaving in 1888. Hon. R.S.A., 1896. Partnership with Simon and Crawford, 1898, dissolved 1902. Partnership with Balfour

Paul, 1903. He helped set up R.I.A.S. in 1916 and was Gold Medallist at J. J. Burnet's recommendation. His life long interest in the building heritage of Scotland and its recording was recognised by the publication in 1921 of the first of four portfolio volumes of drawings many of which he had commissioned for the National Art Survey of Scotland. Others followed in 1923, 1925 and 1933.

ANSON, Peter, Author of *Fashions in Church Furnishing*, London 1960.

ANSTRUTHER, Robert, 1834–1913. 5th Bt. of Balkaskie (one mile south of Kellie Castle), seat of the Anstruthers since 1694 Lt. Col. Grenadier Guards. H.M. Lieutenant of Fife and M.P. for Fife. The terraced garden layed out by William Bruce was an early interest of Lorimer's.

ARMOUR, Hazel (Mrs John Kennedy). Exhibited at the R.S.A. in the nineteen-thirties. Designed 'The Tunnellers' Friends' panel in the Scottish National War Memorial.

ASHBEE, Charles Robert, 1863–1942. Kings College Cambridge, Articled to George Bodley 1886, founded Guild of Handicraft 1888, and Essex house printing press 1902. Writer, designed a number of simple houses. Lorimer told Dods on his election to the A.W.G. 'Suppose I ought to be proud to be associated with C. R. Ashbee, Voysey etc., anyway I accepted.'

BAKER, Sir Herbert, 1862–1946. K.C.I.E., R.A., F.R.I.B.A. Born in Cobham, Kent, educated R.A. School of Design and the A.A. Articled to his uncle Arthur Baker 1879. Assistant to E. George, 1882. Practised in South Africa,

1893–1912, thereafter in London. Architect to the government of South Africa, India and Kenya. Principal architect, 1919–26, to Imperial War Graves Commission where Lorimer came to know him well. Knighted, 1926, Gold Medal, 1927, Hon. D.C.L., Oxford, 1937.

BALFOUR and TURNER, architects, London. Lorimer knew the Balfour family including Eustace, the architect, and was invited to house parties at Whittinghame, the family seat in East Lothian. He was fiercely critical of what he called B. & T.'s 'South African Houses on Park Lane'. Turner (H. Thackeray) was a leading Arts and Crafts figure and first secretary of S.P.A.B.

BAXTER, John, ?–1798. Edinburgh architect. Domestic and ecclesiastical work such as Galloway House, 1730–50. Rebuilt Gordon Castle.

BARRY, Charles, 1795–1860, R.A., F.R.S. articled to Middleton and Bailey, Lambeth surveyors, 1810–16. Began practice in London, 1820. Large extension (with Leslie) to Dunrobin, Golspie, seat of Duke of Sutherland, 1844, (also designed Houses of Parliament with A. W. N. Pugin, 1840, and the Treasury Whitehall, 1845).

BEATTIE, Thomas. A young architectural modeller whom Lorimer instilled with his ideas, and who contributed hand modelled ceilings from 1893 until 1923.

BEGG, John, 1864–1937, F.R.I.B.A. Trained with H. J. Blanc Edinburgh. Hon. mention Pugin Prize, 1889, Pugin Prize, 1890, Ashpital Prize, 1891. Worked with Alfred Waterhouse, London, runner up Soane Medallion, 1892, Silver Medal, 1894. Outstanding draughtsman who drew several of Lorimer's early submissions to the R.S.A. Then worked for Real Estate Corporation in South Africa. Returned to Edinburgh during Boer War and worked part-time for Lorimer. Consulting Agent to Government of Bombay, 1901, and to Government of India; 1908–21. Responsible for large number of public buildings. Partnership with Lorne Campbell in Edinburgh, 1921. Head of School of Architecture, Edinburgh College of Art (of which Lorimer was a governor) 1922. P.E.A.A., 1929. P.R.I.A.S., 1932. One of Lorimer's inner circle of lifelong friends.

BLANC, Hippolyte Jean, 1844–1917, R.S.A. Born Belgium. Pupil of Robert Matheson and David Rhind. Member of most professional committees. P.E.A.A., 1871, 1888–1906. A.R.S.A., 1892, R.S.A., 1896 and Treasurer 1907–17. Large practice in Baronial and Jacobean styles.

BLOMFIELD, sir Reginald, 1865–1942 R.A., F.R.I.B.A. Educated Haileybury and Exeter College, Oxford. Trained by uncle Arthur, 1829–1900 (who had a large ecclesiastical practice), and at Academy Schools, began practice 1884 with mixed commercial and public buildings. Principal architect to Imperial War Graves Commission where he met Lorimer. Author of *The Formal Garden*, 1889, a book which may have helped Lorimer to his views on garden design. Member Fine Art Commission. Member, Board of Ancient Monuments, and of advisory council, Victoria and Albert Museum.

BLOW, Detmar, 1867–1939, F.R.I.B.A. Educated Hawtreys. Pugin Prize, 1892 and started practice with F. Billerey. Lorimer reminded Dods that he 'used to scoff because he was one of the "from the roots upwards" crew, but I don't suppose you ever met him', Blow had carried out the mason's work on Gimson's Leicester Cottages and was a member of S.P.A.B. Lorimer met him in 1896 and was impressed but they did not meet again until 1906.

BODLEY, George Frederic, 1827–1907, R.A., E.P.S.A., F.R.I.B.A. Born in Hull, Yorkshire. Pupil of George Gilbert Scott, 1845–50. Began practice, 1860. Partnership with Thomas Garner, 1869–97. He worked closely with all his craftsmen, especially on ecclesiastical buildings. He gave William Morris his first commission for stained glass (Kings Stanley Church). Established Watt and Co. to produce church fittings. Designed houses and gardens. Gold Medal, 1899.

BONE, Phyllis, 1894–1972, A.R.S.A. 1929. First woman R.S.A., 1944. Sculptor of animals, worked extensively on Scottish National Memorial. Notable series of animal capitals of the piers of the great niches on the exterior. Also stylised lion and unicorn on either side of the entrance.

BONNAR, Thomas, 1810–73. Decorative artist. Principal of Bonnar and Co. Restoration of painted ceilings and measured copies including Earlshall.

BOSE, Finrandra Nath, A.R.S.A. ?–1926. So far as is known, was the first Indian Sculptor to receive official recognition in Britain. Born in Calcutta, came to Britain when 15, trained at Royal Institution School, and College of Art Edinburgh, (under Percy Portsmouth R.S.A.). Travelling Scholarship to Paris to work with Rodin. Married a Scot. He worked from the Dean Studios and exhibited at the R.S.A. (from 1909), the R.A., and in India. (Note by Priscilla Minay, Central Fine Arts Library, Edinburgh).

BRIERLEY, Walter H., 1862–1926. Trained with father and then worked in Yorkshire on Arts and Crafts Tudor houses, Gothic churches and neo-Georgian public buildings. A northern architect showing points of similarity with Lorimer.

BROWN, Gerard Baldwin, 1855–1932, F.S.A. Scot. Educated Uppingham and Oriel College, Oxford, and Fellow of Brasenose College. First Watson Gordon professor of Fine Art, University of Edinburgh, 1880. Prolific author of papers on the arts including architecture. Hon.

A.R.I.B.A., 1887, P.E.A.A., 1889. Commissioner Board Ancient Monuments, 1909, Hon. R.S.A., 1911.

BROWN, Lancelot (Capability), 1719–83, born Northumberland, began career as gardener. Worked at Stowe in 1740 when he met William Kent. Became landscape consultant in 1749. Worked with Robert Adam and Henry Holland.

BROWN, Margaret Smith, 1899–1974. Daughter of a Merchant Navy Captain. Trained Athol Crescent and McAdams Secretarial School. Joined Lorimer as temporary typist, 1916. Stayed on with him and then with Matthew until 1940. Lorimer worked her hard – as he did everyone else – and educated her to beome a dedicated member of his team imbued with a strong sense of mission. Married James Swan, the civil engineer responsible for much work in the East including Raffles Hotel, Singapore.

BROWNE, sir George Washington, 1853–1939, R.S.A., F.R.I.B.A. Trained with Campbell Douglas, Glasgow, to 1857. First winner of J. J. Stevenson prize for measured drawings. Pugin Prize, 1878. Worked for J. J. Stevenson and E. Robson in London, 1881, as well as for Arthur Blomfield and W. E. Nesfield. Then worked with Rowand Anderson becoming chief draughtsman of the Medical School and partner from 1881–4. P.E.A.A., 1884, Partner in Wardrop, Anderson and Browne, 1884–7. Partner with Dick Peddie, 1887–1905. A.R.S.A., 1892, R.S.A., 1902 P.R.S.A., 1924–33. Commercial and public buildings in Francois Premier and neo-Classical styles. His own house is in freely composed Queen Anne, Lorimer deeply respected him 'because he could do the whole thing' and he also shared Browne's liking for French culture.

BRUCE, sir William, c. 1630–1710. Younger son of Robert Bruce of Blairhall, Fife. Enjoyed many years of Royal patronage after playing some part in Restoration of Charles II. In 1665 he bought, extended and remodelled Balcaskie and laid out he terraced garden. The house had plasterwork by Dunsterfield who probably did the decorated ceilings at Kellie c. 1665. He bought an estate at Kinross in 1675 and built a large house for himself. The garden axis terminated by Queen Mary's Castle on an island in Loch Leven, was among the effects particularly liked by Lorimer.

BRYCE, David, 1803–76, R.S.A. Founder of short-lived Architectural Institute of Scotland. Son of Edinburgh builder, trained in father's office with W. Burn, later in partnership with him. Burn moved his practice to London, 1844, Bryce carried on Edinburgh practice becoming leading exponent of revival Baronial. Briefly in partnership with Rowand Anderson and D. Bryce (nephew) in 1873. A.R.S.A., 1851, R.S.A., 1856.

BRYDON, John McKean, 1840–1901, F.R.I.B.A. Trained in Liverpool as well as Edinburgh with D. Bryce and Glasgow with Campbell Douglas. Assistant to Shaw and Nesfield, London. Began practice, London, c. 1880. Public and commercial buildings, interior designs and furniture. Recommended Lorimer for R.I.B.A. associate-ship. Vice President R.I.B.A., 1899–1901.

BURN, William, 1789–1870. Born Edinburgh son of Robert Burn, architect. Trained with Sir Robert Smirke, London. Succeeded to father's practice, 1820. Classical public buildings, neo-Tudor and neo-Jacobean country houses re-introducing also Scots traditional features. Partnership with Bryce until 1844 forming most influential Edinburgh firm. After 1844 transferred his practice to London and thereafter mostly executed domestic buildings.

BURNET, Sir John James, 1857–1938, R.A., R.S.A., F.R.I.B.A. Born Glasgow. Educated Ecole des Beaux Arts, Paris, 1874–77. Partnership with John Burnet, his father, 1878. Moved to London, 1905, and developed a large mixed practice with partners Thomas Tait and Francis Lorn, while remaining a partner in Glasgow, F.R.S., Edinburgh, F.S.A. Scot., A.R.S.A., 1893, R.S.A., 1914, Knighted, 1914, Gold Medal, 1923. A principal architect of Imperial War Graves Commission, 1918–26.

BURRELL, Sir William, 1861–1958. Succeeded to father's shipping business with George his elder brother, 1885. Perhaps Scotland's most opulent collector of the Antique. Lorimer went on three European tours with Burrell, his two sisters and mother, visiting museums and antique shops. He may have played a part in swinging Lorimer away from his Arts and Crafts pre-occupation and the delights of having new – sweet smelling-furniture made towards collecting antiques. Burrell was Lorimer's closest friend after Dods returned to Australia in 1896 and introduced him to other collectors including Sir T. G. Carmichael. Hon. R.S.A., Knighted, 1945.

BUTTERFIELD, William, 1814–1900, F.S.A. Articled to builder London, then with architect in Worcester where he practiced. Transferred practice to London, 1844. Active member of Camden Society (Cambs) for reform of ecclesiastical architecture. Large ecclesiastical practice. Gold Medal, 1884.

CADELL, Francis Campbell Boileau, 1883–1937, R.S.A. Painter of landscapes and still life. A.R.S.A., 1931, R.S.A., 1936. Cousin of Phyllis Bone and J. S. Richardson.

CAMPBELL, John A., 1859–1909. Trained with Burnet and Son, then at École des Beaux Arts, Paris, 1880–83. Partnership with J. J. Burnet in Glasgow, 1886–97, thereafter in practice alone.

CAMERON, Sir David Young, 1865–1945. Born Glasgow. Etcher and painter. Studied in Edinburgh for a short time. A.R.S.A., 1904. Member of Scottish Water Colour Society, Society of Twelve and Berlin and Munich secessionists. He executed figures and landscapes, city scenes and interiors. Knighted, 1927. Knew Lorimer socially. H.M. Painter and Limner for Scotland, 1933.

CARRICK, Alexander, 1882–1966. Sculptor. A.R.S.A., 1918, R.S.A., 1929. Worked on Scottish National War Memorial. Succeeded Portsmouth as head of Sculpture in Edinburgh College of Art.

CARMICHAEL, Thomas Gibson, Bt. of Castlecraig, Peebleshire. Proprietor of Hailes Quarry, Chairman of Board of Trustees National Gallery, Scotland. An influential collector with whom Lorimer had many dealings.

CLARK, James H., 1886–?. A.R.S.A., 1934. Modelled maquettes from which the Clows worked. He also worked with Beattie in Edinburgh.

CHALMERS, Peter MacGregor, 1859–1922. Pupil of Honeyman. A scholar rather than designer. His wife also an architect. Romanesque churches and restorations. Glasgow-based practice.

CHAMPNEYS, Basil, 1842–1935. Trinity College, Cambridge. Articled Llandaff office. Began practice 1867. Gold Medal 1912. Lorimer found his work too 'pretty' for his tastes.

CLOW, W. and A., Woodcarvers who set up shop in 1891, met Lorimer in 1892 and went on to work exclusively for him. The Thistle Chapel Stalls was their first big job. By 1931 Hussey described them as – 'Two identical middle-aged men, looking, in their long grey overalls, like Tweedledum and Tweedledee grown spare and kindly', as they each reiterated each other's thoughts. They were something of linguists and scholars, totally absorbed in their work. They took holidays in Europe only to measure and draw more details from buildings and museums. They achieved a virtuosity unsurpassed since the Middle Ages (Hussey) and often worked from plaster maquettes modelled by Deuchars, Hayes and latterly Meredith-Williams and Pilkington Jackson.

COWIE, Morton, c. 1900–1970. Architect who trained with Lorimer 1920–24. Practised in Edinburgh.

CRAWFORD, R. Hunter, c. 1860–?. Worked for five

years with J. Russell Walker, Edinburgh, for three years with Selden Wornum in London and for six months with L.C.C. Returned to Edinburgh 1891. Partnership with Rowand Anderson, 1899–1902. His harled and tiled cottages in Colinton, a little later than Lorimer's, share their simplicity. P.E.A.A., 1902. (Details provided by Anne Riches).

DAVIS, LOUIS. Stained glass artist, Pinner, London. Probably met Lorimer in Oxford in 1896. An Arts and Crafts figure, who did much of the glass for Lorimer's buildings 1896–1914. A close friend of Lorimer's.

DAWBER, Sir E. GUY, 1861–1938. Worked for Sir Thomas Deane and Sir Ernest George. Began practice 1891. Lorimer met him at A.W.G. meetings in 1896 and Dawbers Cottages, like Lorimer's, rely on an extreme simplicity of detail.

DEVEY, GEORGE, 1820–86, F.R.I.B.A. Born London. Articled to London surveyor Little. Began practice in eighteen forties. Large country house practice.

DEAS, FRANK W., M.A., F.R.I.B.A. Lorimer persuaded him to become an architect rather than an interior decorator, and they were very close friends. Deas was deeply musical and Lorimer used him as a confidant often spending weekends at the house, The Murrel, which Deas built himself near Aberdour. Deas practised from the same addresses as V. Horsburgh and helped Hussey on the compilation of his book.

DEUCHARS, LOUIS, 1871–1927. Sculptor and Painter. Studied Glasgow School of Art, and in London under G. F. Watts, R.A., Continental tour. He exhibited works in the galleries from 1900 to 1920. He modelled the cherubs' heads carved for the Thistle Chapel and several fireplaces for Lorimer, and also 'The Miracle' modelled for a fountain designed by Lorimer (Exhibited R.S.A., 1917). (Note by Louise Boreham.)

DICKSON, Dr. ELDER, 1899–1978. Author of the section on the crafts in the Statistical Account of Edinburgh, 1966. Formerly Vice-Principal Edinburgh College of Art.

DODS, ROBIN SMITH, 1868–1920. Met Lorimer in 1890 in Oxford and became his closest friend. Born Dunedin, New Zealand, of Scottish parents. Came to Edinburgh in 1886 to train with Hay and Henderson. Member of E.A.A. work class committee, 1890, and went to London to work for Aston Webb and Ingress Bell. Worked later for William Dunn. Special Prize in Tite Prize Competition, 1893, medal of mention Soane Prize, 1894. A fine draughtsman, he did some of Lorimer's early exhibition drawings. Returned to Brisbane to partnership with Francis Hall, 1896. They became pre-eminent for houses and churches. Moved to Sydney, 1911, to a commercial practice but his health was failing. Lorimer and he discussed life and every aspect of their design in their letters and he was considering a return to go into partnership with Lorimer as late as 1916.

DUNCAN, JOHN, 1866–1945, R.S.A. Decorative painter. Native of Dundee. The main neo-Celt of the Edinburgh Group seeking a Scots renaissance in art (based on Celtic motives). He contributed to Patrick Geddes's short-lived magazine, the *Evergreen*. His murals included a frieze on the evolution of pipe music for the hall of Geddes's house and seven panels from Celtic and Scots history for Ramsay Lodge, showing rich colour, a sense of movement and a conscious return to the primitive. A.R.S.A., 1910, R.S.A., 1923 and librarian, 1925–45. Assistant Professor Chicago School of Education, 1900–1903.

DUNN, WILLIAM, 1859–1934. Worked with William Flockhart before joining James Maclaren. Partnership with Robert Watson, 1890. They carried on Maclaren's work with less originality but no great change of emphasis. Dunn was an early exponent of reinforced concrete and his influence shows perhaps, in Lorimer's use of it for the floors of most of his country mansions.

Lorimer and he kept in touch after Lorimer['s] return to Edinburgh.

DUNN, JAMES B., 1861–1930. Partner of Finlay P.E.A.A., 1910–12, A.R.S.A., 1918, R.S.A. 1930. Buildings included *The Scotsman* office on North Bridge, Edinburgh, and the east win[g] to Sheildaig earlier built by Lorimer.

ELLIOTT, ARCHIBALD, 1761–1831. Began work i[n] London but returned to practice architecture i[n] Edinburgh. Works include Waterloo Place 1815, St Paul's Episcopalian Church, 1816 Broughton Place Church, 1821 (all i[n] Edinburgh).

FAIRLIE, REGINALD, 1883–1951. c. 1902 trained with Lorimer and became a close friend of J. S[.] Richardson who was in the office at that time Worked in London. Began practice in Edinburgh, 1909. Churches in third pointed period o[f] Gothic, and modified norman. A.R.S.A., 1923[,] R.S.A., 1934.

FLETCHER, MORLEY, Principal of Edinburgh College of Art. Brother of Sir Bannister Fletcher architect. Was closely associated with Lorime[r] through the D.I.A. and through the College Board of Governors of which Lorimer was a member for many years.

GIBSON, THOMAS, Architect. Designed Marchmont, Berwickshire 1750–54. No other work known (*Biographical Dictionary British Architects*, Colvin, 1978).

GILLIES, WILLIAM, 1898–1973, R.S.A. Trained and taught at, and was finally Principal of, Edinburgh College of Art. Landscape and still life painter. A.R.S.A., 1940, R.S.A., 1947.

GOODHART-RENDEL, HARRY STUART, 1887–1959. Articled Charles Nicholson. Began practice in London, 1910. P.R.I.B.A., 1937–39. Numerous writings and works of architectural criticism.

GRAHAM, JAMES GILLESPIE, 1777–1855. Born in

Dunblane. Apprenticed to joiner, married an heiress. Practised architecture in Edinburgh. Gothic revival mansions and layout of Moray Estate in New Town of Edinburgh.

GUTHRIE, Rome. Scottish student, Alex Thomson Prize, 1900. Made the drawings, including those of Earlshall, for H. I. Triggs *Formal Gardens in England and Scotland*, London 1902. (Thomas Ross helped choose Scots examples.)

HAY, William, 1818–88. Worked in 1846 for John Henderson (his partner's father) and later as Clerk of Works for George G. Scott at St John's, Newfoundland. After practising in Montreal, Chicago and Toronto, returned to Edinburgh in 1879 to enter partnership with George Henderson, the younger.

HEITON, Andrew, 1823–94. Pupil of his father and of David Bryce. Domestic practice based in Perth.

HENDERSON, George, the younger, 1846–1905. Practised in Geelong, Victoria, Australia, (houses, schools, factories), 1867–79. Partnership in Edinburgh, 1879, with William Hay. Dods may have chosen to train in this firm because of its Australian connections. (Notes by Robert Riddel.)

HILL, Arthur. Director of Kew Gardens and advisor to the Imperial War Graves Commission in Egypt.

HORSBURGH, Victor, *c.* 1860–?. He witnessed Lorimer's indenture at Wardrop, Anderson and Browne's in 1884. Silver Medal, 1907. Member Advisory Committee on the Town Planning and Housing Supplement of the *Architectural Review* with Lorimer, Ashbee Crane and Macartney, 1910. Drew perspectives for Lorimer. May well have shared offices at 23 Rutland Square and 43 Frederick Street, Edinburgh with F. Deas.

HUSSEY, Christopher, 1899–1970. M.A., F.S.A., Hon. R.I.B.A., Hon. I.L.A. Historian of Scotney Castle, Kent. Educated at Eton and Christ Church, Oxford. Architectural Advisor to *Country Life* Magazine. Historian and writer. Works included *Garden Ornament*, with Gertrude Jekyll, 1927. *The Picturesque* 1927. The job of writing *The work of Sir Robert Lorimer* was passed to him on Weaver's death in 1930. In parts vividly written, the book incorporates large extracts from Weaver's earlier articles.

JACKSON, Charles d'Orville Pilkington, 1887–1973. A.R.S.A., 1956. A sculptor and modeller primarily of military figures. A modest man who told me, 'I may not have been the best sculptor on the Scottish National War Memorial but I was certainly the busiest.'

JACKSON, Sir Thomas Graham, 1835–1924. R.A., F.S.A., F.R.I.B.A. Educated Wadham College, Oxford. Articled to Sir George G. Scott, 1858. Began practice, 1862. Examination schools 1876, Trinity College 1883, Brasenose College 1886, Hertford College 1887 and 1903, were Oxford works for which Lorimer expressed grudging approval after seeing work by other contemporary architects in Cambridge.

JEKYLL, Gertrude, 1843–1932. Studied Kensington School of Art. Visits to France, Italy and Near East. Painter and designer who advised on interior of Eaton Hall. Many artistic friends including William Robinson, to whose journal *The Garden*, she contributed articles. 1885 took up photography. Met Lutyens at Littleworth near Munstead where she was living, 1889, and with whom she collaborated on many garden designs. Increasing myopia ended her painting and embroidery and she turned to gardening, writing a number of books. Her ideas on colour in the flower garden the most influential; also very knowledgeable on crafts of garden construction.

JOASS, John James, 1868–1952. Born Dingwall. Trained with his father, but left Dingwall to enter J. J. Burnet's office as office boy. Studied part-time at Glasgow College of Art. After 1890 he worked in Edinburgh. Pugin Prize, 1893, Owen Jones Prize, 1895, and A.R.I.B.A., 1895. Interested in the formal gardens of Scotland (*Studio* Vol, XI p. 165). Drew several perspectives for Lorimer. Became John Belcher's partner in London, *c.* 1897.

KENT, William, *c.* 1685–1748. Born Bridlington. European tour, Lord Burlington his patron, 1709–19. First he was a historical painter, began architectural career in early 1830. Important influence on English landscape gardening. Work at Stowe included gardens and temples. Also a leading interior designer.

KERR, Robert, 1823–1904, F.R.I.B.A. Born in Aberdeen. Founder member of the First President A.A., London. Professor of the Arts of Construction, King's College, London, 1847–8. District Surveyor of St James, Westminster, 1862–1902. Wrote *The English Gentleman's House*, 1864, which discusses the virtues of houses planned by certain Edinburgh Architects (Burn).

KINROSS, John, 1855–1931, R.S.A. Born Stirling, trained with John Hutchinson, Glasgow. Worked with Wardrop and Reid. European tour, 1882, published *Details from Italian Buildings, Chiefly Renaissance*, then started practice. A.R.S.A., 1893, R.S.A., 1905. In partnership with Seymour and later Tarbolton. Domestic and Ecclesiastic work, some of very high quality. Latterly treasurer of R.S.A., 1924–31.

KIRKWOOD, Elizabeth, Enamellist. Worked with Alex Kirkwood and Son on the later stall-plates for The Thistle Chapel in Edinburgh.

KITSELL, Thomas Rogers, 1864–1914. Attended University of Edinburgh with Lorimer. His declaration for associateship with the R.I.B.A. states he was apprenticed to Rowand Anderson and later his chief draughtsman (1878–87). Tite Prize, 1892, at about which time he started his own practice in London. One of Lorimer's circle of Scottish friends in London.

LAING, William, 1907–   . Last managing director of Nathaniel Grieves, Contractors and Architectural Woodworkers of Washington Lane, Dalry. The firm ran an intricate and thorough system of apprenticeship for their craftsmen and Lorimer used this firm regularly and consistently.

LEIPER, WILLIAM, 1893–1916. Pupil of Boucher and Cousland. Worked for Campbell Douglas, William White and J. L. Pearson. Began practice in Glasgow, c. 1865. A.R.S.A., 1892, R.S.A., 1896.

LETHABY, WILLIAM RICHARD, 1857–1931, F.S.A., F.R.I.B.A. Born in Barnstaple. Articled to local Architect Alexander Lauder, Soane Medallion, 1879. Entered R.A. Schools. Worked for N. Shaw, 1879–91. Founder member of A.W.G., 1886. Associated with S.P.A.B. and D.I.A. Founded and designed for Kenton and Co. furniture manufacturers. Lorimer visited one of his houses at Ringwood and told Dods that it failed in the very particulars against which Lethaby raged, that everything was 'done in the office' and not 'worked out on the spot as in the old days afore time'. Lethaby gave up practice in 1902 and devoted himself to teaching and writing. He was Principal of the Central School of Arts, 1896–1911 and Professor of Design at the R.C.A., 1900–1918.

LLOYD, NATHANIEL. Author of *A History of the English House*, 1934. Commissioned the restoration of Great Dixter from Lutyens, with a topiary garden like Earlshall, c. 1911.

LOCKHART, WILLIAM EWART, 1846–1900, R.S.A. Entered Trustees Academy, 1861. First of several visits to Spain, 1867, from which came costume and domestic paintings. Also painted episodes of Scots history, of literature and portraits. A.R.S.A., 1871, R.S.A., 1878. Lived in Edinburgh until 1887 when Queen Victoria commissioned him to paint her Jubilee Celebrations in Westminster Abbey. His works show a relish for colour and a gusto in handling. Painted portrait of Alice Corbett, *Pl. 95*

LORIMER, JAMES, 1818–90, M.A., LLD, F.R.S.E., M.A., Edinburgh, 1856, LL.D Glasgow, 1882, and Dr Juris, Bonn, Geneva and Berlin. Advocate, 1845. Principal Lyon Clerk, 1848, (office regulating use of heraldic emblems in Scotland). Published *Handbook of the Law in Scotland*, 1859. Professor of Public Law (and law of nature and nations), 1862, and for which he exercised his deep interest in the philosophy of law and politics, and in aspects of moral philosophy. Other publications, listed p 173 *Quasi Cursores*, Constable, Edinburgh, 1884.

He married Hannah Stodart (1835–1916) in 1851 who was a grand-daughter of Robert Stodart founder of the firm which did so much to develop the grand piano early in the nineteenth century, and she was both artistic and musical. She had six children: James born 1853 emigrated and died in South Africa in 1899. Hannah Cassels born 1854, an able modeller, painter and carver in wood, who married Sir E. im Thurm, Governor-General of Fiji in 1856. John Henry born 1856, died 1936, trained at the R.S.A. School and with McTaggart and Chalmers in Scotland and Carolus Duran in Paris. A.R.S.A., 1882, R.S.A., 1900. Portraits, landscapes and genre paintings. Subject painter of distinction. Janet Alice born 1857. Married Sir David Chalmers, she commissioned the designs for some of Lorimer's best early furniture and she embroidered some of his designs. Caroline Louise, born 1861, wrote verse and prose and was a keen gardener. She remained single. She, John and Robert were particularly close. Robert Stodart, born 1864 benefitted from John's abilities in draughtsmanship and painting.

LORIMER, SIR ROBERT STODART, b. 1864. Educated Edinburgh Academy, and University of Edinburgh. Apprenticed to Hew Wardrop in Edinburgh 1884. Worked in London for George Bodley, 1889, and James Maclaren and his successors Dunn and Watson. Returned to Edinburgh 1892. Set up office in 1893, elected to A.W.G., 1896, as A.R.S.A., 1903, in which year he married Violet Wyld. Knighted, 1911, appointed principal architect to Imperial War Graves Commission, 1918, elected A.R.A., 1920 and R.S.A., 1921. LL.D. Edinburgh K.C.B.E. and elected P.R.I.A.S., 1928. Died September 1929.

LUTYENS, SIR EDWIN LANDSEER, 1869–1944. R.A. F.R.I.B.A. Born London. Educated R.C.A., briefly a pupil of Sir E. George, 1887. Began practice 1889, and became Britain's most celebrated architect of his time. Lorimer came to know him very well, probably through the A.W.G. and was very impressed by his work. Whinfold and possibly High Barn, both in Surrey show signs of Lutyen's influence. Lutyens introduced him to G. Jekyll, c. 1895. He and Lorimer dined and wined together on their respective visits south or north. Lutyens probably suggested Lorimer to the Imperial War Graves Commission as another principal architect in 1919. Lutyens was knighted in 1918, was Gold Medallist in 1923, when he recommended Lorimer to Rossall School for the design of their Memorial Chapel.

MACARTNEY, SIR MERVYN EDMUND, 1853–1932, F.S.A., F.R.I.B.A. Educated Lincoln College, Oxford. Pupil of Norman Shaw. Founder member A.W.G. (and its Master 1900). May have met Lorimer at the National Congress in Edinburgh 1889. Recommended Lorimer to R.I.B.A. for Associateship, R.I.B.A., 1890. Resigned R.I.B.A., 1891, rejoined 1906. Member of Kenton and Co. furniture designers and manufacturers, c. 1899. Practice included many houses and gardens (the relationship between which was his particular interest) and church restorations. Editor of the *Architectural Review*, 1905, and began widening its interests to town planning. Its advisory board was largely composed of A.W.G. members. Knighted 1930.

MACKENZIE, IAN, former managing director of Mackenzie and Moncur of Edinburgh; a firm started in 1869 as hot-house builders. As many head gardeners of the day were Scots the work spread throughout the U.K., and to country house heating as well. It entered electrical engineering about 1900, and its foundry produced most of the cast iron lighting standards for Edinburgh. It was another craft firm for whom the sixties were too hard and it closed around 1970.

MACGIBBON, DAVID, 1830–1902. Worked for William Burn at same time as Shaw and Nesfield. Started practice Edinburgh c. 1855. P.E.A.A., 1882–4. A better writer than designer he began his authoritative *The Castellated and Domestic Architecture of Scotland* in 1887 after unsuccessful speculations in building virtually ended his practice.

MACKINTOSH, CHARLES RENNIE, 1869–1928, F.R.I.B.A. Born Glasgow, educated Glasgow College of Art. Articled to John Hutchinson, 1884. Joined Honeyman and Keppie as draughtsman, 1889. Alex Thomson Prize, 1890. Early work included office buildings and his domestic work after 1896 shows strong Art Nouveau influence. Partner with Honeyman and Keppie, 1904. Moved to London in 1913 and from there to France. Lorimer seems to have found nothing in common with him.

MACLAREN, JAMES MARJORIBANKS, 1843–90. Born Stirling. Articled James Salmon Sr., Glasgow. Worked for Campbell Douglas and Stevenson before moving to E. Godwin and Richard Coad's office, London. Started practice in London. Member A.W.G., 1886. Addressed E.A.A. on 'ancient ecclesiastical remains', 1889. Article by him in A.A. Notes Vol. 4, p.56 says that if architects 'are to succeed', they, 'are bound to good construction and proportion first before [taking] the liberty of a single ornament', which reinforced views earlier put to Lorimer by Hew Wardrop.

MACKMURDO, ARTHUR H., 1851–1942. Trained for one year with T. Chatfield Clarke, moved to Oxford where he met Ruskin with whom he travelled to Italy in 1874. Briefly with James Brooks in London in 1875. Started practice the same year. Founded the Century Guild, 1883, the first of the Art and Crafts Movement Guilds.

MATTHEW, JOHN FRASER, 1875–1955, F.R.I.B.A.,

F.R.I.A.S., F.S.A., SCOT. Trained at Edinburgh School of Applied Art and the Heriot Watt College. Articled to Lorimer, 1893. Served with Edinburgh Volunteers in South Africa in Boer War, and as Major in Signals in the First World War. Partner with Lorimer by 1927, after running office as manager for a quarter of a century. 'He was an inveterate humorist with a keen awareness of the ridiculous and seemed never too busy to enjoy a joke.' (Harry Hubbard).

MAXWELL, HERBERT EUSTACE, 1845–1932, BT., Born Edinburgh. Educated Christchurch College, Oxford. Rhind lecturer 1893–1911. Lecturer in Scots History, Glasgow University, 1910. President Society Antiquaries Scotland. Chairman Royal Commission on Scottish Historical Monuments. Lord Lieutenant, Wigtonshire. M.P.

MAXWELL, JOHN MAXWELL STIRLING, 1866–1945. 10th Bt. of Pollock House, Glasgow. Educated Trinity College, Cambridge. Chairman, Fine Art Committee. Trustee National Galleries of Scotland. Chairman of Ancient Monuments Board Scotland. *Shrines and Homes of Scotland*, 1937. Hon. R.S.A., Hon. R.I.B.A., Hon. R.W.S. M.P., College Division Glasgow (1895–1906).

MITCHELL, ARNOLD B., 1863–1944. Articled to E. George, London. Soane Medallion, 1885. Began practice which included many cottages, 1886. Practised from Harrow and Chiswick before retiring to Lyme Regis.

MITCHELL, ARTHUR GEORGE SYDNEY, 1856–1930. Pupil of Rowand Anderson. Practised in partnership with Wilson. Lorimer was unimpressed with their work and kept silent on Mitchell's fine house for himself – 'The Pleasance', Gullane (as Muthesius did not).

MORRIS, WILLIAM, 1834–96. Educated Exeter College, Oxford. Worked in office of G. E. Street and studio of Dante G. Rossetti. He revitalised the building crafts. Founded Morris Marshall and Faulkner, decorators, furniture designers and makers, of tiles, tableware and wall paper

manufacturers, 1861, the Kelmscott Press, and S.P.A.B.

MUTHESIUS, HERMAN, 1861–1927. German architect. Worked in Berlin. Commissioned by German Government to study low cost housing in Britain, 1896–1903. Author of *Das Englische Haus*, Berlin, 1904–5 and was the guiding influence of the Deutsche Werkbund, founded 1907.

NESFIELD, WILLIAM EDEN, 1835–88. Pupil of William Burn 1851–3 and of A. Salvin (his uncle) 1853–6. Began practice, 1858. Shared offices with N. Shaw, 1803–78. Executed gardens and ornamental parks as well as buildings and their furnishings.

NEWTON, ERNEST, 1856–1922, O.B.E., R.A., F.R.I.B.A. Articled to N. Shaw, 1873. Began practice, 1879. Founder member A.W.G., 1884, and early member of Arts and Crafts Society. Domestic practice including many cottages. Author of *A Book of Country Houses*, London, 1903, gives nineteen examples of his design. P.R.I.B.A., 1914–17. Gold Medal, 1918. Later work neo-Georgian.

NICHOLSON, SIR CHARLES, 1867–1949. Educated New College, Oxford. His father was Speaker in New South Wales House of Assembly and Chancellor of Sydney University. Articled to John Sedding, 1890. Worked with Henry Wilson, 1890. Began practice and won Tite Prize, 1893. Partnership with H. C. Collette, 1895–1914 succeeded to baronetcy, 1903. Partnership with Rushton, 1927–49. Large ecclesiastical practice. His *Recent Ecclesiastical Architecture* c. 1911 included two Lorimer churches.

NOBBS, PERCY ERSKINE, 1885–1964. M.A., Edin. Became Lorimer's pupil, c. 1896. Tite Prize, 1900, Owen Jones Prize, 1903. Worked for L.C.C. Succeeded Henbest Capper as McDonald Professor in Architecture at McGill University c. 1903. Partnership with Hyde. F.R.I.B.A., 1910, R.C.A., 1919. A very able but irascible man some of whose work in Canada is strongly Baronial.

PLAYFAIR, WILLIAM HENRY, 1789–1857. Son of James, a Scots architect practising in London and Scotland. Educated Edinburgh and under William Stark of Glasgow. Worked for Robert Smirke and James Wyatt in London. Started practice in Edinburgh and won 1815 competition for completion of Robert Adam's scheme for The University of Edinburgh. Other classical works, the R.S.A. and National Gallery of Scotland, also many Baronial mansions introducing Scottish features after 1830.

PORTSMOUTH, Percy H., 1873–1953. Studied under Walter Crane and Morley Fletcher. A.R.S.A., 1906, R.S.A., 1923. Head of Department of Sculpture at the Edinburgh College of Art. Carried out phoenix arising from the ashes in the deep cusped recess over the entrance to the Scottish National War Memorial in Edinburgh.

RICHARDSON, James Smith, 1883–1970, F.S.A., Scot, F.R.I.A.S., HON R.S.A. Born in North Berwick, trained with McIntyre Henry. Worked for Lorimer, c. 1903–6 F.S.A., Scot., 1912. H.M. Inspector of Ancient Monuments, Scotland, 1913–46, except for service as Captain in Royal Scots in the First World War. Chair of Antiquities of the R.S.A., 1953. Member, Societé Prehistoric Francaise. British Representative, League of Nations International Institute, department of Art and Architecture. F.R.I.A.S., 1922. Curator National Museum of Antiquities of Scotland, 1925. His work led to discovery of Skara Brae and the recovery of the Traprain Silver in East Lothian. Rhind lectures, 1948. Hon. LL.D University of St Andrews and Edinburgh. Designed formal gardens at Pitmedden and Edzell (also a gramophone driven by weights). Continued to bicycle until two years before his death at eighty seven.

ROSEBERY, Archibald Philip Primrose, 5th Earl of 1847–1929. K.C.G.K.T., P.C., D.C.L. An implacable critic of the designs for the Scottish National War Memorial and Lorimer felt that although

'Rosebery was shooting these poisoned arrows at him' he could not hit back at so old and so great a public figure. The public controversy sapped Lorimer's strength and contributed to his relatively early death.

ROSS, Thomas, 1839–1930, F.S.A., Scot., HON. R.S.A., 1918. Apprenticed to Kirkland and Charles Wilson in Glasgow. Assistant to D. MacGibbon, 1862, later partner. P.E.A.A., 1897–9. LL.D Edinburgh, 1910. Professor of Antiquities, R.S.A., 1918. Associated with Lorimer as Editor of the *National Art Survey for Scotland*, for volume 2, 1923, and volume 3, 1925.

SALVESEN, George, little has yet come to light about this sculptor who exhibited intermittently at the R.S.A. (1921, 1924, 1925), and who worked on the Scottish National War Memorial.

SCHULTZ, Robert Weir, 1861–1951. Born Scotland. Trained with Rowand Anderson, Edinburgh then worked for N. Shaw and Sir E. George in London. Began practice in London, 1891. Member A.W.G. (later its Master). Like Lorimer most of his work is domestic and strongly influenced by the Arts and Crafts. A friend of Lethaby. Study tours in Italy and Greece. Changed his name to Weir, 1914. Troup was his closest friend but Lorimer was close for a while before being alienated by Schultz's aggressive ways. His office had four or five assistants but he did not ever delegate design.

SCOTT, George Gilbert, the younger, 1837–97. Fellow of Jesus College, Assisted his father G. G. Scott R.A. (1811–78) and brother of John Oldrid. With Bodley and Garner established Watt and Co. to produce church fittings of pre-Raphaelite design. Later withdrew from practice. Lorimer liked his New Buildings for Pembroke College, Cambridge, 1883.

SCOTT, Sir Giles Gilbert, 1880–1960, O.M., R.A., F.R.I.B.A. Second son of George Gilbert Scott, the younger. Articled Temple Moore. Began practice, 1903. Won Liverpool Cathedral com-

petition. Large and varied practice. President, A.A., 1920. Knighted 1924. Gold Medal, 1925.

SEDDING, John Dando, 1835–91, F.R.I.B.A. Articled to G. E. Street. Pupil of his brother, 1865–8, practising in Penzance. Set up practice in London with Henry Wilson, 1875. Church restorations and all furnishings. Delivered paper at National Art Congress Edinburgh, 1899. His *Garden Craft Old and New* (1891) has all the poetic overtones adopted by Lorimer in his paper on Scottish Gardens (*Architectural Review*, 1899).

SHAW, Richard Norman, 1831–1912, R.A. Born Edinburgh. Educated at the Academy in Hill Street, the street in which Lorimer was born. Articled to William Burn (after Burn's move to London). R.A. Schools Medal. Travels in Europe. Published *Architectural Sketches* from his tour, 1858. He worked for A. Salvin briefly, and after 1858 for G. E. Street as draughtsman. Began practice, 1862, in offices shared with W. E. Nesfield. Member R.I.B.A. but resigned over its policies. Lorimer visited him regularly, and the Colinton Cottages may reflect a little of his influence. Hon. R.S.A., 1911.

SIMON, Frank W., 1862–1933. Trained with J. Cotton, Birmingham, then 1883–6 at Atelier Pascale, École des Beaux Arts, Paris. Professor in School of Applied Arts, 1892. Practice, 1894. Partnership with C. E. Tweedie 1899 also 1899 with Rowand Anderson and Hunter Crawford until 1902. Then moved to Canada.

SPARROW, Walter Shaw, 1862–c. 1935. Joined Charles Holmes as Assistant Art Editor for the *Studio Magazine* in 1899 and found Holmes was biased in favour of Art Nouveau, and after 1904 Sparrow as an independent editor pushed the craft side of architecture in a number of books featuring the cottages of Lutyens, Lorimer, Bidlake, Guy Dawber and E. Newton.

STATHAM, H. Heathcote, 1839–1924. Editor of *The Builder* and author, *Modern Architecture*, London, 1897.

STEVENSON, John James, 1831–1908. Started as student of theology but after Italian visit became pupil of David Bryce, Edinburgh (1856–8) then worked in office of Gilbert Scott in London. Joined Campbell Douglas in Glasgow as partner in 1860. Partnership with E. R. Robson, London, 1869. Continued to build in Scotland as well as churches, houses, university buildings in England. Pioneered Queen Anne Revival in his own house. His office became the Scotsman's stepping-stone to London. In 1891 he proposed Lorimer for associateship with R.I.B.A.

STRACHAN, Douglas, 1875–1950. Hon. LLD., Hon. R.S.A. Born Aberdeen. Apprentice lithographer to Aberdeen Free Press. Short period at Life School of R.S.A. Worked in Manchester on several papers as a black and white artist. Two wall panels on Ancient and Modern Labour for Aberdeen Trade Hall, 1898, followed by additional murals. Transferred to London, 1904. Returned to Edinburgh where he concentrated on design of stained glass windows. A strong colourist who was nevertheless a close friend of Lorimer's who shared his tastes in music and Chinese Art.

SWAN, Mrs Margaret. See BROWN, Margaret Smith.

TALBOT, Silversmith used by Lorimer. The only late Victorian or Edwardian silversmith of that name recorded in *English Goldsmiths and Their Mark* (Sir Charles Jackson, 1921) is of Crook, Darlington.

TAPPER, Sir Walter, 1861–1935. Born Devon. Articled Rowell and Son, Newton Abbot. Worked for B. Champneys, and then George Bodley where Lorimer met him. Began practice, 1900 was knighted and became P.R.I.B.A. Ecclesiastical and domestic practice. Lorimer was a life long friend of his and his wife Katie.

THOMSON, Alexander (Greek), 1817–75. Born Balfour, Stirlingshire. Worked for Robert Foote, Glasgow, and John Baird, the elder c. 1844. Entered partnership with John Baird, the younger, 1847, and later with his own brother George. Particularly known for his Neo-Greek houses and churches (including Great Western Terrace house remodelled by Lorimer for Burrell).

TRAQUAIR, Phoebe Anna, (née Moss) b. Dublin 1852–1936. Married Ramsay H. Traquair, 1873 for whom she illustrated articles on fossils. Later took up mural painting and manuscript design. She helped establish the Scottish Society of Arts and Crafts in 1898. She contributed jewellery and enamelwork to its exhibitions. She taught in School of Art set up by Patrick Geddes. Hon. mem. R.S.A., 1920.

TRAQUAIR, Ramsay, 1874–1952. Educ. University of Edinburgh and Bonn and under Capper at School of Applied Art 1896. Travelled abroad. Worked for Lorimer. Lecturer in College of Art. Emigrated to Canada 1913. McDonald Professor in Architecture, McGill 1914–39. Author of numerous papers and two main books on Architecture of Quebec and its Silverware. A keen sportsman. (Notes on Phoebe and her son Ramsay by Elizabeth Cumming, the City Art Centre Edinburgh).

TROUP, Francis W., 1859–1931. Born Barnstaple, articled locally before working for N. Shaw 1879–90. Began practice 1891. Lorimer met him at Tapper's house in 1896 and became friends. Lorimer used Troup's builder in Surrey and c. 1901 'lugged him (FWT) off to dine at the dear old SKM (Victoria and Albert Museum). Quite like the old days . . . a wander open mouthed into the tapestry court and oh Lord in heaven, what a place it is!! I still think that these allegorical Flemish 15th century tapestries are the most marvellous things that have ever been produced.' Troup later Master of A.W.G.

VOYSEY, Charles Francis Annesley, 1857–1941. Born Hessle. Articled J. P. Seddon. Worked for Saxon Snell and George Devey. Began practice 1881. He lived for some years largely off his wallpaper designs and had built very little by 1893 when Lorimer's first cottages were started.

WARDROP, Hew Montgomery, 1856–87. Succeeded to his father's practice, Wardrop and Reid, 1884, taking Rowand Anderson and G. Washington Browne as partners as well as Lorimer as apprentice (upon whom he had a strong influence). He died at the early age of thirty one in 1887 but Lorimer continued working on Tilliefour, one of Wardrop's few recorded jobs. The lodge is half-timbered.

WARDROP, James Maitland, 1824–92. Born London. 1849 partner with Thomas Brown and from 1874 with Charles Reid. His will 1887 witnessed by Lorimer. Revival Baronial houses and Gothic churches.

WATERHOUSE, Alfred, 1830–1905, R.A., F.R.I.B.A. Begg worked for him c. 1891. P.R.I.B.A., 1888–91. Visited Aberlour House in 1896 and commented favourably on Lorimer's plasterwork designs.

WATSON, George Mackie, 1859–1948, L.R.I.B.A. Articled to Rowand Anderson and later his principal assistant. Worked on McEwan Hall, Edinburgh. Began practice 1892. Built the small house of Bardrochat for the McEwans. First architectural teacher in the School of Applied Art.

WATSON, Robert, 1865–1916. Trained with Paterson of Edinburgh. Worked for H. J. Blanc. Assistant to Wardrop, Anderson and Browne, then to James Maclaren in London. Joined William Dunn 1890 as partner, to continue Maclaren's practice after which Lorimer (and Dods) worked for them. A fairly close friend of Lorimer's.

WEAVER, Lawrence, 1930, F.S.A., Hon. R.I.B.A., F.R. Historical society. Began as an ironmongery salesman, articled for three years but never practised. Joined Edward Hudson at *Country Life* magazine. Began writing articles on Lorimer's work 1905. 'To the younger architects of any spirit he was always readily accessible and a perpetual fount of wise and practical advice' (C. Williams-Ellis). He was influential at the D.I.A. and worked at the office of Controller of Food Production in the First World War. Lorimer kept in touch while visiting him on his journeys to and from the War Cemeteries. Director-General of U.K. Exhibits, Wembley Empire Exhibition. He had done some preparatory work on a book on Lorimer when he died and then Hussey took over the job.

WEBB, Sir Aston, 1849–1930, K.C.V.O., C.B., R.A., F.R.I.B.A. Born Clapham. Articled to Banks and Barry. Continental tour. Began practice London 1873. Collaborated with Ingress Bell, with whom in 1882 he was appointed consulting architect to the Crown Agents for the Colonies. Dods worked for him and was proposed for associateship with R.I.B.A. by him. P.R.I.B.A., 1902. Knighted 1904. Gold Medal, 1905, Gold Medal A.I.A., 1907. P.R.A., 1919. Works included Christ's Hospital, Horsham, 1893, upon which Dods worked.

WEST. T. W., Wrote not altogether satisfactory book on the history of Architecture in Scotland 1967, which nevertheless accurately reflects the general opinion of Lorimer's work at that time, and its anti-historical bias.

WILLIAMS, MEREDITH, M. and A. Both exhibited regularly at the R.S.A. (and are listed as Williams), Maurice exhibited as a painter, and Alice as a modeller-Sculptor. He taught art at Fettes College. Her work for the Scottish National War Memorial was based on his sketches, many made while serving in the war.

WILLIAMS-ELLIS, Clough, 1883–1978. Like Lutyens he was largely a self-taught architect. Although he and Lorimer were prominent members of the D.I.A. the Stowe Competition of 1926 was the only time they seem to have come together.

WILMOTT, Ernest. Author of *English House Design*

London 1911, which included Ardkinglas, Barton Hartshorn, Lympne Castle, and Wemyss Hall (since called Hill of Tarvit).

WILSON, J., ?–1959. Pupil of G. Washington Browne. Studied School of Applied Art, Edinburgh. Travelling Scholarship. Government service 1911. Chartered Architect to Department of Health Scotland 1928. P.R.I.A.S.

WILSON, Samuel. Architectural modeller who, with Beattie, did most of Lorimer's decorated hand modelled ceilings.

From a letter.

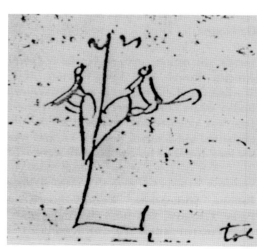

List of Works

The list of dates in Hussey's book was that provided by Lorimer's office. Its own inaccuracies show that the account books and records were not meticulously kept, but enough have survived to provide more than enough dates to make the initiatory work of each scheme hard to pin down. Lorimer worked intermittently on a number of buildings for decades and the list which follows records the present state of research on them. Lorimer's revival transitional Baronial works are listed under the description he used himself – 'Scotch'.

1 1891 FIELDHEAD, 43 Arthur Road, Wimbledon, London S.W. 19.
New Queen Anne brick house for uncle George Wyld M.D.

2 1892 EARLSHALL, Leuchars, Fife.
Restoration of sixteenth-century stone tower house, layout of new garden, new sewing pavilion, garden store and gate lodge for R. W. Mackenzie.

3 1893 ABERLOUR HOUSE, Banff.
Alterations to drawing room (new plasterwork within a classical country house) and Wrought Iron gates for J. R. Findlay.

4 WESTBROOK, Balerno, Edinburgh.
Addition of small wing to rear of classical country house, for J. H. Sang.

5 COLINTON COTTAGE, 23 Pentland Avenue, Colinton, Edinburgh.
New harled house in 'cottage' style with garden layout for Miss Guthrie Wright.

6 THE GRANGE, North Berwick, East Lothian.
New harled house for Lord Trayner. Walled garden and stable block. Extended 1899 and separate studio, dynamo house and garden pavilion built for Captain Armitage in 1904.

7 BUCKINGHAM TERRACE, 8, Queensferry Road, Edinburgh.
Alterations (remodelling of interior) of Victorian terraced house for Lady Chalmers (his sister).

8 1894 MINTO HOUSE, Roxburghshire.
Alterations, including ceiling plasterwork and stone bridge 1897, alterations to Fatlips Castle 1899, garden terracing 1904, new servants' wing 1906 for Lord Minto.

9 ST MARNOCKS, County Malahide, Ireland.
Old country house remodelled, extended and given a new garden for John Jamieson.

10 STRONACHULLIN LODGE, Ardrishaig, Argyll.
New harled house and stable court, small garden, for Graham Campbell.

11 ELLARY, Ardrishaig, Argyll.
Restoration after fire of David Bryce revival Baronial house with the tower heightened and new billiards room added for J. Fox Tarrat.

12 1895 GRANDTULLY CASTLE, Perthshire.
New gates for Lady Stewart.

13 ORMELIE, Kinellan Road, Edinburgh.
Minor alterations to existing house for J. Stirling Boyd.

14 CLOUSTA HOTEL, Shetland (Destroyed).
New hotel for fishermen, largely carried out in timber, since burnt down.

15 ROXOBEL, 14 Gillespie Road, Colinton, Edinburgh.
A new harled house and garden layout for P. Ronay Dougal.

16 1896 TORDUFF, Lanark Road, Juniper Green, Edinburgh.
Large additions and alterations to existing house for Miss Bruce.

17 BRUNTSFIELD CRESCENT, 12, Marchmont, Edinburgh.
Alterations to revival Baronial stone terraced house for J. Duddingston Herdman R.S.A.

18 BALCARRES, Colinsburgh, Fife.
New 'Holyrood' gate lodge and wrought iron gates for the Earl of Crawford and Balcarres.

19 1897 MOUNIE CASTLE, Daviot, Aberdeenshire.
Scheme for large additions and new garden layout (not carried out). Interior remodelled, and Doocot remodelled as a garden pavilion for Major Seton.

20 EILEAN SHONA HOUSE, Eilean Shona, Loch Moidart, Argyll.
Alterations for Spencer C. Thomson.

21 GOOD SHEPHERD, Church of, Murrayfield Avenue, Edinburgh.
New stone church, tower not completed, for J. M. Tod.

22 HALLYARDS MANOR, Peeblesshire (Not executed).
Scheme for totally remodelling and extending house with large walled garden layout for Dr Anderson (who was a 'sort of cousin').

23 BINLEY COTTAGE, 42 Pentland Avenue, Colinton, Edinburgh.
New harled 'cottage' and garden layout for Lord Pearson.

24 WESTFIELD, 40 Pentland Avenue, Colinton, Edinburgh.
New harled 'cottage' and garden layout for Miss Guthrie Wright.

25 PENTLAND COTTAGE, 21 Gillespie Road, Colinton, Edinburgh.
New harled 'cottage', stable block and garden layout for Dr Downie.

26 THE MANSE, West Wemyss, Fife.
A new harled manse for Randolph Wemyss.

27 WEMYSS CASTLE, Fife.
Undercroft remodelled as chapel for Randolph Wemyss. Scheme for new gate lodge not carried out.

28 1898 TEVIOTDALE, Abbotsford Road, North Berwick, East Lothian.
A new harled house for J. C. Stewart (formerly called Greyhome).

29 ORMIDALE, Murrayfield, Edinburgh.
Alterations for Col. Burnley Campbell.

30 PRINCES STREET, 124, Edinburgh. (Destroyed).
Alterations for Messrs Henry Darling & Co.

31 DREGHORN LOAN, Colinton, Edinburgh.
Layout of feuing plan and scrutiny of design proposals for sites for the McFie Trust.

32 FETTERCAIRN, Laurencekirk, Forfarshire.
Remodelling of library for the Hon. Charles Trefusis.

33 WHINFOLD, Hascombe, Surrey.
A brick and tiled 'cottage', garden layout and gardeners lodge, for E. P. Benson.

34 NEWARK CASTLE, near Elie, Fife. (Not executed).
Scheme for extensive additions and alterations for William Burrell.

35 1899 NEWARK CASTLE, near Elie, Fife. (Not executed).
Smaller scheme for additions and alterations for W. A. Baird.

36 COLMONELL CHURCH, Ayrshire.
New pulpit and stained glass windows for R. F. McEwan.

37 ELIZABETSGATEN, 13 (St Andrews) Helsinki, Finland.
Design only for a stone house for Ossian Donner.

38 ACHARRA, 3 Spylaw Avenue, Colinton, Edinburgh.
A new harled 'cottage' and garden layout for Major Meares.

39 ALMORA, 49 Spylaw Bank Road, Colinton, Edinburgh.
A new harled 'cottage' and garden layout for P. Guthrie.

40 ST ANNE'S CHURCH, Dunbar, East Lothian.
Internal woodwork including pulpit and kneelers.

41 FURSEFIELD, Winkworth Hill, Surrey.
A new house for R. F. Pinks.

42 INVERALMOND, Dunkeld Road, Perth. (Not executed).
Terrace of four artisans' cottages for H. T. Fairweather.

43 CORNER COTTAGE, 4 Spylaw Park, Colinton, Edinburgh.
Project only for a harled house (not carried out), for Stuart Silver.

44 THE HERMITAGE, 26 Gillespie Road Colinton, Edinburgh.
A new harled 'cottage' and garden layout (formerly L'Ermitage, since extended and partially stripped of its harling), for Charles Sarolea.

45 BRIGLANDS, Rumbling Bridge, Kinrossshire.
Large harled additions to classical house, garden courtyard and new lodge for the Rt. Hon. Lord Clyde Billiard room and guest bedrooms added in 1908.

46 RAITH HOUSE, Fife.
Alterations to library and garden layout.

47 LINLITHGOW BRIDGE, Linlithgow, West Lothian.
Terrace of harled flatted cottages, assembly hall and playground (at various dates) for Charles Chalmers.

48 1900 PITCAIRNFIELD, Perthshire. (Not executed).
Project for a model village for Henry Darling (a cottage design only survives).

49 LONGFORGAN CHURCH, Perthshire.
Internal woodwork (memorial panels).

50 SPYLAW PARK, 10, Colinton, Edinburgh.
A harled house for Mr Walker (harling omitted). The west wing was deferred but added to original design in 1906 and stables built for Mr Drysdale who renamed the house called Dilkusha, Hartfell.

51 KELLIE CASTLE, Pittenweem, Fife. (Now National Trust for Scotland).
A stone garden-house for Mrs Lorimer.

52 BAVELAW CASTLE, Near Balerno.
'High corbelled turret to improve

172

circulation on the attic floor by *Robert Lorimer c.* 1900. He also added the boat shaped dormers, reconstructed the existing outhouses to the N.E. and W., joining them to the house with a balustraded screen, and laid out a small formal garden. Indoors he made the vaulted basement habitable, supplemented the existing woodwork, and added a thin-ribbed geometric ceiling in the drawing room', p. 99. *Lothian*, Colin McWilliam, London, 1978.

53 1901 INCHDREWER HOUSE, Colinton Road, Edinburgh.
New stone billiards room extension to existing house for J. Galletley.

54 HIGH BARN, Hascombe, Surrey.
New stone house and garden layout for the Hon. Stuart Bouverie.

55 HUNTLY, 32 Gillespie Road, Colinton, Edinburgh.
A new harled 'cottage' and garden layout, for Miss Paterson. A west wing and stable block since added.

56 THE ROWANS, 21 Pentland Avenue, Colinton, Edinburgh.
A new harled 'cottage' and garden layout, for Miss Guthrie Wright (her fourth and last).

57 RUSTIC COTTAGES, (1–3) Colinton Road, Edinburgh.
A terrace of three harled artisans' cottages for J. Galletly.

58 CHURCH OF OUR LADY, STAR OF THE SEA, North Berwick, East Lothian.
Interior woodwork in Lady Chapel.

59 GLENLYON, 47 Spylaw Bank Road, Colinton, Edinburgh.
New harled 'cottage' garden layout and garage, for S. C. Thomson.

60 GREAT WESTERN TERRACE, 8, Glasgow.
Complete internal remodelling of existing Victorian terraced house for William Burrell (much altered since he left).

61 BRIDGE OF TEITH, Doune, Perthshire.
A new harled house and garden layout for J. Burn Murdoch.

62 BRACKENBURGH, Near Penrith, Cumberland.
(North wing demolished).
New stone Tudor mansion, garden layout, lodge, cottages, stable and farm buildings for Joseph Harris.

63 WAYSIDE, St Andrews, Fife.
A new stone house and garden layout for C. E. Todd.

64 RISOBANK, Mandal, Norway.
Design only, new wooden house with outbuildings for Lord Salvesen.

65 1902 RUSTIC COTTAGES, (4–7), Colinton Road, Edinburgh.
Two pairs of semi-detached harled artisans' cottages for J. Galletly.

66 FOXCOVERT, Clermiston Road, Edinburch. (Demolished).
Large harled additions to small existing house and garden layout and walls for Lady Chalmers.

67 PITKERRO, Broughty Ferry, Dundee.
Large additions to sixteenth century house, harled, and new lodge house and garden layout for Col. Douglas Dick.

68 WEAPONESS PARK, Scarborough, Yorkshire.
A new brick and tiled house and garden layout for the Rt. Hon. A. H. D. Acland.

69 LUNDIE, Arncroach, Fife.
Existing cottage, remodelled (additions of bays and attics) for James Bennet.

70 GLENCRAIG PUBLIC HOUSE, Lochelly, Fife.
A new building which does not appear still to exist, for the East of Scotland P. H. Trust.

71 ETON TERRACE, 7, Edinburgh.
Alterations to a terraced house.

72 MARLY KNOWE, North Berwick, East Lothian.
A new harled house and garden layout, cottage and stables, for Professor Edward Schaeffer.

73 PEEBLES, Peeblesshire.
(Not executed).
A house for Mrs Bruce.

74 CRAIGMYLE, Torphins, Aberdeenshire. (Destroyed).
Large additions and alterations to sixteenth century granite house, terraced garden, remodelling of farm courtyard and new west lodge, for B. P. Robertson-Glasgow.

75 ALDOURIE, Inverness.
New dining room and scullery wing added to existing house, for A. Fraser-Tytler.

76 ROWALLAN, Kilmaurs, Ayrshire.
A Scots Baronial Mansion, lodge, stables court, cottages and garden layout with pavilion and gardeners cottage, for A. Cameron Corbett, M.P.

77 BARTON HARTSHORN, near Buckingham, Buckinghamshire.
Large stone additions to 16th century manor for Col. Trotter. (Further additions and garden layout in collaboration with Gertrude Jekyll, 1908).

78 1903 BALCARRES, Colinsburgh, Fife.
New stone estate office for the Earl of Crawford and Balcarres.

79 HALLYBURTON, Coupar Angus, Perthshire.
Large new wing added to Baronial

House by A. Heiton, also layout of adjoining garden with wrought iron gates for W. Graham Menzies.

80 DUNDERACH, 1 Craiglockhart Park, Edinburgh.
A new harled house for Walter J. Murray.

81 HYNDFORD, North Berwick, East Lothian.
Additions and alterations for F. J. Tennant.

82 COLSTOUN HOUSE, Near Haddington.
Old harled house, smoking room remodelled, 1903, also some work to rooms along W. Side, p.142 *Lothian* Colin McWilliam, London, 1978.

83 OLIPHANT Memorial gateway, St Andrews, Fife.

84 1904 BUNKERSHILL, North Berwick, East Lothian.
A large stone Tudor house and lodge for Robert Craig.

85 BANCHORY, Aberdeenshire. (Not executed).
Harled 'cottage' in pine wood, for Mrs Fergusson.

86 EYRE TERRACE, Henderson Row, Edinburgh.
Block of four tenements with pend giving access to stable block and storeroom for Robert Graham.

87 ARDGOWAN, Inverkip, Renfrew.
Alterations for Sir Hugh Shaw Stewart, Bt.

88 1905 CHARLTON, Colinsburgh, Fife.
Observatory for Col. & Mrs Anstruther.

89 MORAY PLACE, 27, Edinburgh.
Alterations to a terraced house for the Rt. Hon. Lord Clyde.

90 THE GLEN, Innerleithen, Peeblesshire.
Restitution of burnt out Baronial Mansion by David Bryce for Sir Charles Tennant, Bt.

91 CARMICHAEL BURYING GROUND, Thankerton, Lanarkshire.
Ground works.

92 AUCHENTRAIL, Upper Largo, Fife. (Not executed).
Large harled house scheme for himself.

93 ST MARY'S R.C. CATHEDRAL, Edinburgh.
Donlevy Memorial.

94 1906 WHITEHOLM, Gullane, East Lothian.
New harled house and garden layout, for A. Spottiswoode Ritchie.

95 LESLIE HOUSE, Markinch, Fife.
Additions and alterations for the Earl of Rothes.

96 LORETTO, Musselburgh, East Lothian.
Extension to North Esk House.

97 ST PETER'S CHURCH, Falcon Avenue, Edinburgh.
New stone church, church hall and priest's house, for M. Raffalovich (and Rev. Father John Gray).

98 ARDKINGLAS, Cairndow, Argyll.
New stone Baronial Mansion house, terraces, hydro-electric power house and dam, also new farm yard, cottage, kennels and remodelling existing house, for Sir Andrew Noble, Bt.

99 SHEILDAIG, 24 Hermitage Drive, Edinburgh.
New stone house and garden layout for E. C. Jack. (East wing added by J. B. Dunn since).

100 SKIRLING HOUSE, Peeblesshire. (Not executed).
Design for large 'Scotch' house for Sir T. Gibson Carmichael.

101 SKIRLING GREEN, Peeblesshire. (Not executed).

New harled house for the Maclehoses.

102 BARGUILLEAN, near Taynuilt Argyll.
Large harled house, garden layout and stables for T. Martin Macdonald. (Formerly known as Achnahanit, now Lonan House).

103 BARDROCHAT, Colmonell, Ayrshire.
Large harled additions and alterations (to small house designed by George M. Watson) for R. F. McEwan.

104 HARMENY, Marchbank, Balerno, Edinburgh.
Large additions and alterations to east and west of a house designed by R. Rowand Anderson and built to replace Harmony, (which was sited a little to the east) with garden layout, chauffeurs cottage and garage block, for Col. W. M. Younger.

105 1907 CRAIGROYSTON, West Shore Road, Granton, Edinburgh.
New east wing for existing house, for M. L. P. Jardine.

106 KIRKLANDS, Ancrum, Berwickshire.
Additions and alterations for Lord George Scott.

107 ESKHILL, Inveresk, Midlothian.
Alterations and additions for R. Craig Cowan.

108 WEMYSS HALL, near Cupar, Fife, (now Hill of Tarvit, National Trust for Scotland).
Large additions and alterations to existing house and new garden, landscaping and gardener's cottage and laundry house for F. B. Sharp.

109 AITHERNIE, Lundin Links, Fife.
Additions and alterations for G. Lumsden.

110 LYMPNE CASTLE, Kent.
Restoration of old castle, large new

west wing, walled garden and cottages, for Frank Tennant.

111 MARSHILL, Alloa.
Alterations for A. P. Moir.

112 CARNEGIE LIBRARY, University of St Andrews.
New stone building for University.

113 AYTON, Glenfarg, Perthshire.
Alterations (interior woodwork), for R. W. Seton Watson.

114 RHU-NA-HAVEN, Aboyne, Aberdeenshire.
New granite house, terraced garden, cottage and lodge, for J. Herbert Taylor.

115 THE KNOLL, North Berwick, East Lothian.
Alterations, new garage and cottage for Dr G. A. Berry.

116 BALGILLO, Broughty Ferry, Dundee. (Destroyed).
Garden laid out for J. C. Buist at existing mansion.

117 ST JOHNS, Plumpton, Cumberland.
A new stone church and lytch gate, for Joseph Harris.

118 1908 ST MARK'S, Scotland Street, Glasgow. (Destroyed).
A new harled church for Rev. Knox.

119 ESSENDRY HOUSE, Near Blairgowrie, Perthshire.
Additions and alterations for Rev. W. Fraser.

120 NEW CLUB, 86 Princes Street, Edinburgh. (Destroyed).
Interior remodelling and new woodwork, 1906, 1908, & 1913 (some woodwork reinstated in new building on the site).

121 WOODHILL, Barry, Forfarshire.
A new harled house, garden layout and lodge for D. S. Milne.

122 SWANSTON COTTAGE, Swanston, Edinburgh.
Alterations for the Hon. Lord

123 Guthrie.
MUIRFIELD, Royal Scottish National Hospital, Gullane, East Lothian.

124 Two storey administration block with single storey wards canted forward on each side.
MONZIE CASTLE, Perthshire.
Burnt out castellated house reinstated with alterations and all furnishings, for C. M. Makgill Crichton.

125 FORMAKIN, Bishopton, Renfrewshire.
New 'Scotch' mansion, lodge, garden, landscaped grounds and farm buildings for John A. Holms.

126 PITTENCRIEFF HOUSE, Pittencrieff Glen, Dunfermline, Fife.
Restoration of sixteenth century house for the Dunfermline Carnegie Trust.

127 1909 LOGIE, Dunfermline, Fife.
Additions and alterations for Col. Hunt.

128 DAWICK, Peeblesshire.
Additions to William Burn house for Mrs Balfour.

129 THE ORDER OF THE THISTLE, St Giles, Edinburgh.
New Chapel (extension) for the Order, with all the furnishings and fittings.

130 GALLOWAY HOUSE, Wigtonshire.
Extensive internal remodelling for Sir Malcome McEachern.

131 1910 CARBERRY TOWER, near Inveresk, Midlothian.
Alterations for Lord Elphinstone.

132 SKINBURNESS TOWER, Silloth, Cumberland.
Alterations for J. E. Carter.

133 GLENDALOUGH, North Berwick, East Lothian.
Extensive remodelling for Sir W. Gardiner-Baird.

134 GILMERTON, Strathvithie, Fife.
Additions and alterations for Captain R. W. Purvis.

135 HERIOT ROW, 6, Edinburgh.
Remodelling of interior for Alexander Maitland.

136 1911 DUNDERAVE CASTLE, near Inverary, Argyll.
Restoration of, and additions to, sixteenth century castle, also garden and landscaping for Sir Andrew Noble, Bt.

137 GREYWALLS, Gullane, East Lothian.
Additions (kitchen and dining room on the north since burnt out) to a Lutyens house for William James.

138 BISHOP DOWDEN MEMORIAL, St Mary's Cathedral, Edinburgh.

139 GILLINGSHILL, Pittenweem, Fife.
Alterations for J. C. Pitman.

140 LEXHAM GARDENS, 39, West London.
Alterations for Sir E. Im Thurn.

141 KING EDWARD VII MEMORIAL, Holyrood Palace, Edinburgh.
(Not executed).
Competition entry (Sir George Washington Browne won).

142 ANCHOR VILLA, North Berwick, East Lothian.
Alterations internally for Rev. W. Houldsworth.

143 1912 BELHAVEN HOUSE, Dunbar, East Lothian.
Alterations for K. R. Maitland, including iron gates.

144 CORNMILL SQUARE, Galashiels.
Layout for site of former mill, for the burgh.

145 CORNER HOUSE, Gullane, East Lothian.
New stone house and garden layout, for R. O. Pitman.

146 ST LEONARD'S, Murrayfield, Edinburgh.
Alterations for W. R. Macmillan.

147 LAVEROCKDALE HOUSE, Dreghorn Loan, Colinton, Edinburgh.
New 'Scotch' house, lodge and garden layout, for J. A. Ivory.

148 DUNBLANE CATHEDRAL, Perthshire.
Internal woodwork including, reredos, choir stalls and organ.

149 LENNOXLOVE, Haddington, East Lothian.
Restoration and remodelling of front door of east wing also 'Duchess of Lennox's room' and new fireplace in hall for Major W. A. Baird.

150 MELVILLE STREET, 54, Edinburgh.
Alterations and addition of attic storey for Sir R. S. Lorimer.

151 BALCASKIE, Pittenweem, Fife.
New gates for R. Anstruther.

152 ST MARY'S EPISCOPAL CHURCH, Broughty Ferry, Dundee.
Additional bay added and woodwork (Bishop's chair and kneelers).

153 LORETTO SCHOOL, Musselburgh, East Lothian.
New gymnasium for the Trustees.

154 1913 GLENMAYNE, Galashiels, Selkirk.
Entrance gateway and library for H. S. Murray.

155 WESTERLEA, Ellersly Road, Corstorphine, Edinburgh.
House (by J. J. Stevenson) remodelled and garden layout, for John J. Cowan.

156 LORETTO SCHOOL, Musselburgh, East Lothian.
New cricket pavilion.

157 ROSEBERY THEOLOGICAL COLLEGE, Grosvenor Gardens, Edinburgh.
Alterations and additions.

158 INVERAWE, near Taynuilt, Argyll.
Additions and alterations to harled country house, for James Currie.

159 DUNCRAGGIE, Brora, Sutherland.
New harled house for C. H. Akroyd.

160 KINELLAN, Murrayfield Road, Edinburgh.
Alterations to house and garage block for J. Herbert Herdman.

161 HUNTERSTON, West Kilbride.
Alterations for General Sir Aylmer Hunter-Weston.

162 KIRKSIDE, St Cyrus, Montrose.
New wing (in Hill of Tarvit style) added to 18th century house.

163 ZOOLOGICAL PARK, Edinburgh. (Destroyed).
New bandstand.

164 1914 STONEHOUSE, 1 Pentland Road, Colinton, Edinburgh.
New stone house and garden layout, for J. F. Will.

165 DOUGLAS CRESCENT, 4, Edinburgh.
Alterations for Douglas Strachan.

166 ST JOHN'S EPISCOPAL CHURCH, Alloa.
Memorial for Mrs Younger.

167 ST ANDREW'S EPISCOPAL CHURCH, Aberdeen.
Rood screen and other furnishings.

168 GRANGE PARK, Dick Place, Edinburgh.
Alterations for C. M. Pelham Brown.

169 GATTONSIDE, Melrose, Roxburghshire.
Large alterations for E. H. Ebsworth.

170 MARCHMONT, near Duns, Berwickshire.
Interior and exterior remodelling of classical mansion and some landscaping for R. F. McEwan.

171 MIDFIELD, Lasswade, Midlothian.
Restoration of house and new east wing and garden layout, for J. A. Hood.

172 BRAMPTON HOUSE, Brampton, Cumberland. (Not executed).
New house for James Morton.

173 1915 WHITEKIRK CHURCH, East Lothian.
Restitution after fire. S transept much restored, the new crossing follows the old design. Wagon roof over nave and transcepts. 'The texture of the wood makes it appear older than it is', p. 468, *Lothian*, Colin McWilliam, London, 1978.

174 MORTON SUNDOUR FACTORY, Carlisle.
New weaving shed for James Morton.

175 DUNROBIN CASTLE, near Brora, Sutherland.
Restoration of roof for the Duke of Sutherland (additional internal remodelling 1919).

176 FOSS HOUSE, near Pitlochry, Perthshire.
Alterations for Sir A. Aberfeldy.

177 1916 BALMANNO CASTLE, Glenfarg, Perthshire.
Remodelling of castle and new garden, Belvedere, gardener's store-house and gate lodge for W. S. Miller.

178 HUTTON CASTLE, near Duns, Berwickshire.
Addition of new kitchen quarters and bedrooms and remodelling of old castle, for Sir William Burrell.

179 CONHEATH, Dumfriesshire.
New farmhouse, and existing chapel remodelled for R. Y. Pickering.

180 1917 ST BALDRED'S EPISCOPAL CHURCH, North Berwick, East Lothian.
New south porch.

1918

MEMORIALS:

Additions and alterations for Sir Benjamin Faudel Philips, Bt.

245   HURWORTH HALL, near Darlington, County Durham.
Additions and alterations for Miss Forster.

246   1926   LORETTO SCHOOL, Musselburgh, East Lothian.
New classrooms.

247   MEMORIAL, MORTON at Darvel, Ayrshire.

248   CRAIGIEHALL, Cramond, Edinburgh.
Alterations for James Morton.

249   ST ANDREW'S CHURCH, Aldershot.
New brick built church.

250   1927   GLENCRUITTEN, Oban, Argyll.
Library wing added for Alexander Mackay.

251   STOWE SCHOOL, Chapel, Buckinghamshire.
Stone chapel and all internal woodwork (won in competition).

252   1928   MEMORIAL, WORKINGTON, Cumberland.

253   TOUCH, Stirling.
Alterations and gates for Charles A. Buchanan.

254   JORDANSTONE, Meigle, Perthshire.
Large alterations and additions for J. L. Duncan.

255   OLD FARM, Corniche du Paradis Terrestre, Cannes, France.
Extensive remodelling of old 'Provencal' buildings for Mr Playfair.

256   ST GILES CATHEDRAL, Edinburgh.
Alterations for the Shrine of Youth.

257   KINFAUNS CASTLE, Perthshire.
New dairy.

258   1929   MEMORIAL, RUSSELL ALLEN, Davenham.

259   PLACE OF PAISLEY, Renfrewshire.
Remodelling of mediaeval house near Abbey.

260   BRAIDWOOD, near Carluke, Lanarkshire.
Additions for Major John Colville, M.P.

261   CRIEFF SOUTH CHURCH, Perthshire.
Alterations.

262   ALLOWAY BURNS INSTITUTE.
Large harled additions in traditional style for Lord Glentanar.

263   ST MARGARET'S CHURCH, Knightswood, Glasgow.
A new stone church finished posthumously (by J. F. Matthew). 🍎

From a letter.

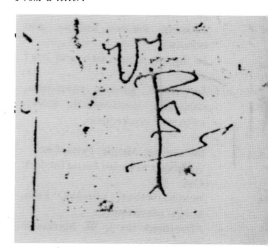

178

List of Woodwork

...orimer was celebrated for his Church wood-
...ork. The following list comprises items from
...he accounts of the office.

...BERDEEN, ST ANDREW'S EPISCOPAL CHURCH, re-
...edos, wall panelling and pendant cross for Very
...ev. Prior Erskine Hill.

...RBROATH, ST MARY'S, Rood Cross and panelling
...or Rev. Millar.

...ROUGHTY FERRY, ST MARY'S EPISCOPAL CHURCH,
...eredos, Bishop's chair and kneeler for Rev. A.
...C. Dow.

...ARNBEE, Fife, Pulpit for Rev. George Thomson.

...ELLARDYKE PARISH CHURCH, Communion table
...nd chairs for Miss Oliphant.

...UPAR, ST JAMES EPISCOPAL CHURCH, Reredos and
...vall panelling for Mrs Culroy.

...OAVENHAM, Kneeler.

...OARLINGTON, HOLY TRINITY CHURCH, panelling,
...Bishop's chair, credence, table and sedilia for
...Rev. F. Peacock.

...OALSTON CHURCH, Cumberland, Font cover.

...OUNBAR, ST ANNE'S CHURCH, Choir stalls and
...oulpit for Rev. James Kirk.

...OUNINO CHURCH, Font cover.

...EDINBURGH, ST MARY'S MISSION, Bells Brae, Re-
...edos (removed).

...EDINBURGH, ST GEORGE'S UNITED FREE CHURCH,
...Communion table.

...EDINBURGH, ST MARY'S CATHEDRAL, pedestal
...Bishop Teviot's bust.

...GLASGOW, ST MARY'S CATHEDRAL, woodwork for
...Very Rev. Prior Lethbridge.

...GLASGOW, ALL SAINTS CHURCH, woodwork for
...Rev. Henderson Begg.

...HAWICK, ST CUTHBERT'S EPISCOPAL CHURCH, wood-
...work for Rev. E. T. S. Reid.

...NVERNESS CATHEDRAL, Screen.

...KILDONAN, Prie dieu.

LASSWADE, ST LEONARD'S CHURCH, reredos for Mr
Hood of Midfield.

LATTINGTOWN, LONG ISLAND, ST JOHN'S CHURCH,
lectern font, panelling, etc.

LITTLE SOMERFORD CHURCH, woodwork for Mr
Fitzgerald.

NORTH BERWICK, ST BALDRED'S CHURCH, Houldsworth Memorial doors, etc.

OXFORD, CHRIST CHURCH, Trinity Rood and
carved oak pulpit, kneeler and font cover for
Rev. P. M. Herford.

PITTENWEEM CHURCH, panelling etc.

RINGFORD CHURCH, woodwork for Rev. Peter
Fisher.

ROSSALL CHAPEL, reredos and pulpit for Dr
Houghton.

SELKIRK, ST JOHN'S EPISCOPAL CHURCH, woodwork
for Rev. W. Perry.

SOUTH QUEENSFERRY, PRIORY CHURCH, oak font
cover.

STIRLING, HOLY TRINITY CHURCH, screen for Vis-
count Younger.

WHITEKIRK CHURCH, communion table and font,
pulpit and seating for Lady Grissell Baillie
Hamilton.

179

From a letter.

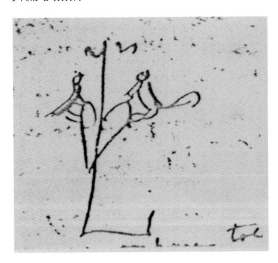

Bibliography

bibliography

ooks

DAMS, Maurice. Modern Cottage Architecture. nd ed. 1912

NDERSON, R. R.. Examples of Municipal Archiecture in France and Italy. N. D. c1856

PTED, M. R.. The painted ceilings of Scotland 550–1650. 1966

OX, E. H. M.. A history of gardening in cotland. 1935

OODHART RENDEL, H. S.. English Architecture ince the Regency. 1953

ALDANE, Elizabeth S.. Scots Gardens in Old imes. 1934

AY, Ian. Their Name Liveth. 1931

USSEY, christopher. The work of Sir Robert orimer. 1931

ERR, Robert. The English Gentlemans house. 856

ONGWORTH, philip. The unending Vigil. 1967

ORTON, Jocelyn. Three generations in a family irm. 1971

UTHESIUS, Herman. *Das Englische Haus.* 1904–5

NICHOLSON, sir chas. (and Spooner). Recent Ecclesiastical Architecture. N. D. c1911

NICOLL, James. Domestic Architecture in Scot-

land. 1908

SPARROW, walter. shaw
The British home of today. 1904
The Modern home. 1906
Our homes. 1909
Hints on home furnishing. 1909

STATHAM, H. heathcote. Modern Architecture. 1897

STEVENSON, J. J.. House Architecture. 1888

STIRLING MAXWELL, sir John. Shrines and homes of Scotland. 1937

Studio Year Books of Decorative Art. 1906 and 1907

TRIGGS, Inigo. Formal gardens in England and Scotland. 1902

TURNER, Laurence. Decorative plasterwork in Great Britain. 1927

WEAVER, sir lawrence.
The house and its equipment. N. D. c1912
Country life book of cottages. 1913
Small country houses their repair and enlargement. 1914
Memorials and monuments. 1915
Small country houses. 2nd series. 1919

Papers and Pamphlets

Catalogues of Royal Scottish Academy, Edinburgh Central Library (Fine Art Dept.)

DEAS, Frank. Review of Lorimer's work. RIBA

Journal 21.2.1931 and 7.3.1931

HMSO command 279. 1919

MITCHELL, Arnold. Plans for the home, in The British Home of today, edited Shaw Sparrow. 1904

SIMPSON, W. Douglas. The tower houses of Scotland, in Building History, edited E. M. Jope 1961

THOMSON, L. G.. Review of Lorimer's work. Quarterly RIAS. Autumn 1929

181

Index

ADDENDA

The List of Works should include: